Migration and Insecurity

This book presents an inter-disciplinary investigation into contemporary migration and social inclusion through an examination of migrant and refugee experience.

In this edited volume, contributors discuss new understandings of individual and community security in a world where legal borders and definitions of citizenship no longer adequately capture the reality of migration. Distinguished contributors approach questions of social belonging and inclusion from diverse perspectives. Drawing its primary examples from Australia, *Migration and Insecurity* is framed by the wider experience of the Global North, with examples from Europe, the United Kingdom and United States woven throughout the collection. An inter-disciplinary approach to migration studies, this book integrates local, national and transnational spaces in its discussion of new constructs of inclusion and security. It considers questions of historical memory, ontological security, transnational communities, the role of civic institutions and social relationships in local spaces to guide the reader towards the wider conceptual questions of migration studies using expertise from the fields of sociology, gender, historical and political studies.

Migration and Insecurity will be of interest to students and scholars of transnationalism, migration politics and international relations.

Niklaus Steiner is the Director of the Center for Global Initiatives at the University of North Carolina – Chapel Hill, USA.

Robert Mason is a Lecturer at the University of Southern Queensland, Australia.

Anna Hayes is a Senior Lecturer at the University of Southern Queensland, Australia.

Routledge research on the global politics of migration

1 **Globalization, Migration, and the Future of Europe**
   Insiders and outsiders
   Edited by Leila Simona Talani

2 **Citizenship, Migrant Activism and the Politics of Movement**
   Edited by Peter Nyers and Kim Rygiel

3 **Migration and Insecurity**
   Citizenship and social inclusion in a transnational era
   Edited by Niklaus Steiner, Robert Mason and Anna Hayes

Migration and Insecurity
Citizenship and social inclusion in a transnational era

Edited by Niklaus Steiner, Robert Mason and Anna Hayes

LONDON AND NEW YORK

First published 2013
by Routledge
2 Park Square, Milton Park, Abingdon, Oxfordshire OX14 4RN

Simultaneously published in the USA and Canada
by Routledge
711 Third Avenue, New York, NY 10017

First issued in paperback 2014

Routledge is an imprint of the Taylor & Francis Group, an informa business.

© 2013 Niklaus Steiner, Robert Mason and Anna Hayes for selection and editorial matter; individual contributors their contribution.

The right of Niklaus Steiner, Robert Mason and Anna Hayes to be identified as the authors of the editorial material, and of the authors for their individual chapters, has been asserted in accordance with sections 77 and 78 of the Copyright, Designs and Patents Act 1988.

All rights reserved. No part of this book may be reprinted or reproduced or utilized in any form or by any electronic, mechanical, or other means, now known or hereafter invented, including photocopying and recording, or in any information storage or retrieval system, without permission in writing from the publishers.

Trademark notice: Product or corporate names may be trademarks or registered trademarks, and are used only for identification and explanation without intent to infringe.

British Library Cataloguing in Publication Data
A catalogue record for this book is available from the British Library

Library of Congress Cataloging in Publication Data
Migration and insecurity : citizenship and social inclusion in a transnational era / edited by Niklaus Steiner, Robert Mason and Anna Hayes.
   p. cm. – (Routledge research on the global politics of migration ; 3)
   Includes bibliographical references and index.
   1. Emigration and immigration–Social aspects. 2. Social integration.
   3. Immigrants–Cultural assimilation. 4. Immigrants–Social conditions.
   5. Immigrants–Civil rights. 6. Transnationalism. I. Steiner, Niklaus.
   II. Mason, Robert, 1981– III. Hayes, Anna, 1977–
   JV6342.M53 2012
   305.9'06912–dc23   2012007178

ISBN: 978-0-415-66549-0 (hbk)
ISBN: 978-1-138-82218-4 (pbk)

Typeset in Times New Roman
by Wearset Ltd, Boldon, Tyne and Wear

Contents

Notes on contributors vii

Detailed synopsis 1

1 Securing twenty-first century societies 3
  ANNA HAYES AND ROBERT MASON

2 A comparison of asylum-seekers in Europe and illegal
  immigrants in the United States 17
  NIKLAUS STEINER

Receiving strangeness 29

3 Legacies of war and migration: memories of war trauma,
  dislocation and second generation Greek-Australians 31
  JOY DAMOUSI

4 An invitation to inclusion: museums and migration 48
  KAY FERRES

5 Negotiating migration, sentiment, and insecurity:
  encounters with sadness and shame in Australia 64
  SARA WILLS

Negotiating integration 85

6 Would-be citizens and 'strong states': circles of security and
  insecurity 87
  PAUL JAMES AND ANNE McNEVIN

7 Negotiating integration: refugees and asylum seekers in
   Australia and the UK 108
   SUSANNE SCHECH AND SOPHIA RAINBIRD

8 Transnational practices, social inclusion, and Muslim
   migrant integration in the West 127
   FETHI MANSOURI

Securing long-term belonging 147

9 Equal valued status: belonging, identity and place 149
   HURRIYET BABACAN AND ALPERHAN BABACAN

10 Citizens of nowhere: refugees, integration criteria, and
   social inclusion 169
   EILEEN PITTAWAY

Index 188

Contributors

Alperhan Babacan is the Deputy Head, Accounting, Economic, Finance and Law at Swinburne University. He has held numerous university positions including as Director for the Juris Doctor Program, RMIT University. Alperhan holds degrees in Law and Political Science and a PhD. Alperhan has worked as a lawyer, a researcher and as an academic. Alperhan's research mainly revolves around human rights law, counter terrorism, racism and migration. He has published in national and international journals and has written several books in these areas.

Hurriyet Babacan is the Director of the Cairns Institute at James Cook University. Previously, Hurriyet held other key positions including Director of the Institute for Community, Ethnicity and Policy Alternatives at Victoria University, Executive Director, Multicultural Affairs, Women's Policy and Community Outcomes Branch in the Department of Premier and Cabinet (Queensland), Commissioner with the inaugural Ethnic Affairs Commission in Victoria and Victorian Manager, and in the Department of Prime Minister and Cabinet. Hurriyet has led numerous national and international research and development projects. She has recently been a member of two Council of Europe and OECD working parties. Hurriyet has published nationally and internationally on the issues of health, welfare, multiculturalism, immigration, identity, social policy, gender, racism, settlement and community development. Her work has been recognized by awards such as the Bicentennial Medal by the Prime Minister, Multicultural Services Award by the Premier of Qld and Telstra (Business Women's Awards).

Joy Damousi is a Professor of History in the School of Historical and Philosophical Studies at the University of Melbourne. She has published widely in the fields of Australian cultural history, feminist history, political history, history of emotions, war and memory, and the history of psychoanalysis. She is the author of numerous books and articles, including *The Labour of Loss: Mourning, Memory and Wartime Bereavement in Australia* (Cambridge, 1999), *Living with the Aftermath: Trauma, Nostalgia and Grief in Post-war Australia* (Cambridge, 2001), *History on the Couch: Essays in History and Psychoanalysis* (co-edited with Robert Reynolds, Melbourne University

Press, 2003), *The Transnational Unconscious: Essays in the history of Psychoanalysis and Transnationalism* (co-edited with Mariano Plotkin, Palgrave Macmillan, 2008), *Freud in the Antipodes: A Cultural History of Psychoanalysis in Australia* (University of New South Wales Press, 2005; Winner of the Ernest Scott Prize, 2006) and *Colonial Voices: A Cultural History of English in Australia* (Cambridge, 2010). Her current research explores the connections between war, memory and migration in Greek war stories: transnationalism, war trauma and migration.

Kay Ferres is a Professor in the School of Humanities, Griffith University. Her research is concerned with culture and citizenship. She has published on women's participation in the public sphere, the role of cultural institutions in creating emergent public spheres, and the representation of migrant experience in literary and visual formats. Her current project is focussed on mobilities, memory and creative placemaking. Her most recent books include *An Articulate Country: Reinventing Citizenship in Australia* (co-authored with Denise Meredyth, University of Queensland Press, 2001) and *Deciphering Culture: Ordinary Curiosities and Subjective Narratives* (co-authored with Jane Crisp and Gillian Swanson, Routledge, 2000).

Anna Hayes is a Senior Lecturer in International Relations at the University of Southern Queensland. She has published a number of articles examining the human security dimension of the HIV/AIDS epidemic in China. More recently, she has conducted research on the Uighur diaspora in Adelaide Australia, and their experiences of living outside of the Chinese state. Findings from this research can be found in her chapter titled 'Uighur Transnationalism in Contemporary Australia: exile, sanctuary, community and future' in the forthcoming book titled *Cultures in Refuge: Seeking Sanctuary in Modern Australia* (co-edited with Robert Mason, Ashgate, 2012).

Paul James is the Director of the Global Cities Institute (RMIT University) and Director of the United Nations Global Compact, Cities Programme. He is Professor of Globalization in the Globalism Research Centre, on the Council of the Institute of Postcolonial Studies, and a Fellow of the Royal Society of the Arts. He is an editor of *Arena Journal*, as well as an editor/board-member of nine other international journals, including *Globalizations* and *Global Governance*. He has delivered invited addresses in over 20 countries and is author or editor of 24 books including most importantly, *Nation Formation* (Sage, 1996) and *Globalism, Nationalism, Tribalism* (Sage, 2006). His other recent books include *Global Matrix* (co-authored with Tom Nairn, Pluto, 2005) and the first 12 volumes of a projected 16-volume series mapping the field of globalization (Sage, 2006–2010). He has been an advisor to a number of agencies and governments including the Helsinki Process, the Canadian Prime Minister's G20 Forum, the National Economic Advisory Council of Malaysia, and the Commission on Reception, Truth and Reconciliation in East Timor. His work for the Papua New Guinea Minister for Community Development became the basis for their Integrated Community Development Policy.

Contributors ix

Fethi Mansouri is the Director of the Strategic Research Centre for Citizenship and Globalisation, holds a Chair in Migration and Intercultural Studies, School of Humanities and Social Sciences, Deakin University. He is the editor of the highly rated *Journal of Intercultural Studies* (Routledge) and an expert advisor to the United Nations (Alliance of Civilisations) on cultural diversity and intercultural relations. His recent authored and co-edited publications include *Political Islam and Human Security* (co-edited with Shahram Akbarzadeh, Cambridge Scholars Publishing, 2008), *Islam and Political Violence: Muslim Diaspora and Radicalism in the West* (co-edited with Shahram Akbarzadeh, Tauris Academic Studies, 2007), *Identity, Education, and Belonging: Arab and Muslim Youth in Contemporary Australia* (co-authored with Sally Percival Wood, Melbourne University Press, 2008), *Youth Identity and Migration: Culture, Values and Social Connectedness* (Diversity, 2009), *Australia and the Middle East: A Frontline Relationship* (Tauris Academic Studies, 2011, second edition); and *Migration, Citizenship and Intercultural Relations: Looking Through the Lens of Social Inclusion* (co-edited with Michele Lobo, Ashgate, 2011). His recent books include: *Muslims in the West and the Challenges of Belonging* (co-edited with Vince Marotta, Melbourne University Press, 2012); and *The Arab Revolutions in Context: Socio-Political Implications for the Middle East and Beyond* (co-authored with Benjamin Isakhan and Shahram Akbarzadeh, Melbourne University Press, 2012). His forthcoming book is entitled *Reframing Multiculturalism for the 21st Century* (University of Toronto Press, 2013). His 2004 book *Lives in Limbo: Voices of Refugees under Temporary Protection* (co-authored with Michael Leach, University of New South Wales Press, 2004) was short-listed for the 2004 Human Rights Medals and Awards.

Robert Mason is a Lecturer in History in the School of Humanities and Communication at the University of Southern Queensland. His research is in the areas of Australian multiculturalism, Hispanic populations in the Asia-Pacific, and legacies of trauma and loss in the public space. His most recent publications investigate transnational social movements in local contexts, focusing particularly on the effect of political memories on Australia's Spanish-speaking migrant communities. With Anna Hayes, he is the editor of the forthcoming book *Cultures in Refuge: Seeking Sanctuary in Modern Australia* (Ashgate, 2012).

Anne McNevin is a Research Fellow at the Globalism Research Centre, RMIT University, Melbourne. She is author of *Contesting Citizenship: Irregular Migrants and New Frontiers of the Political* (Columbia University Press, 2011), co-editor of *Global Ideologies and Urban Landscapes* (Routledge, 2011) and associate editor of the journal *Citizenship Studies*. Her research is focused on irregular migration as a window into the contemporary transformation of geopolitics, security, governance and citizenship. She has published articles in *Globalizations*, *Review of International Studies*, *Local-Global*, and *Australian Journal of Political Science*.

Eileen Pittaway is the Director of the Centre for Refugee Research, University of New South Wales, Sydney, Australia. In the past decade she has conducted research, provided training to refugees, UN and NGO staff in refugee camps and urban settings, acted as technical advisor to a number of projects and evaluated humanitarian and development projects in Kenya, Thailand, Ethiopia, Bougainville, Egypt and Sri Lanka. She was also involved in tsunami relief projects in Sri Lanka. This work has been variously funded by UNHCR, UNFPA, UNIFEM, the Ford Foundation, the Japan Foundation, the Asia Development Bank, the Australian Research Council and public subscriptions.

Sophia Rainbird is an anthropologist who specialises in the field of migration and in particular, asylum seekers and refugees and their interaction with host communities. She is predominantly interested in how settlement services and integration are conceptualized and implemented, and how broader themes of narrative, ethnicity, whiteness, identity and social justice intersect. Sophia has conducted ethnographic research with applied outcomes for NGOs, government and ethnic community groups in both in Australia and the UK. She holds the position of Senior Postdoctoral Research Fellow at Central Queensland University's Appleton Institute in South Australia.

Susanne Schech lectures in development studies and is the director of the Centre for Development Studies at Flinders University, South Australia. She has researched and published on the social and cultural geographies of race and whiteness in Australia over more than a decade. In recent years she has studied these issues in the context of refugees from developing countries settling in Australia.

Niklaus Steiner is the Director of the Center for Global Initiatives at the University of North Carolina – Chapel Hill (USA). A native of Switzerland who moved to the US in his youth, Steiner has had the good fortune of moving between cultures all his life, and this experience shapes his academic focus. His research and teaching interests include migration, refugees, nationalism, and citizenship, and his publications include *Arguing About Asylum: The Complexity of Refugee Debates in Europe* (St. Martin's, 2000); *The Problems of Protection: UNHCR, Refugees, and Human Rights* (co-edited with Niklaus Steiner, Mark Gibney and Gil Loescher, Routledge 2003), *Regionalism in the Age of Globalism* (co-edited with Lothar Hoennighausen, Marc Frey, James Peacock, and Niklaus Steiner, Wisconsin, 2005); and *The Age of Apology: The West Confronts its Past* (co-edited with Mark Gibney, Rhoda E. Howard-Hassmann, Jean-Marc Coicaud and Niklaus Steiner, University of Pennsylvania Press, 2008). His most recent book *International Migration and Citizenship Today* (Routledge, 2009) is a textbook aimed at facilitating classroom discussions on admission and membership.

Sara Wills is a Senior Lecturer in Australian Studies in the School of Historical and Philosophical Studies, and currently the Associate Dean (Advancement) in the Faculty of Arts. She has been the Director of the Australian Centre (2009–2010) and, alongside her academic career, has worked in museums and publishing. She has published on refugee issues and Australian national memory, immigration and Australian historiography, memory and British migration, representations of migrancy and national identity, the performance and cultural dynamics of Britishness and on other issues relating to migration and multiculturalism. She has most recently contributed chapters to the international edited collections *Places of Pain and Shame: Dealing with 'Difficult' Heritage* (Routledge, 2009) and *Diasporas: Concepts, Identities, Intersections* (Zed Books, 2010).

Detailed synopsis

1 Securing twenty-first century societies

Anna Hayes and Robert Mason

The chapters in this collection explore differing approaches to migrants' insecurity, emphasizing the mutually constituted notions of both individual and social attitudes to security for formerly displaced populations. Rather than reprise state-based approaches to security, contributors instead consider experiences of insecurity that recognize the dual importance of both legal borders and less-visible barriers to community engagement. Under the influence of new technologies, constructs of community and security have undergone profound change throughout the Global North. Many of the authors highlight an increasing tension throughout the first decade of the twenty-first century, whereby states' tightened control of international borders has rendered participation in local communities increasingly fraught and contested. Therefore, local spaces have become vital sites, providing space in which to enact identifications with multiple localities beyond that immediately experienced. As multiple contributors argue, this has had a profound implication for modern forms of civic identity and community inclusion.

Underlying this tension are the substantial changes in the nature of world migration that have occurred in recent decades. Following the Second World War, the dominant image of the irregular migrant in the Global North was of white refugees, displaced from their homes by the devastation of war and the onset of the Iron Curtain. Many of these Europeans settled within states of the Global North, such as Australia, where they were welcomed as valuable additions to their hosts' credentials as cultivated nations. By the end of the twentieth century, this image had given way to one of irregular migrants from the Global South seeking to gain entry into developed nations. Such arrivals raised new questions regarding the relationship between asylum and pragmatic concepts of nation-building, focusing attention on appropriate responses to the presence of visibly different and disadvantaged minorities in local communities.

Adding to this, the accelerating technological revolution that continued throughout the first decade of the twenty-first century has transformed questions about how best to ensure visibly different migrants are effectively integrated in local communities. Residents' negotiation of multiple identities, including those associated with spaces not directly experienced physically, has become central to contemporary Australian citizenship. The social norms governing this process may be seen as a newly emerging form of cosmopolitan ethics, albeit one rooted in local space, but which is at odds with the ascribed ethnicities of multiculturalism. Rather than reinforce a static notion of ethnic identity, an ethics grounded in local experiences of cosmopolitan sentiment emphasizes the fluidity of identity and the inevitable presence of difference in local space.

It follows that traditional notions of Australian nation-building and community inclusion are increasingly challenged within local spaces. As James (2006) intimates, globalization resulted in an intensified awareness of difference at thresholds of passing into the local community. The tension lies in formulating a shared community based on cosmopolitan sentiment, but which does not negate deeply held historical memories for either host or immigrant, as described here by Damousi (Chapter 3). In an era of increasingly fluid migration and identification, this demands renewed emphasis on cultural citizenship rather than increasingly arbitrary parameters of legal citizenship. With cosmopolitan sentiment, these new forms of community extend beyond local space to encompass the notion of human rights so that irregular migrants need not be legal citizens to be full members of the local community (Kymlicka 2003). As Steiner discusses (in Chapter 2), such tensions are at the heart of the Global North's attempts to reconstitute community and security in the twenty-first century.

Human insecurity and the state

New formulations of citizenship and everyday multiculturalism are pressing and frequently appear to be in contrast to the continued state-based rhetoric of governments and border protection. According to the United Nations High Commissioner for Refugees (UNHCR 2010), current statistics on migration movements demonstrate that 220 million of the world's 6.7 billion people are living outside of their country of birth. Following a number of conflicts worldwide, there was a peak in the number of refugees globally in 1995. Since this time, refugee numbers have decreased and the UNHCR (2011: 5) estimated at the close of 2010 there were 15.4 million refugees worldwide (this figure included 4.82 million Palestinian refugees under the care of the United Nations Relief and Works Agency for Palestine Refugees in the Near East). Additionally, 837,500 applications for asylum remained under consideration and there were 27.5 million internally displaced peoples (UNHCR 2011). Thus, the number of refugees remains small in a global sense and state responses can be construed as disproportionate to the challenges posed by displaced populations. In considering displaced populations, the authors of the collection have addressed groups as diverse as asylum seekers, recognized refugees, and those who have been obliged to leave their home in order to seek sanctuary. Factors prompting their decision to leave their home country could include economic or environmental crisis, social or political violence, and situations in which conflict affects their human security.

Each of the contributors in this collection reflected on the changing relationship between the individual and the state. Their contributions have aligned with the human security paradigm by situating the individual as the primary reference point for their discussions of security. Human security provides a useful theoretical base for the analysis of displaced people and social inclusion. Using the United Nations' definition of human security, which is based on the twin notions of 'freedom from fear' and 'freedom from want', human security incorporates components such as economic, food, health, environmental, personal, community, and political security (United Nations Development Programme, UNDP, 1995: 229). This definition asserts that human security is centred on four key characteristics; namely that it is a universal concern, its components are interdependent, it is best achieved through prevention rather than intervention, and it is people-centred (UNDP 1995: 232–4).

The human security paradigm provides a more inclusive approach to considerations of migration, since the referent of security is the individual rather than the state. The theory offers a powerful critique to statist responses to displaced populations, particularly if states' responses deliberately contravene or hinder the pursuit of human rights or refugee conventions in the name of state security. The Commission on Human Security (2003) rightly argued that migration is necessary for many people to attain or to protect their human security. Given the process of forced migration may involve fleeing conflict situations and reliance on people smugglers, however, those involved may temporarily experience heightened human insecurity. By adopting a human security approach to the movement of peoples across borders, migration appears as one component for the attainment of individual security. This places it in contradistinction to the statist approach, which views displaced people as potentially disruptive threats to the security of the state.

While there are undeniable similarities between refugees and irregular migrants, there are specific legal obligations towards refugees that have been articulated by the UNHCR. Refugees experience particular vulnerabilities above and beyond those of economic migrants. Frequently lacking established networks and social capital to settle in their new homes, they are rendered temporarily reliant on the state. According to Edwards (2009), the people-centred focus taken by human security theorists can offer a more holistic approach to state responses to refugees and non-citizens. Sen (2002) agrees, arguing that states' vested interests are often diametrically opposed to the interests of the individual refugee and rarely foreground an ethics based on notions of fairness. Edwards highlights that feminist scholars have long questioned the state-based focus that has dominated international relations and that human security has much in common with development discourse central to a holistic response.

Despite the corrective offered by human security's focus on the individual, the framework has some flaws with regards to the security of internationally displaced populations. While gender issues have been given some attention, the defining documents on human security, such as the UNDP article 'Redefining Security: the Human Dimension' (1995) and the *Human Security Now* report (Commission on Human Security 2003), are not wholly inclusive of a gendered analysis. The absence of a genuine effort to consider how men and women's security is affected is important, and human security discourse and policy documents must include gender as a mainstream rather than a secondary consideration. Forced migrants may experience vulnerabilities on the basis of their gender at every stage of their migration experience.

As Pittaway discusses in this collection (Chapter 10), women and children have a heightened vulnerability to rape during times of war and conflict, and this has long-term implications for their settlement. Rape in times of war and conflict is not only perpetrated by military forces as a weapon, but can also be perpetrated by predatory members of the civilian population and by peace-keeping forces (Hynes and Cardoza 2000). Sexual assault against women and children is not limited to combatants, nor is it limited to pre-displacement. Recent studies have shown that internally displaced or refugee women and children are also vulnerable to sexual assault and exploitation by peacekeepers, humanitarian and aid workers, and community leaders (Ferris 2007). A combined study by UNHCR and Save the Children UK, conducted in 2002, found sexual exploitation was widespread in refugee camps, with boys and girls being victimized from five years and over. Girls and young women aged between 13 and 18 were the most vulnerable and those perpetrating the violence acted with impunity (Ferris 2007). Thus, female refugees face heightened insecurity due to their sex, as it can make them particularly vulnerable to sexual abuse and assault pre-displacement, en route to safer destinations and in refugee camps.

In line with the work of other scholars aligned with human security approaches (Love 2011), Pittaway goes on to argue that the effects of this violence can cause an erosion of 'the sense of self and hope for the future' among affected women and girls. Indeed, women continue to be impacted by trauma from exposure to sexual violence and abuse during their settlement process. The ongoing impacts of this trauma can directly affect women's ability to form relationships based on trust, frequently impairing the relationships within family. This can range from the family not understanding the victim's emotions if they do not know about the rape, through to the rape being viewed as a source of family shame and dishonour. Male authority and control within the family relationship may hinder victims' access to their social networks and other supports for the traumas caused. In addition to these gender-based vulnerabilities, women, like men, experience vulnerabilities as they seek to cross international borders. This is largely because a statist approach remains central to the construction of border control regimes.

Securing the border

According to Dauvergne, in an increasingly globalized world, laws controlling the movement of people across borders represent 'the last bastion of sovereignty' (2008: 169). On the one hand, states find themselves obliged to facilitate the flow of ideas and capital as part of a post-Washington consensus, while on the other, the state acts to control the flow of populations across its border. This tendency has become particularly pronounced among the nations of the Global

North, where so-called 'non-entrée regimes' (Chimini 1998) restrict entry to safety and services within the state's borders. Therefore, for displaced people, a state's border both becomes physical obstacle and site of desire.

Against this backdrop, the state's border has become a site both of legal distinction and of culturally contested hybridity. The border is simultaneously present within wider society as the point at which the nation, and those excluded from it, is negotiated and imagined to be determined. The effects of this negotiation resonate throughout society as primary determinants for displaced population's sense of social inclusion or 'otherness'. The fact that so much of this negotiation is assumed to occur at the geographical border reflects the continued influence of statist approaches to concepts of migrant security, which fail to reflect the twenty-first century reality of irregular migrants' presence or notions of contemporary community.

Conscious of the need to be seen to defend the border, and aware of community concern regarding signs of weakness at the border, governments are swift to deploy the rhetoric of national security against irregular migrants, particularly those who are characterized as entering the state illegally. As Babacan and Babacan argue in this collection (Chapter 9), the increasingly prominent rhetoric of border security post-9/11 has focused attention on social threats that originate from outside the state. Displaced people have found themselves victim of the increased tightening of entry across the border. However, the increased rhetoric of 'homeland security' has also profoundly impacted on visibly different residents within the developed states of the Global North. This has had an acute effect on such migrants' lived experience within communities and has tended to prompt an intensified articulation of the resident society's fear of the 'other'.

Within the Global North, Muslim immigrants have experienced these effects with particular intensity following 9/11 and have become increasingly vulnerable by virtue of their perceived otherness and the discourse of state security (Kabir 2007). The consequences of 9/11 restricted Muslim immigrants access to public space as some members of the wider community felt enabled to give voice to anti-Muslim prejudice. This not only fractured a sense of personal security but also reduced their capacity for full civic participation. In response, and as discussed by Mansouri in this collection (Chapter 8), Muslim residents have sought new ways to affirm their various identities that integrate local and transnational contexts. New configurations of solidarity and support have been articulated in local and online spaces as communities seek security. Despite these acts, their vulnerability demonstrates the correlation of border security with both individual and community security.

Gender adds an additional complexity to the various insecurities and perceived otherness experienced by displaced populations as they settle in the Global North. As Pittaway and Pittaway (2004) demonstrated in previous discussions, refugee women assume or are ascribed multiple subaltern identities during their settlement. Each identity may compound the discrimination they experience and affect their ability to participate within the wider community. For example, female African refugees in Australia may experience race, gender, and class-based discrimination, all of which threaten an affirmative female identity. While the compounded discrimination may aggravate their vulnerability, 'intersectionality' between marginalized groups also offers opportunity for solidarity. Displaced women continue to experience particular insecurities based on their sex throughout their settlement in new homes. This can include traditional expectations of their domestic role, which may prevent them from engaging in social or civic life in their new community. Relegation to the domestic sphere may also limit their capacity for language acquisition, hampering their ability to access social support services provided by the state. As this collection has discussed, such barriers to engagement in civic society must necessarily complicate notions of vulnerable migrants' experience of inclusion in local communities.

Securing Australia

Australia has experienced a particularly forthright state response with regards to displaced populations and asylum seekers, which has directly impacted on social inclusion. This is exemplified by indefinite mandatory detention and the opening of off-shore processing centres in response to refugees arriving by boat without visas. By processing refugees off-shore, the government has been able to restrict and control access to mainland Australia by non-authorized boat arrivals. In common with other states within the Global North, this has reinforced the notion of the border as a defensive line that needs to be tightly controlled as part of a necessary 'non-entrée regime'. While there has been a bipartisan reluctance to receive refugees arriving by boat since at least the 1970s, the introduction of the 'Pacific Solution' (2001 to 2007) has been the clearest articulation of Australia's political determination to prevent asylum seekers reaching the Australian mainland.

Reflecting Australia's continued state-centric approach, the Pacific Solution consisted of three main strategies. First, in 2001 the Federal Parliament passed both the *Migration Amendment (Excision from Migration Zone) Act* and the *Migration Amendment (Excision from Migration Zone) (Consequential Provisions) Act*. These changes resulted in some external territories being excised from Australia's migration zone, meaning that asylum seekers who land there had no right to apply for a visa and Australia had no obligation to grant them temporary or permanent visas. The territories excised included Christmas Island, Ashmore Island, Cartier Islands, and Cocos Islands. In effect, the strategy distanced potential asylum seekers from accessing pathways to the Australia community and limited the duty of care beholden on the Australian state.

The second strategy employed under the Pacific Solution was the involvement of the Australian Defence Force, known as Operation Relex, to detect boats transporting asylum seekers into Australian waters. As Wills discusses in Chapter 5 of this collection, this strategy has endangered individual security without addressing the fundamental causes of those individuals' movement. Once detected, the third strategy of the policy involved asylum seekers being sent to Christmas Island (or other detention centres in countries such as Papua

New Guinea and Nauru), where their claims for asylum were assessed. New Zealand also received some asylum seekers for processing at this time. While controlling the border received substantial support from mainstream Australians, the Pacific Solution was highly contentious policy in the international political landscape. Indeed, it led to strong international criticism that Australia was not upholding its international obligations and was aggravating the personal insecurity of the displaced persons.

The Pacific Solution was recognized to have wrought significant damage to asylum seekers and to local community relations and was consequently abandoned in 2007 by the incoming Australian prime minister, Kevin Rudd. However, a rapid increase of unauthorized boat arrivals occurred the following year. Amid escalating fears among the electorate, concerns for the integrity of the border returned to the fore and support for Rudd's humanitarian reforms fell away. Faced with this collapse in political support, Rudd sought to reframe the question of 'state border security' as an ethical question focused on people smuggling. The regional solution to people smuggling that was initiated in 2002, known as the 'Bali Process', continued to receive bipartisan support, but Rudd's ethical frame has since eroded and there has been a return to the state border security paradigm.

Frequent invocations of the border and vilification of asylum seekers have tended to frame the presence of irregular migrants and refugees in terms of legality, criminality, and threat. Within an Australian nation where whiteness forms an important component of historical memory, this threat is nonetheless more usually constituted as moral rather than physical. Indeed, Neumann (2004) has shown that humanitarianism has only ever been a peripheral issue to Australia's migration programmes. The presence of displaced migrants and rapid social change form part of an ongoing tension in the construction of communities and power relations. While there is a general recognition of the moral obligation to provide temporary humanitarian aid to those deemed needy, this rarely constitutes full inclusion within the wider Australian community.

Within Australia, the presence of visibly different migrants has continued to increase, challenging Australians' sense of national community. Sections of Australia have experienced what Castells (2004) termed accentuated 'resistance identities', due in part to the economic globalization that occurred in the 1980s. This has been accompanied by disorientation caused by the legitimate presence of 'historical others' within the national borders, prompting many established Australians to question their own cultural security. In this collection, Schech and Rainbird (Chapter 7) demonstrate the impact of changing social discourse regarding race and multiculturalism on visibly different migrants who had not previously considered themselves to be marginalized. As they discuss, vulnerable migrants have viewed these occasional, but public, expressions of hostility towards non-Caucasians with alarm, resulting in a profoundly reduced sense of community security.

Australia has invested considerable prestige in its multicultural framework as a means of preventing migrants' social exclusion, but notions of 'intercultural citizenship' remain underdeveloped. Although Kymlicka's (1995) work on the collective rights of minorities has limited resonance within Australia, the lack of attention paid to his comments on the importance of 'interculturalism at the level of the individual citizen' is noteworthy. In part this derives from the function of Australian multiculturalism, which has tended to sustain the dominance of the white imaginary by marginalizing other experiences (Hage 1998). Thus, while legal naturalization remains relatively straightforward for many migrants, identification within the national community remains more problematic for those who are visibly different. Australian citizenship remains predicated on replicating characteristics of white Anglo-Celtic heritage and many of the country's white citizens struggle to articulate new ways of cultural thinking that do not imply a loss of their own culture (Hage 1998). Such sentiment points to Australia's relative failure to develop a dynamic model of citizenship, one that is responsive to the presence of difference in local space, particularly as this has become commonplace in the twenty-first century.

Securing civic space

Strengthened public support for Australia's statist approach to border control is closely connected to the media's portrayal of displaced populations and asylum seekers. Increasingly, the dominant media portrayal has communicated a surge of people travelling to Australia from its regional neighbours. Their movement without visas has led the public to associate them with illegality, threats to national security, and the accusation of being 'queue jumpers'. Christmas Island, and the people processed there, garners significant media and political attention within Australia. Highly provocative headlines communicate to the electorate that the country is threatened by a horde of asylum seekers, arriving by boat without visas. Examples include 'Invasion – Boat people armada sails for Australia' (McPhedran 2010), 'Navy swoops on more boat people' (Reardon 1999), and 'Refugee pool threat to Australia' (Heinrichs 1999), combined with political slogans such as '[S]top the boats', used by Tony Abbott, leader of the opposition Liberal Party (Abbott 2010). Such statements should be viewed in the wider global context of accelerated globalization and changes to sovereignty that has been discussed throughout the collection. Such changes, accompanied by an increased connectedness through innovations in communication technologies, have led to increasingly problematic questions of how to formulate new expressions of civic incorporation and everyday multiculturalism within Australia.

In common with most other states, membership of Australia's national community is most formally defined through being designated as 'citizen'. Ideally this is taken to encompass some sense of belonging and capacity to engage, although substantial cohorts of the population, such as women, may be disadvantaged within this. The notion of 'identity citizenship' adds greater depth to Australian civic membership, encompassing a sense of shared belonging and affinity with the body politic. The relationship between legal and identity citizenship has become increasingly complex in multicultural Australia. It is certainly possible for a long-term resident to lack citizenship, for example, but to identify with the body politic. Conversely, and significantly, it is also possible for a citizen to identify with sentiments deemed inappropriate by federal, state or local authorities. The globalized movement of people and real-time international communication has challenged traditional notions of citizenship and demanded that multicultural advocates recognize the new formulations of identity that exist beyond the relatively static conceptions of legal citizenship. As Ferres discusses in Chapter 4, the local space offers important opportunities to reflect on dynamic formulations of community and to integrate multiple narratives of belonging.

Transnationalism offers further opportunities to challenge the power structures inherent in Australian civic space. There is a legacy of a highly masculinized and militarized sense of national identity in Australia that has historically fixated on perceived threat and fear of the other. The ongoing legacy of this has led to visibly different migrants experiencing disorientation as they seek to enter a public space. Within Australia's multicultural framework, the 'ethnicisation' (Humphrey 1998) of debates relating to the migrant presence can potentially accentuate migrant women's vulnerability by reasserting traditional patriarchal structures. Increasingly, however, communication technologies and globalization offer women the opportunities to develop intersectional relationships from within domestic spaces. Drawing on similar experiences, developing networks of support and freely accessing information provides women with the capacity to learn how to enact civic values in local contexts. Through the development of intersectional interests, therefore, vulnerable migrants, such as women, are able to transcend the multicultural framework that may inadvertently confine them.

Global communications technologies have revolutionized the Australian public sphere, producing a space that has become less hierarchical in its knowledge and information-sharing. This has led to more points of access for the general population in the constitution of the public sphere, albeit requiring digital skills and resources to participate fully in this new domain. This development has profound implications for contemporary patterns of settlement and local community experiences, potentially enabling a more democratic and participatory model of civic activity. Within Australia, as with much of the Global North, public concern regarding these debates has focused on Islamic immigrants, often castigated as a radicalized and threatening social other. The Internet has provided information and facilitated discourses that enable users to draw parallels across multiple locales, suggesting moral and practical lessons from one place are replicable in another. For populations fearful of domestic terrorism, the accessibility of online radical sites has shocked many Australians (including long-term Muslim Australians). Yet, questions of transnationalism and facilitating sites of identification need not be problematic for sustaining inclusive local communities. In addition to reducing a sense of isolation, access to such sites can provide important skills for citizenship and awareness of the subjectivity of ethics and lived experience off-line.

As Australian citizenship is progressively reconceptualized into various disaggregated acts of cultural and community affirmation, its enactment at critical localities has been revisited. Although migrants' civic activities are likely to focus on their immediate surroundings, they are increasingly able to reference multiple localities beyond state borders. While these experiences may increase migrants' capacity to engage in the civic life of their new locale, it also poses new questions for settlement as populations are influenced by civic models from beyond the border and seek to participate in events overseas. It is no longer sufficient to see migration and citizenship as conditioned by statist assumptions of loyalty and circumscribed experience. Instead, everyday interactions in civic spaces point to important new directions for multiculturalism's development. By thinking about inclusive relationships in local spaces, rather than institutionalized states, new opportunities for intersectional solidarity and community security may be constructed that will more fully incorporate the disparate needs of displaced populations who seek residency in the Global North.

Competing dynamics of settlement

This collection is predicated on the stages, and corresponding experiences, of migrants' settlement in their new homes. Its narrative differs from traditional approaches by taking migrants' individual perspectives as its reference point, rather than privileging the views of states and international organizations. In doing so, the collection opens up a space in which to consider new formulations of migrant security. In conceptualizing three broad stages of migrant settlement, the book seeks to trace the tension between local space and transnational sites of identification and discourse. To do so, it draws on scholars from diverse disciplinary backgrounds who consider migrants' experiences within three interconnected stages of their settlement.

Questions of settlement are particularly pertinent within the countries of the Global North, as they seek new formulations of national identity and community inclusion. The desire to mitigate the tensions of multicultural societies has created a tendency for strict border control and the reassertion of the principles of non-entrée at the border. Steiner begins the collection by considering irregular migrants within the context of the Global North. On the one hand, he discusses asylum seekers and the problems of *non-refoulement* within the European Union, highlighting the duty of care towards those within the state's border. On the other hand, he juxtaposes the European experience with the presence of irregular immigrants within the US in order to demonstrate the need for pathways to legal citizenship and a more wide-ranging social inclusion. These questions have broad application throughout the Global North and for Australia, which provides the case study for the remainder of the chapters.

The first part, 'Receiving strangeness', explores the effects of migrants' early arrival in their new homes. The three authors seek to reclaim migrants' personal narratives in order to better appreciate how their past experiences influence their ongoing reception. Joy Damousi's chapter begins the section by demonstrating how the legacies of war trauma affect individuals' capacity to comprehend their new homes and personal biographies. Damousi focuses on the oft-overlooked impact of the Greek Civil War on the very large Greek Diaspora living in Australia. Her piece gives voice to migrants' memories of traumatic events that are frequently displaced from public space. Significantly, her chapter highlights the inter-generational construction of memories within immigrant communities, and the devastating impact on children's sense of personal security in their new homes.

Kay Ferres approaches the question of narrating migrant inclusion from the perspective of local civic space and museums. Considering how to structure a public space that might foster tolerance, she discusses ways to create museums that might reflect on the stories Damousi has identified as lacking public resonance. Ferres situates her discussion of museums within the context of the recognized importance of democratic communication, which facilitates the sharing of different narratives, and sees museums as key sites of local reconciliation and civic strengthening. Migrants' presence in exhibitions would not, in Ferres piece, be defined by their otherness and exoticism, but rather by their legitimate stake in a public space defined by tolerance and difference.

Sara Wills' chapter offers a substantially different perspective on how the construction of public space can affect migrants' security. Focusing on the well-publicized Australian experiences of Cornelia Rau and Vivienne Alvarez Solon, Wills demonstrates the importance of fostering understanding within communities rather than stoking divisive nationalist discourse that alienates migrants. As Wills shows, such debate threatens to cloud the real vulnerabilities experienced by migrants and, in particular, female migrants. The cases of Rau and Alvarez Solon demonstrate the need to foster community empathy, and the importance of effect, if inclusive civic spaces are to be constructed.

The second part shifts the collection's emphasis from the intersecting realms of personal biography and civic space. In 'Negotiating integration', authors consider the spaces in which individual migrants seek to enact and attain a sense of security. Paul James and Anne McNevin's chapter opens the section by viewing Australia within the context of an increasingly interconnected Global North. Taking irregular migrants as their focus, they look at the intersection of individuals' security with material inequality and embeds this relationship in local spaces. Developing the position of authors in the previous section, James and McNevin disrupt traditional notions of state security to refocus attention on the importance of migrants' everyday experiences in the creation of secure local civic spaces.

Susanne Schech and Sophia Rainbird focus their analysis of how migrants negotiate their new settlement by looking at two case studies in Australia and the United Kingdom. Schech and Rainbird demonstrate the social importance of the label 'refugee', and its complex relationship with migrants' visible difference. Notwithstanding the differences between Australia and the United Kingdom, the chapter points to shared shifts away from the rhetoric of multiculturalism as government attempt new ways to generate stable societies. Importantly for the authors, such a shift remains reliant on cultural literacy in order to mitigate racism and disorientation in local populations.

Fethi Mansouri takes many of the findings in Schech and Rainbird's chapter and applies them within a framework of transnational practices. Building on an emerging scholarship that integrates local and online civic spaces, Mansouri questions the levels of transnational identification experienced by Muslim citizens in multiethnic cities in Australia, France and the United Kingdom. His findings point to the fluid negotiation of cultural and religious identities within a context of heightened tension and social anxiety. The tension between non-Muslims' frequent fear of Islam and reservations about multiculturalism places renewed emphasis on the importance of the local belonging despite transnational practices.

The collection's final section, 'Securing long-term belonging', considers migrants' ongoing search for a sense of security in the medium to long-term. Hurriyet Babacan and Alperhan Babacan discuss the changing relationship between the construction of states, and the socialized articulation of racism and multiculturalism. The authors question an individualistic and neoliberal approach to multiculturalism, arguing for a reconceptualization of the state's role in migrant welfare and security. Like other authors Babacan and Babacan point to the importance of public discourses that vilify visibly different residents, but also to migrants' frequent vulnerability in public space. Without denying the role of individual identities, the chapter argues for the importance of group identity in a multicultural framework in order to better consolidate groups and protect them from perceptions of otherness and threat.

Eileen Pittaway continues the analysis of how to consolidate a sense of belonging in her focus on refugees. She examines the experience of resettled refugees and asylum seekers living in Australia and argues that successful resettlement is predicated on both a climate of social inclusion, and structures that facilitate both social inclusion and citizenship. Pittaway argues that such frameworks are necessary as they ensure the centrality of human well-being and self-determination. Furthermore, such a framework is important as it is focused on entitlement, rather than charity, and articulates the specific duties of governments and service providers. This enables resettled refugees both the potential and willingness to contribute significantly to Australian society.

All contributors point to migrants' diverse experiences of insecurity, and to the increasing characterization of visibly different migrants as irregular and potential threats to state security. Public debate and discourse can be profoundly destabilizing to migrants, limiting their capacity to pursue connections with society that can safeguard a sense of security and offer recognition of past experiences. The collection argues for the centrality of local civic spaces as key locales where diverse practices of citizenship can be enacted. In this way, the immediate locality need not be constructed in opposition to transnational identification, but rather as the site at which tensions are resolved.

Conclusion

The study of migration has been transformed in the twenty-first century. Globalization has radically altered the movement of people throughout the globe and international migration has become increasingly visible. At the same time, rapid changes in technology have altered how irregular migrants may experience local inclusion. The authors in this collection have all explored differing approaches to migrants' insecurity and experiences of inclusion or 'otherness'. In doing so, they have considered experiences of insecurity that recognize the dual importance of both legal borders and less-visible barriers to community engagement. Citizens' social experiences and experience of citizenship have transformed over the past decade. The disaggregation of citizenship has become progressively more pronounced as diverse social networks reach across and beyond the borders of the nation state. At the same time, increasing focus has been placed on the enactment of citizenship within the immediate physical locale. This has the effect of cultivating social relations that inculcate Western notions of civic values, nonetheless significantly influenced by the enmeshment of different cultural practices into how the host societies imagine themselves to be.

Bibliography

Abbott, T. (2010) 'Federal election statement: a message from Tony Abbott', Liberal National Party.

Anderson, B. (2006) *Imagined Communities: Reflections on the Origin and Spread of Nationalism*, 2nd edn, London: Verso.

Basch, L, Schiller, N. and Szanton Blanc, C. (1993) *Nations Unbound: Transnational Projects, Postcolonial Predicaments, and Deterritorialized Nation-States*, Langhorne: Gordon and Breach.

Castells, M. (2004) *The Power of Identity*, Malden: Blackwell.

Chimini, B.S. (1998) 'The geopolitics of refugee studies: a view from the South', *Journal of Refugee Studies*, 11(4): 350–74.

Commission on Human Security (2003) *Human Security Now*, New York: United Nations Publications.

Dauvergne, C. (2008) *Making People Illegal: What Globalization Means for Migration and Law*, Cambridge: Cambridge University Press.

Edwards, A. (2009) 'Human security and the rights of refugees: transcending the territorial and disciplinary borders', *Michigan Journal of International Law*, 30: 763–807.

Ferris, E. (2007) 'Abuse of power: sexual exploitation of refugee women and girls', *Signs: Journal of Women in Culture and Society*, 32(3): 584–91.

Hage, G. (1998) *White Nation: Fantasies of White Supremacy in a Multicultural Society*, Sydney: Pluto Press.

Heinrichs, P. (1999) 'Refugee pool threat to Australia', *The Sunday Age*, 14 November.

Hollifield, J.F. (ed.) (2000) *The Politics of International Migration: How We Can Bring the State Back In*, New York: Routledge.

Humphrey, M. (1998) *Islam, Multiculturalism and Transnationalism: From the Lebanese Diaspora*, London: The Centre for Lebanese Studies in association with I.B. Tauris.

Hynes, M. and Cardoza, B. (2000) 'Sexual violence against refugee women', *Journal of Women's Health and Gender-Based Medicine*, 9(8): 819–23.

James, P. (2006) *Globalism, Nationalism Tribalism: Bringing Theory Back In*, London: Sage.

Kabir, N. (2007) 'Muslims in Australia: the double edge of terrorism', *Journal of Ethnic and Migration Studies*, 33(8): 1277–97.

Kymlicka, W. (1995) *Multicultural Citizenship: A Liberal Theory of Minority Rights*, Oxford: Oxford University Press.

Kymlicka, W. (2003) 'Immigration, citizenship, multiculturalism: exploring the links', *The Political Quarterly*, 74(1): 195–208.

Love, M.C. (2011) 'People on the move. Refugees, IDPS, and migrants', in M.C. Love (ed.) *Beyond Sovereignty: Issues for a Global Agenda*, 4th edn, Boston: Wadsworth.

McPhedran, I. (2010) 'Invasion – Boat people armada sails for Australia', *Sydney Daily Telegraph*, 24 July.

Neumann, K. (2004) *Refuge Australia: Australia's Humanitarian Record*, Sydney: UNSW Press.

Pittaway, A. and Pittaway, E.E. (2004) 'Refugee woman: a dangerous label', *The Australian Journal of Human Rights*, June: 119–36.

Putnam, R.D. (2000) *Bowling Alone: The Collapse and Revival of American Community*, New York: Simon & Schuster.

Reardon, D. (1999) 'Navy swoops on more boat people', *The Age*, 8 November.

Sen, A. (2002) 'Justice across borders', in P. De Greiff and C. Cronin (eds), *Global Justice and Transnational Politics: Essays on the Moral and Political Challenges of Globalization*, Cambridge: MIT Press.

United Nations Development Programme (UNDP) (1995) 'Redefining security: the human dimension', *Current History*, 94(592): 229–36.

United Nations High Commissioner for Refugees (UNHCR) (2011) *Global Trends 2010*, June. Available at: www.unhcr.org/4dfa11499.html (accessed 9 November 2011).

United Nations High Commissioner for Refugees (UNHCR) (2010) *Global Report 2009*, June. Available at: www.unhcr.org/4c08f2ee9.html (accessed 15 March 2011).

United Nations High Commissioner for Refugees (UNHCR) and Save the Children UK (2002) Sexual Violence and Exploitation: The Experience of Refugee Children in Liberia, Guinea, and Sierra Leone. Available at: www.savethechildren.org.uk/resources/online-library/sexual-violence-exploitation-the-experience-of-refugee-children-in-guinea-liberia-and-sierra-leone (accessed 14 May 2012).

2 A comparison of asylum seekers in Europe and illegal immigrants in the United States

Niklaus Steiner

Introductory remark

To the important discussions in this book, I would like to offer some thoughts and a warning regarding the marginalization of two types of migrants in Europe and in the US: asylum seekers and illegal immigrants. While, of course, important differences exist between these two, there are also striking similarities. Unlike other migrants, such as those who liberal democracies crave because they make up the 'creative class' (Florida 2006), asylum seekers and illegal immigrants are not actively sought and indeed face considerable barriers to entry. Yet they enter anyway, raising concerns about national security, political stability, economic harm and cultural degradation. And once they have entered, Europe and the US, as liberal democracies, find it surprisingly difficult to either deport them or integrate them. This inability to deal with them satisfactorily leaves liberal democracies frustrated and migrants marginalized. Regrettably, on neither side of the Atlantic does the situation appear near resolution and, in fact, I fear that the US is now in danger of making the same mistake Europe has long made.

Asylum seekers in Europe

As liberal democracies, all European countries readily accept the obligation to grant asylum to refugees. The controversy that has been roiling Europe for well over two decades stems not from this general principle but rather from two specific questions that arise when countries seek to grant asylum. First, what exactly constitutes a refugee worthy of receiving asylum? Second, how should countries fight abuse of the asylum process by people whom they do not consider refugees? While seemingly straightforward on the surface, these two questions are fraught with complexities that have caused much skepticism about and resentment towards asylum seekers, which in turn have led them to feel significantly insecure and marginalized.

European countries all have slightly different processes for determining whether an asylum seeker ought to receive asylum, but the principle is fairly consistent: an asylum seeker applies for asylum and the case is reviewed by a government official who then decides whether asylum should be granted. If asylum is granted, the individual is allowed to remain in the country and is commonly put on the road to citizenship. If asylum is rejected, there is usually an appeals process, although the chance of successfully appealing this negative decision is small. When a final rejection is made, the asylum seeker faces deportation.

However, governments often hesitate to deport rejected asylum seekers for fear of violating the principle of *non-refoulement*, an important international standard that forbids returning rejected asylum seekers back into dangerous situations (see Article 33 of UNHCR 1951). Instead, rejected asylum seekers are often allowed to remain in the country but without the full status and rights given to those who receive asylum. This legal limbo contributes significantly to their marginalization.

Unlike the US, Canada and Australia, which have long been destinations for foreigners, Europe has a long tradition of people emigrating, not immigrating. It does not see itself (and does not want to be seen) as a destination, which therefore makes it difficult to formally immigrate. Precisely because it is so difficult to enter Europe through formal immigration processes, the asylum process has become a roundabout form of immigration and some asylum seekers do indeed misuse it for that purpose. The extent to which it is being used as a form of immigration is central to the controversy over asylum. On the government side, the perspective is generally that the asylum process is heavily abused by those who are not really refugees but rather immigrants and who, if an immigration policy existed, would come through that process. Because of this perspective, European governments have been rejecting the large majority of asylum seekers; in 2009, for example, the EU-27 countries rejected three-quarters of asylum applicants. On the other side, critics of these restrictive government policies acknowledge some abuse of the asylum process but argue that governments exaggerate the amount of abuse in order to impose restrictive policies, which negatively affect genuine refugees.

The asylum process can take months or even years, which raises the question of what to do with the asylum seekers as they await their decisions. One policy has been to allow them to work while they wait, with the justification that this policy allows asylum seekers to help support themselves and relieves the government of some of the welfare costs. Critics of this policy, however, charge that such a policy encourages abuse of the asylum process, because it gives asylum seekers temporary access to the labour market and allows them to earn more money in a few months than in several years at home.

In response to such criticism, governments have also tried to withhold work permits from asylum seekers during the process. This policy, however, leaves asylum seekers with little to do, which in turn fuels charges that asylum seekers are lazy, unproductive and misusing public services. A similar Catch-22 situation arises with regards to housing and public assistance: if the housing of asylum seekers is too nice and assistance too generous, critics argue that this encourages abuse and fuels resentment among citizens, but if these services are too stingy, other critics argue that they are inhumane and a violation of human rights and dignity.

Because of these problems, shortening the time it takes to decide an asylum case has been a major goal of governments. One approach has been to use 'safe country' and 'safe third country' rules. With the former, a government declares a certain country to be free of persecution and anyone applying from that country is rejected out of hand or fast-tracked toward a negative decision. With the latter, a government declares a country through which an asylum seeker came to be a safe third country and deports the asylum seeker back to that country with the argument that the asylum seeker could have applied for asylum there.

Another effort to shorten the asylum process in European countries has been to harmonize their asylum policies. Here the idea is that all countries adopt the same standards and share information about asylum seekers, so that if they are rejected in one country they will be rejected by all. Such harmonization is intended to discourage what is sometimes called 'asylum shopping', whereby an asylum seeker asks for asylum in one country after being rejected in another and repeats this process with the hope of eventually getting it somewhere.

While these policies may well be sensible in principle, critics charge that, in practice, such policies are fraught with pitfalls. Shortening the length of time to make an asylum decision, for example, may mean a rush to judgment and an inability to thoroughly investigate each case. Likewise, declaring a country free from persecution might be done over-zealously by government bureaucrats more eager to reduce their case-load than fairly consider an asylum seeker's claim. Critics argue that at least external parties such as the United Nations High Commissioner for Refugees (UNHCR), the Red Cross, Amnesty International or Human Rights Watch should be involved in deciding which countries are safe. The safe third country principle runs the risk of being an obfuscating trail back to danger. It may indeed be reasonable to send a Pakistani asylum seeker who entered Switzerland through Austria back to Austria to apply for asylum there. But if they did not fly straight from Karachi to Vienna but instead came overland through Hungary, Romania, Bulgaria, Turkey and Iran, which of these third countries is safe enough to guarantee a fair asylum process?

As noted earlier, importantly there is little controversy over whether Europe should grant asylum to refugees; rather the controversy lies over who exactly is a refugee worthy of protection. To understand this controversy, it is noteworthy that European countries all recognize the UNHCR's widely recognized definition of 'refugee', which is laid out in Article 1 of its 1951 Convention. Here, a refugee is defined as any person who 'owing to a well-founded fear of being persecuted for reasons of race, religion, nationality, membership of a particular social group or political opinion, is outside the country of his nationality and is unable or, owing to such fear, is unwilling to avail himself of the protection of that country'. By the end of 2010, about 10.5 million refugees fell under this definition (UNHCR 2010). At first glance, this refugee definition appears to be fairly straightforward but, upon closer examination, it is open to interpretation in several key respects, and this is where the controversy lies.

For example, in order to be granted asylum as a refugee, an individual must only demonstrate a 'well-founded fear' of being persecuted. After all, proof could be fraudulent (scars that an asylum seeker attributes to torture could have been self-inflicted) so it is sufficient for asylum seekers to demonstrate credibly that they have a well-founded fear of persecution. But of course the demonstration of a well-founded fear can also be fraudulent: an asylum seeker could be a good liar who can spin a compelling story and produce tears as well.

Another important aspect of the refugee definition is that, in general, a person seeking asylum must demonstrate an individualized fear of persecution. It is therefore in principle not enough for that person to argue that their minority group was persecuted in another part of the country and that they thought they would be next. The problem with this individualized principle is that persecution can spread rapidly and, by the time they themselves had a well-founded fear of persecution, it may be too late. Important exceptions to this general principle of individualized fear have been made in situations like Bosnia in the 1990s, where large numbers of civilians fled ethnic cleansing. In such cases, European governments tend to acknowledge a threat to an entire group and not insist on examining each case individually.

Furthermore, asylum is meant to protect individuals from abuse by their government and classic cases include journalists tortured for criticizing the president or religious leaders jailed for setting up an underground place of worship. But what if the persecution is committed by non-government actors, whether they be pro-government paramilitary groups (Colombia) or anti-government forces (Pakistan)? In such situations, governments may be unable or unwilling to protect civilians from harm.

And then there are extreme examples like Somalia, which simply has no government to speak of, in which case the question of whether the government can or should offer protection is moot. Such lack of government capacity raises the question of at what point do European governments have the obligation to step in and offer asylum. While some governments argue that civilians who fear persecution by non-state actors should not be given formal refugee status, UNHCR's position is that it is not the origin of the persecution that should be decisive in determining refugee status but, rather, whether a person deserves international protection because it is not available in the country of origin (UNHCR n.d.).

Asylum is especially complicated when considering protecting people being harmed for reasons other than 'race, religion, nationality, membership of a particular social group or political opinion', which raises the question of broadening the definition of a refugee. Among the most commonly mentioned elements that should be included in a broader definition is gender, in order to address gender-based persecution. Advocates for this position argue that asylum should be granted to women who refuse to adhere to social rules, such as dress codes or arranged marriages, or who fear practices such as forced sterilization and abortions, domestic violence, forced prostitution and female genital cutting. Furthermore, some people point out that homosexuals face persecution in numerous countries around the world and that therefore sexual orientation should also be grounds for asylum and be included in the refugee definition.

Broadening the refugee definition further, what about people who are displaced by a dramatic change in their environment? Now, it is perhaps too much to ask European governments to grant asylum to victims of a natural disaster; after all, governments cannot control rainfall and therefore cannot be held responsible for a subsequent drought that kills farmers' crops and forces them to flee their land. But what if a home government is connected to the deterioration of the environment? Take, as an example, Brazil turning a blind eye to illegal gold mining or logging in a remote area of the Amazon rainforest that forces an indigenous people like the Yanomami to change or abandon their traditional way of life. And government policy can be directly responsible for a dramatic change in the environment, as is the case with the Three Gorges Dam project in China, which has displaced over 1 million people.

The most significant controversy arises over the issue of economic hardship. As mentioned earlier, asylum is sometimes sought by people who claim to be persecuted but in fact are fleeing economic hardships. European governments decry such practices as abuses of the system, vow to crack down on them and feel no obligation to accept such cases. Critics argue that the issue is not always so clear-cut, because politics and economics are often so intertwined that it is hard to see where the political ends and the economic begins. A worker may be unemployed for years because she has been blacklisted by the government for being a labour activist.

Even the harshest critic of European asylum policies must concede that they cannot possibly expand the definition of a refugee to such a point that it accepts all poor people from around the world. The World Bank estimates that over one billion people live in 'extreme poverty', defined as living on $1 per day, while almost three billion people live on under $2 a day. The challenge Europe faces is whether and how far it is willing to open asylum to such people.

Much of the above discussion hinges on the fact that, perhaps surprisingly, 'persecution' is not specifically defined by UNHCR, which has written that there is no universally accepted definition of the term. This lack of a definition is likely due to governments not wanting to be boxed in by such a definition and instead wanting flexibility in applying the term. This absence leaves us pondering the fundamental question of just what kind of action an individual must have suffered, or feared to suffer, in order to be considered a refugee. Saudi Arabia denying women the right to drive may not strike us as a policy that is severe enough to warrant being declared persecution, although we may consider it a form of discrimination. But what about Saudi Arabia denying women the right to vote? Surely being tortured because of one's political beliefs is a form of persecution, but how about being fired from one's job for expressing such beliefs? There appears to be a continuum from discrimination to persecution and Europe's challenge is to decide where to draw the line. This is a matter of interpretation and therefore of controversy.

In sum, much of the controversy over asylum in Europe stems from disagreement over the extent that asylum is abused by people not really persecuted at home but rather simply seeking a better life. Remarkably, this has been a controversial issue in Europe since the 1980s, with little progress toward resolution. It is therefore time to consider bolder action: countries that are suffering from asylum abuse should, if they have not already done so, make immigration opportunities much more accessible. Giving people an opportunity to enter through such channels would divert many from trying to get in through false asylum claims. By cutting down on the number of people seeking asylum, governments could then focus more time and resources on the asylum caseloads they are carrying and these cases would then get a much fairer and more thorough hearing. And by making the asylum process fairer and having all sides agree that it is fair, everyone would be more likely to be able to accept the decisions made and thereby reduce the controversy and resultant marginalization of asylum seekers.

Illegal immigrants in the US

As with asylum in Europe, in the US there is broad agreement that illegal immigration is a problem, but fiercely different proposals exist to address it. As of 2010, about 11 million illegal immigrants were living in the US, 58 percent of whom are from Mexico (Passel and Cohn 2011). One side emphasizes the illegal nature of this immigration, arguing that it undermines the authority and credibility of the country's laws and policies, harms native workers and their culture and is unfair to law-abiding immigrants. This side advocates more punitive action toward illegal immigrants, such as tighter border control, increased deportations, employer sanctions and cutting education and health services in hopes of discouraging future illegal flows.

The other side focuses on the exploitive nature of illegal immigration. It points out the harm that comes to both the immigrants and the natives by having immigrants live in the shadow of society where they are exposed to exploitation by smugglers and employers. This side also stresses the harm that comes to the host society if such marginalized immigrants do not have access to proper health care and education. Having unhealthy and uneducated people living on the fringes of society is a financial, practical and moral drain.

In other words, both sides want to get rid of illegal immigrants, but how? One suggestion that quickly rises to the surface is tighter border control, including lengthening the existing barrier along the US–Mexico border. Currently, the US is working to complete a 700-mile fence that was approved by the federal government in 2006 (although one wonders about the remaining 1,300 miles). From a technical point of view, the US could, of course build a Berlin-type wall along the entire Mexican border. It could build it 30-feet high, run a lethal amount of electricity through it and, just for good measure, mount it with motion-sensing machine guns pointing outward that would kill anyone moving within 100 yards.

Of course, not even the most ardent anti-immigrant advocate would support such a monstrous construction, which would violate every possible democratic principle, not to mention raising environmental concerns. As much as liberal democracies may complain about illegal immigration and argue for border controls, they all acknowledge that there are limits to how far a democracy can go to control borders. They simply do not have, and indeed cannot have, the will to put up truly effective walls.

Considerable effort has been put into controlling the US–Mexican border and yet illegal immigration continues. What conclusion can be drawn from this paradox? On the one hand, it can be argued that the US needs to allocate even more resources for border control until the flow of illegal immigrants is stemmed. On the other hand, some argue, counter-intuitively, that the tightening of the border is in fact the cause for the rise in illegal immigration. Interestingly, this position is shared by people from diverse ideological positions. The migration scholar Doug Massey and the libertarian Cato Institute, for example, both agree that, before this significant tightening of the border, there had been a circular flow of illegal immigrants, with male workers coming and going while their families remained behind in the sending country. With the border becoming harder to cross, this circular migration of individuals has been replaced by entire families coming once and then settling (Massey 2005). In addition, building up the border has had the unintended consequence of driving more migrants to rely on professional smugglers, who have a higher success rate of getting them into the country. Not only has this shift made interdiction more difficult, it has also significantly raised the price that smugglers charge (Roberts *et al.* 2010).

It is important to note that about 40 percent of people in the US illegally originally entered through legal channels but then overstayed their visa. Indeed, it is easy to overstay as there is no systematic process for confirming when a visa holder has left the country, which is a considerable problem given that in 2008, for example, 39 million people entered the US on some kind of temporary visa (*New York Times* 2009).

If border controls fail to keep unwanted people out, a country may consider deporting them. However, significant practical, financial, ideological and moral barriers stand in the way of finding and forcibly removing 11 million people from the US. The US deports large numbers of illegal immigrants each year: in 2010, 390,000 were deported (*New York Times* 2010b). But this number is relatively small compared with the total number of illegal immigrants living in the country, especially when a substantial number of these deportees had simply crossed the border. If the US wants to significantly reduce the number of illegal immigrants, it would have to increase dramatically the number of deportations. While this idea gets airtime on talkback radio, no serious politician or policy maker suggests it as it is not worthy of further discussion.

Failing keeping illegal immigrants out and deporting them in significant numbers, another option is to treat illegal immigrants in ways that make them feel unwelcome so that they decide to leave on their own accord. Such an approach may stress enforcing existing laws, imposing new ones or withdrawing social services. Sometimes referred to euphemistically as 'self-deportation', in essence this approach seeks to marginalize illegal immigrants. Supporters of this approach believe that it will have the added benefit of discouraging new arrivals as well. Federal, state and local governments are using various types of measures in their attempts to discourage illegal immigrants. As there are too many methods to discuss here, I will consider a few that have received attention. Despite their tactical differences, they all follow the same strategy: send a clear and unwelcoming message to illegal immigrants.

Beginning in the mid-1990s, a long list of such initiatives has been implemented, often at the state and local level and partly out of frustration with inaction at the federal level. Proposition 187 in California, for example, barred illegal immigrants from receiving many government services, including public education and non-emergency health care, and required public service providers to report to government authorities any illegal immigrant using these services. This law was subsequently challenged and overturned in federal court as being unconstitutional.

By the mid-2000s, scores of local communities were drawing up and passing ordinances that sought to discourage illegal immigrants from settling among them by, for example, prohibiting business owners and landlords from hiring or renting to illegal immigrants. These local efforts have also been repeatedly challenged and struck down in court. More successful have been efforts by states to ban issuing driver's licences to illegal immigrants so that currently only three of 50 states in the country still do so.

Current high profile efforts at discouragement include Arizona State Bill 1070 and a federal program known as 287(g). Passed in summer 2010, Arizona 1070 has attracted considerable controversy, especially the provision that compels law enforcement agents to stop and check the immigration status of anyone if there is 'reasonable suspicion' that the person is in the country illegally. The law was immediately challenged in court because of fear of racial profiling. The day before it was to go into effect, a federal judge blocked the most controversial parts of it as unconstitutional. Nonetheless, numerous other states have since followed by introducing similar measures, Alabama's being the most recent and far-reaching one.

Through 287(g), federal officials train and authorize state and local law enforcement agencies to check the immigration status of people they have arrested. If the arrested person is in the US illegally, then the local official can detain that person until federal officials deport them (local authorities do not have the authority to deport) and as of January 2011, 72 jurisdictions had joined this program (Capps *et al.* 2011).

That the US deports illegal immigrants who committed crimes may be reasonable, but how significant must the crime be to warrant such action? The *New York Times* recently reported of an illegal immigrant whose car was hit by another car. Because she had no driver's licence, the immigrant was arrested for this violation and then faced deportation after having lived in Georgia for 17 years. An estimated 4.5 million illegal immigrants drive regularly in the US without licences: this woman became one of at least 30,000 illegal immigrants who over the last three years have been stopped for common traffic violations and ended up in deportation (*New York Times* 2010a).

Critics charge that the woman's case illustrates that the 287(g) program is less concerned with reducing serious crime (its stated purpose) and more with reducing illegal immigration. The Migration Policy Institute (cited in Capps *et al.*

2011), for example, reports that, nationally, half of all detainees committed only misdemeanours and traffic offences. It concludes:

> State and local officials operate 287(g) programs according to priorities shaped largely by political pressures. In many communities in the Southeast and Southwest, the immigrant population grew rapidly during the 1990s and the 2000s, leading to a public backlash and putting pressure on sheriffs and other elected officials to pursue a set of enforcement strategies. These strategies include pursuing a 287(g) program alongside adoption of state and local laws that directly target unauthorized immigrants, such as Arizona's Senate Bill 1070 and laws in Georgia imposing mandatory jail time for driving without a license.
> (Migration Policy Institute, cited in Capps *et al.* 2011)

While such measures may well have the desired local effect, one wonders whether they have the national effect of returning these illegal immigrants to their home countries; perhaps they simply move to another less hostile community. Local politicians may not care where they move to as long as they are no longer in the politicians' communities. In terms of a national solution, however, such discouraging measures are unlikely to rid a country of illegal immigrants. More likely is that squeezing illegal immigrants is like squeezing a balloon – the pressure only moves them around rather than forcing them out. And through this pressure, they are pushed further and further to the margins of society.

Citizenship, membership and marginalization

The commonality of asylum seekers in Europe and illegal immigrants in the US is striking, especially in the resentment and marginalization they face. One striking difference between Europe and the US is that this marginalization has had a stronger impact on the politics and culture of Europe, in part because Europe does not see itself as a destination and does not have the long tradition of dealing with outsiders seeking entry. To be sure, the US has had and continues to have significant tensions over foreigners, but the issue does not roil society as profoundly as in Europe. The list of European tensions is longer and the issues are ongoing and seemingly intractable: third generation Turks and North Africans, Danish cartoons, bans on burkas, prominence of anti-immigrant parties, provocative campaign posters of minarets shaped like missiles and restrictive conceptions of citizenship, identity and belonging.

However, recently I have been struck by the potential risk of the US slipping in the direction of Europe. My concern does not stem from measures like Proposition 187, SB 1070 or 287(g), which I consider ugly but passing knee-jerk reactions to difficult economic times. As the economy improves, so will the US's attitude towards illegal immigration.

Instead, my concern stems from recent discussions about changing 'birthright citizenship', which grants US citizenship to anyone born in the US, including children of parents in the country illegally. In 2009, about 350,000 children became citizens as a result of being born to families in which at least one parent was an illegal immigrant (Passel and Cohn 2011). This situation has led to around 73 percent of the 5.5 million children of illegal immigrants being citizens (Passel and Cohn 2009a).

This birthright citizenship stems from the 14th Amendment to the US Constitution, which, when ratified in 1868, for the first time formalized US citizenship. Interestingly, this Amendment had nothing to do with immigration; instead, it addressed freed slaves and others of African descent, who, through the Supreme Court's infamous 1857 Dred Scot Decision, had lost the opportunity to become citizens. With the end of the Civil War and the end of slavery, the 14th Amendment assured them their citizenship by declaring:

> All persons born or naturalized in the United States, and subject to the jurisdiction thereof, are citizens of the United States and of the State wherein they reside. No State shall make or enforce any law which shall abridge the privileges or immunities of citizens of the United States; nor shall any State deprive any person of life, liberty, or property, without due process of law; nor deny to any person within its jurisdiction the equal protection of the laws.
>
> (14th Amendment to the United States Constitution)

While there have been periodic calls from the political fringes to challenge birthright citizenship, the issue is suddenly receiving mainstream attention, in part because the well-respected journalist George Will wrote an opinion piece in the *Washington Post* in March 2010 suggesting a reinterpretation of the phrase 'subject to the jurisdiction thereof'. A reinterpretation of the Amendment is more feasible than changing it, which would require approval of both chambers of the federal legislature by a two-thirds majority and then approval by three-quarters of state legislatures.

Acknowledging that changing the Constitution is extremely difficult, critics of the 14th Amendment are instead planning a different line of attack. At least five states plan to draw up laws to create two kinds of birth certificates: one for children of legal parents and one for children of illegal parents. The constitutionality of this move is questionable, not only because of the 14th Amendment but also because citizenship is a federal, not a state issue. And that is exactly the point – critics hope these laws will be challenged in court and taken all the way to the Supreme Court, in the hope of bringing about a favorable reinterpretation of the 14th Amendment.

While sharp legal minds on both sides are now debating the issue, I urge the US to take a broader view and to consider the potential ramifications of such a change: the profound marginalization of a significant section of society through the creation of a second class citizenry. This move, I fear, is a fast track to having the *banlieues* of Los Angeles burning, the headscarves in Dearborn removed, political posters depicting foreigners as black sheep or third generation immigrants never becoming part of the *demos*. As a democracy in which the *demos* rules, we, the people, must have an inclusive conception of who 'we' are. Birthright citizenship has been a clear and simple marker for who is to be included in the US *demos*: this clarity has been a strength for democracy in the US and its lack has been a great weakness in Europe.

Concluding thought

I suggest going in the opposite direction. Far from restricting citizenship for illegal immigrants, the US ought to put them on the path to citizenship. With the stroke of a pen, the US Congress could rid the country of all its 11 million illegal immigrants. Congress has in fact already done this several times. Such a move was a cornerstone of the 1986 immigration law (IRCA), by which about 2.7 million illegal immigrants were given legal status. Subsequently, six other targeted efforts legalized another three million by 2000.

In the short term, such legalization programs do get rid of illegal immigrants by simply getting rid of their illegality, without getting rid of the immigrants themselves. The long-term effect is less clear. In the US, for example, within a few years of the 1986 legalization, the number of illegal immigrants was back up to the original numbers. This resurgence leads to one of the most common charges against such programs: they encourage more illegal immigrants to come in the hopes that sooner or later they will also be granted legal status. The anti-immigration backlash of the 1990s, epitomized by California's Proposition 187, reflects this critique.

Much of the opposition to legalization is rooted in deep frustration with an immigration system that is widely perceived to be broken. By declaring illegal immigrants to now be legal, a country is acknowledging its system has failed. While this declaration may be frustrating, it may also be refreshingly realistic, given the alternatives for dealing with illegal immigrants. Such a declaration recognizes that illegal immigrants are here and are unlikely to leave soon. Indeed, despite the increasingly restrictive measures and the profound economic downturn of the last few years, the number of illegal immigrants in the US remained largely unchanged from 2009 to 2010 (11 million) but down from a high of about 12 million in 2007 (Passel and Cohn 2011). As bad as things are in the US, they still appear to be better than in the countries of origin.

Thus, while the US and Europe have sought to impose over the last two decades ever more restrictive admission policies, they have at the same time faced labour shortages for jobs no longer deemed acceptable by native workers. Unsurprising, both places now have a population of foreigners who have entered without authorization to fill these labour needs. These foreigners find themselves in the unenviable position of being needed but not wanted. They are a part of the economic fabric but are apart from the larger society.

Perhaps a democracy that attracts such unauthorized migrants must accept that, periodically, it must fully legalize and routinize their status, not in the hope of solving the problem of illegal immigration or of asylum abuse but in the hope of managing it. For if a democracy is unwilling to accept them and unable to get rid of them, then it creates a permanently marginalized, exploited, unassimilated segment of society whose costs are much higher than if it had made them true members.

Bibliography

Capps, R., Rosenblum, M.R., Rodríguez, C. and Chishti, M. (2011) *Delegation and Divergence: A Study of 287(g) State and Local Immigration Enforcement*, Washington DC: Migration Policy Institute.

Florida, R.L. (2006) *The Flight of the Creative Class: The New Global Competition for Talent*, New York: HarperBusiness.

Massey, D. (2005) 'Backfire at the border: why enforcement without legalization cannot stop illegal immigration', *Trade Policy Analysis*, 29, Cato Institute. Available at: www.freetrade.org/pubs/pas/tpa-029es.html (accessed 23 April 2012).

New York Times (2010a) 'Unlicensed drivers who risk more than a fine', 12 January.

New York Times (2010b) 'Immigration vote leaves Obama's policy in disarray', 18 December.

New York Times (2009) 'U.S. can't trace foreign visitors on expired visas', 12 October.

Passel, J. and Cohn, D. (2009a) *Trends in Unauthorized Immigration: Undocumented Inflow Now Trails Legal Inflow*, released 14 April, Washington DC: Pew Hispanic Center. Available at: www.pewhispanic.org/files/reports/107.pdf (accessed 28 October 2010).

Passel, J. and Cohn, D. (2009b) *A Portrait of Unauthorized Immigrants in the United States*, Washington DC: Pew Hispanic Center.

Passel, J. and Cohn, D. (2011) *Unauthorized Immigrant Population: National and State Trends*, Washington DC: Pew Hispanic Center.

Roberts, B., Hanson, G., Cornwell, D. and Borger, S. (2010) *An Analysis of Migrant Smuggling Costs along the Southwest Border*, Washington DC: Department of Homeland Security, Office of Immigration Statistics.

United Nations High Commissioner for Refugees (UNHCR) (2010) *Global Trends*. Available at: www.unhcr.org/4dfa11499.html (accessed 18 October 2011).

United Nations High Commissioner for Refugees (UNHCR) (1951) *Convention Relating to the Status of Refugees*.

United Nations High Commissioner for Refugees (UNHCR) (n.d.) *The 1951 Refugee Convention: Question and Answer*, The UN Refugee Agency, Regional Office for Belarus, Moldova, Ukraine.

Will, G. (2010) 'An argument to be made about immigrant babies and citizenship', *Washington Post*, 28 March. Available at: www.washingtonpost.com/wp-dyn/content/article/2010/03/26/AR2010032603077.html (accessed 28 October 2010).

Receiving strangeness

3 Legacies of war and migration
Memories of war trauma, dislocation and second generation Greek-Australians

*Joy Damousi**

> It's almost like I led this bizarre existence. We will put history over there and then there is life. Leave that behind, we will put that behind us.[1]
>
> (Peter)

A common refrain among immigrants when asked about the motivation for migrating is that they wish to leave the life in the old country behind them and to reinvent themselves and their prospects in a new society. But how do you leave your identity and self, indeed, your biography, in another place? What happens to the memories that are carried into another cultural setting? Which memories form a part of the family narrative and which are forgotten or repressed in the host community? How do these memories circulate within the family when these are memories of trauma or violence? In what ways do these memories shape immigrant identity and raise challenges for negotiating integration within host societies?

The hidden memories and impact of wartime experience generationally remain an area in need of further examination by historians, especially in relation to the impact of war on the waves of immigrants who settled in countries, like Australia, far removed from the sites of world wars. A central aspect of war migration – not of refugees but of those who willingly migrated – is that of the emotional and psychological aspects of this migration away from sites of the violence of world wars. In tandem with this question is that of the enduring legacies of war and migration on the second generation. There is an absence in the literature on second generation migrants in ethnic communities in general, but Greek migrants in particular.

My aim in this chapter is to consider these questions of transnationalism in the context of memories of war among Greek immigrants and how these stories shaped the identities of those who migrated to Australia during the post-war period. This perspective offers a new dimension in transnational discussion of migration studies which have not incorporated issues of emotions and memories into studies of social inclusion and dislocation.[2] This case study aims to consider how war has shaped the family memory of migrants and how the intergenerational transmission of war experiences to children who inherited the war stories of the Second World War (1940–44) and the Greek Civil War (1944–49) can be seen as a prism through which themes of migrant relocation and dislocation can be examined.

The connections between memory and history are instructive when considering the question of the intergenerational transmission of grief, trauma and its impact on social inclusion. The observations which emerge from Holocaust literature illuminate the ways in which children carry many of the emotional burdens of their parents. Some of the observations of these studies regarding the permeation of war trauma stories are useful in considering how families deal with trauma and war in conveying war stories. The 'conspiracy of silence' is where there is a non-verbal agreement in the family of keeping some traumatic experiences unspoken and detached from everyday life. It arises not only from the parents' need to forget and to adjust to new social contexts, but also from their belief that withholding information about the horrors of the Holocaust was crucial to their children's development. As a result, a 'double wall' of silence developed that was mutually maintained by both generations, where 'parents do not tell and children do not ask'. Studies have shown the ways in which the intergenerational communication of trauma was considered in relation to children's social emotions of anger and guilt in response to their parents.[3]

Parents also saw their children offering 'new hope and meaning and expected them to be a form of restitution for the families, aspirations and communities that were lost in the Holocaust' (Wiseman *et al.* 2006: 177). The direct and indirect transmission of trauma, the importance of resisting a homogenous response of children and the paradox of both silence and noise – 'the background music' of conflict – inform the framework of understanding adopted in this chapter to consider the place of memories in the experience of migration (Wiseman *et al.* 2006: 183).

Crucial to this aspect is the reception given to immigrants by the host societies. In the context of Australian post-war migration, the assimilation policy of the 1950s could not accommodate differences or allow for the expression of such stories, which was a part of the immigrants' identities. There have also been long-term effects of unresolved traumas. Over the course of 20 years, there has emerged a body of scholarship which has considered issues of depression and anxiety within migrant communities and of their hopes and the demands of cultural adjustment. Studies of Greek communities around the world have revealed many lives were fragmented by this experience and by the emotional impact of migration. While studies in psychology and psychiatry have considered the incidence of depression in the Greek community, especially among the elderly and among women, much of this is examined without reference to the historical and cultural context from within which it emerges. This study will provide an historical context to further extend our understanding of the current phenomenon in Australia of migrants arriving with traumatic pasts by emphasizing how the second generation has inherited these stories and their enduring legacy in family history, dislocation and cultural inclusion (Damousi 2010: 7–25).

Oral testimonies provide the archive through which to explore these themes of psychological displacement through the place and legacy of war stories. In recent times, scholars working in the fields of oral histories and memory studies have identified the key commonalities in their methodologies (Hamilton and Shopes 2008; Portelli 2003). These oral histories also speak to the multicultural present in that this second generation raises issues of how broader themes of transnationalism, citizenship and migration remain ever present, even when contemporary conditions have become more accommodating of difference and inclusion.

This chapter serves as a case study of where migrants have arrived in their host society, Australia, having experienced trauma and violence. There is a long history of this and it continues to the present day. The transnational circulation of the experience and narration of war trauma, coupled with migration and social inclusion and dislocation in the construction of the self and identity, form the central concern. In taking specific cases of witnesses to the violence and trauma of an historical event, this chapter seeks to explore the paradox that past stories need to be integrated in new ways for migrants, while simultaneously memories return through internalization, repression and displacement in the next generation.

Post-war migration and the Greek diaspora

In the context of Greek history, war stories within the Greek diaspora and the enduring war experience that affected different communities as they migrated have also not been a major focus of research. The Second World War and the Greek Civil War have been the subject of much debate and discussion over the past 30 years, but much of this has taken place outside Greece. During the 1980s, in the context of political reconciliation, the debate continued to be conducted in terms of diplomatic history or the Cold War, with blame attributed to the British and Americans or to the actions of the Communist Party. With the end of the Cold War, historians of Greece have moved towards considering issues of nationalism, ethnicity, memory and the psychological repercussions of war. These discussions, however, have largely been conducted within Greece and little research has extended these considerations to immigrant communities outside of Greece (Mazower 2000: 3–23). These events remain in family history, but they have also defined ethnic identity in Australia and shaped processes of integration for second generation Australians.

The post-war migration from Greece to Australia emerged from wartime circumstances. During the Second World War Greece was defeated by Germany. What followed was an armistice, or capitulation, as the German army occupied Athens and the first collaborationist government of occupied Greece was formed. The struggle for survival during the wartime occupation of Greece was intense, as was the five years of uninterrupted civil war that followed it. This period was arguably the most devastating in modern Greek history.

The experiences of war were compounded by the protracted civil war that took place simultaneously with, and then following, the Second World War.

Two forms of civil conflict emerged at this time: the first between the collaborators (usually on the right) and the resisters (on the left). In the years that followed and until 1949 when the civil war finally ended, casualties rose dramatically and the country was in turmoil. By 1950, a strained peace set in and it was not until the collapse of the military junta in 1974 that there was genuine harmony. While estimates vary on the numbers of violent deaths over this period, there appears to be an even greater loss of population caused by emigration; the total numbers of exiles amounted to 136,000 people (Iatrides 1995: 1–30).

In the years which followed the civil war, this mass migration spread throughout the world, as Greeks looked beyond a ravaged Europe to rebuild their lives. Mass migration took place to the US and Canada, but it was Australia that attracted a significant numbers of Greek immigrants. The massive post-war migration of Greek immigrants to Australia was one of the largest in Australia's history to that time. The post-war immigration policy implemented after the Second World War saw large numbers of assisted and non-assisted Greek immigrants arrive in Australia. In the period from 1947 to 1972, a total of 214,304 Greek immigrants arrived in Australia (Doumanis 1999: 58–70; Dimitreas 1998: 158).

What has the Greek child of post-war migration had to absorb? Which memories have been retold into family history and which have been repressed? How has this impacted on their identities as Greek-Australians and on their sense of belonging and inclusion within Australian society?

Following the immediate post-war period, as I have argued elsewhere, the assimilationist policies developed during the 1950s were based on the denial of an immigrant's past: the suppression of individual and collective memory of that past was vital to it. Consistent with the assimilation policies of the day, the expectation was that Greek immigrants who may have experienced this war would excise it from their memories and their identities in adjusting to a new life in Australia (Damousi 2010: 7–25).

In the writings of most assimilationist theorists, migrant children were identified as the liaison officers between Old and New Australians. There was then recognition in some discussion of 'adjustments' of migrants, but what is striking is the lack of recognition of the past experience of migrants and why they migrated in the first place. Although there were passing references to the war, the impact of these experiences was not further considered. In expecting that migrants would readily and seamlessly 'adopt' their new country, assimilationist policy effectively aimed to construct a nation-building discourse by denying the life stories,[4] the narratives and the memories of migrants which are central to the creation and maintenance of an identity and one's sense of self. The assumption that the migrant would readily merge or be subsumed in Australian cultural life ignored the ways in which past narratives, stories and memories fundamentally shape the self and are indeed vital for adjustment in a new society (Smith and Sparkes 2006: 169–92; Smith 2007: 391–8). For some growing up in Australia, the family history they brought to a new land was central to their identities.

While second generation Greeks have been energetic in the community and have taken a leading and active role in establishing educational and cultural institutions, subliminal issues remain regarding the nature of Greek-Australian identity (Tamis 2005).

Stephen's story

Stephen's story is one of the paradoxes of silence, where silence can create the circumstances for the most painfully enduring war trauma in family memory and create an intense burden for those asked to carry it.

Born in August 1951 in Chalkis, the major city of Evia about 60 kilometres north of Athens, Stephen arrived in Australia in 1954. In 1948 during the Greek Civil War, his grandmother and pregnant aunt were executed by leftist guerillas. His uncle died attempting to avenge these deaths. Following the war, Stephen's family decided to migrate to Australia, which his father did in 1952, with the family following in 1954.

What stories were told within the family about these events? The first narrative Stephen tells of the decision to move was based on the hope of a better future in Australia and of 'fundamental opportunity'. His father took the decision so that his three sons would have a 'better future'. Circumstances had deteriorated so badly in post-war Greece that the decision to migrate was 'for the future of his sons ... [to] live [a] better life, [a] more peaceful life'. His father also believed that conditions would deteriorate in Greece, so he made the life changing move of migrating to a foreign land. In the second narrative, the story was one of stoic survival and of the war experience that had 'hardened' his father, who aimed to pass on these values to his sons. A physically very strong and authoritarian figure, he impressed on his sons the importance of moral courage and physical strength.

But for the intelligent, sensitive and impressionable Stephen, the youngest son, close to and adoring of his mother rather than his father, the paternal figure represented a form of authority to be feared. Stephen felt being 'constantly [under] the gaze of [that] authority figure; he had a dreadfully penetrating eye. I couldn't engage as a small child. I couldn't look at him'. Stephen's fear of his father was in some ways understandable, given the intensity of his father's authority, which had been shaped by the experience of war. His father had served in the regular army in Greece and fought against the Germans and Italians.

> He had grown in an environment where if you didn't really know how to deal with pain then you couldn't cope with life ... [My father's message was] you have got to be strong. Otherwise ... you will not be able to cope with the difficulties of life.
>
> (Stephen)

The role model of toughness, perhaps appropriate for conditions in wartime Greece, continued in the peace of Australia, a model Stephen 'suffered ... as a child'.

The experience of these wars was the defining experience of his father. How were these told to his Greek-Australian sons? His father was:

> so deeply formed [by the war]; it was the foundation of his way of being in the world, that that couldn't be changed.... He could relax himself here, but at the same time he had been so significantly affected by his experiences, he couldn't become another person.
>
> (Stephen)

While Stephen's father was not a storyteller, he felt it was important to impart the family history to his sons.

> I think he felt it was very important.... He was not a storyteller.... He didn't speak, he didn't talk. Mostly he was silent. He did not speak easily. He would not be drawn out. Nobody could actually make him speak. He spoke when he wanted to speak. He spoke in very blunt and very direct and very unembellished terms. The stories he told never changed. The narrative never changed. It was very blunt.... He was the most silent man [regarding the burdens of his experience].
>
> (Stephen)

In other small ways, this violent past would break through in his language and in his demeanour:

> One of the things my father used to say when he got very angry at me was ... 'I will cut your throat'. I come from [this] lineage ... I have observed the degree of control my father exercised over the intensity of his emotion and the way that can very easily lead to a physical expression and encounter. You ... couldn't take anything for granted. You really had to stand by your actions ... You had to account for yourself...
>
> (Stephen)

The war stories explicitly defined Stephen's own identity as Greek. It was important to analyse how these stories defined his 'Greekness' in Australia and:

> the degree to which I am framed by that history.... It permeates me. It's woven into me, my sense of who I am, so profoundly that I am intensely emotional about it ... I am Greek. I am nothing but Greek ... I am not Australian. The reason I am not Australian is that ... in the most profound influences, the deepest influences, the really emotional formation has been drawn from my relation to my mother and my father and the presence of their history. One thing is to talk about the stories and to talk about the narrative and what they related to me about that. But growing up in the 1950s ... [The stories and history] was present in their presence. My father's silence, his intensity, the intensity of his emotion is scary. My mother's vulnerability ...

the dual of the male–female presence. Both of equivalent intensities; both compelling, both really compelling; both expecting of me that level of recognition and contact, emotional engagement ... very primal.

(Stephen)

His father reminded Stephen of the need not to:

carry on as though suffering didn't exist. I can remember him turning on me on a couple of occasions. 'You think it's like that ... you think it's all that easy. It's not. I am evidence of it and my relation to you is expression of it.... You can see it in [my] face, you can hear it in my voice.' The fierceness of it [was compelling].

(Stephen)

For Stephen, the migration experience was one of a sharp dichotomy between two competing emotional worlds. The emotional intensity of the home where this history permeated their lives on a domestic everyday level was in sharp contrast with the outside world and the novelty of white Australia, which had its own tragedies. As Stephen poignantly recalls:

Every time I stepped out of the house I stepped into Australia; every time I stepped back into the house I was in Greece. And who I was, I couldn't really identify with what was happening outside, because what was happening outside was nothing.... It was nothing compared to the intensity of the emotional experience that I engaged in the presence of my parents. The outside was peculiar, it was fascinating, it was rich in other ways, it was mystifying. There were also traumatic aspects of it. I grew up in Smith Street in Collingwood in the '50s.... There were a lot of alcoholics, there were a lot of Aboriginals [sic]. I went to state school with Aboriginal children. I could see the trauma everywhere.... There were a lot of traumatic.... Indigenous Australians. If you like, it had a kind of Dickensian [feel].

(Stephen)

Post-war Australia did not comfortably accommodate these narratives and stories. The assimilation policy which framed migration objectives after the Second World War did not allow for recognition of an immigrant's past. The discourse of the nation-state was premised on a denial of past connections to home and indeed a repression of these memories. There was an expectation that these memories and experiences would be subsumed in integrating within Australian cultural life and in assuming a cultural identity which negated recognition of these experiences.

Another powerful motif in Stephen's story is his parents' decision to migrate and his own guilt about his parents' sacrifice that is interconnected with the war stories. His unflinching belief is that they made the wrong decision in migrating and that, in doing so, they lost the very essence of their being and indeed his own sense of self. Reinventing a new life did not involve embracing the host culture in Australia. 'It was clear my parents didn't fit and therefore I didn't fit. There was this distance.... There was no connection ... I don't think it [the new was] integrated very well'. Despite the accolades and achievements he has received over many years as a renowned artist and that he is fully 'integrated', at 'another level, at a personal level, I am not Australian'.

In other words, he retains a fierce commitment to maintaining a Greek identity as a way of being loyal to his parents for their own sacrifice in migrating in the first place.

> I won't accept anyone telling me I am not Greek, that I am Australian. I don't accept that at all ... I don't have a sense of humor about it all.... They made the decision. I think they made the wrong decision.... What they won if you like through their sacrifice ... my achievements ... I would easily negate everything I've done if it could actually reclaim their lives and what they lost. Because I think they lost too much. How could you equate a 60-hour week in a factory with the life they would have had in Greece...
>
> (Stephen)

He is reflective of the way in which he has internalized the lack of compensation for his parents' decision:

> At a personal level, I have taken it on totally. I accept it ... I am absolutely adamant about the rightness of it ... I have made the complaint. My parents made the wrong decision. None of the advantages that I have experienced in my life can compensate for what I know as the sacrifice of my parents.... In a sense I lost something. I also lost something. That life I would have had in Greece...
>
> (Stephen)

The position in which he was placed was as a witness especially to his mother's own traumatic pain and the losses and frustrations of migration, almost as an affirmation of her predicament: 'My mother did voice it more. There was pressure also from her. She spoke about it especially to me. She needed me to be a witness to her pain, to affirm it.'

In the present time, the war stories for Stephen both create a connection with Greece and yet a distance from it; he feels at once cultural inclusion and exclusion:

> It both separates – isolates, even alienates me – and at the same time it connects me. I have a sense of what happened in Europe at that time – an intimate sense of it – and I have a sense of the distance from it being here. And I also can reflect on Australian culture in relation to what my parents brought here as migrants, the condition they were in and then the difficulties

that they encountered and what they had to actually sustain to conform to Australian culture and the expectations. One of the things they were absolute about: we had to present always in relation to Australians in a respectful and well-mannered way. They were aware they were guests.... There was a lot of humility in my parents and in their approach.... We had to behave in an appropriate way [and] accord with Australian protocols.

(Stephen)

Stephen carries their past with him but he does not see this as oppressive in any way, but as a part of his identity: 'I am carrying it on their behalf. It is not a burden'.[5]

Stephen's story takes us through an experience of bearing psychological witness to the trauma of his parents, within a cultural and political climate which did not allow for its expression. Furthermore, the demands of the post-war assimilation policies, where migrants were expected to adopt the 'Australian Way of Life', allowed for no accommodation of this emotional burden. In recent times, rather than seeing this as oppressive, Stephen has appropriated this responsibility almost as a badge of honour. As the youngest son, he has internalized the expectation to compensate for his parents' inability to mourn or grieve and done so quite consciously.[6]

Peter's story

A similar protective silence engulfed Peter's upbringing. Although stories were told, specific details of violence were left unspoken. Peter's family migrated in 1957 to a migrant hostel in Newcastle. They moved from there to Sydney when his father found work there. Born in 1910, his father, an educated man and mayor of the village, was in his late forties when he migrated, unusually older than the average male immigrant of the day, who would have been in his twenties. Stories of the war were part of conversing with relatives:

We grew up on the stories, on the war stories.... When relatives would come over we would go over the same ground and once upon a time I could recount the stories because Dad had a limited repertoire of stories.

(Peter)

In preparing for the interview, Peter confessed he had been 'dysfunctional for the past two days' and realized what was happening as he recalled the violence at the heart of the family tragedy:

I was dissociating. I just didn't want to access those stories again. The pain is horrific. I was trying to think. I can't even recall anymore who executed my grandmother. My grandmother was lined up against the wall. I don't know anymore whether it was the Germans, or the *ardantes* [Communists].... It's all lost in a great big blur. My father faced executions three times ... I can recall the stories where he said they got fucked over by the Germans, they got fucked over by the *ardantes*...

(Peter)

His father experienced a 'vicious trauma'. His business was wiped out three times and after that experience he decided it was time to leave. It was his father who was the 'verbal one'; his mother remained in the shadow in these conversations.

She did not want to talk about the war experience. She has never really wanted to talk about them. Because I suspect horrible things have happened.... She never wanted to go [back] to Greece ... I have never asked. I have respected her silence about it.... I was dying to say, "Mum, I know something terrible has happened. Do you want to talk about it?" But she has never shown any signs.... Said never wanted to talk about it.

(Peter)

The paradox is of the silence of these war stories which yet had a profound impact. But these were stories which remained within the family, having no place outside of it:

What happens to trauma is that it is not an easy thing to talk about outside of Greek culture. It is easy to talk about it in Greek.... My Greek is not good enough to talk about ... I have consciously compartmentalized it.... There was this deep pain about things that was profound. I understood it to be the pain that was conveyed to me through the stories of my father and my mother's silence was profound. It is absolutely profound ... I realized [I] consciously avoided it. And yet it informs everything that I do but not in that conscious [way] ... what I understand about trauma allows me to be deeply empathic to people aka of the stories I grew up with but it is obviously correct – that kind of trauma.

(Peter)

The theme of execution is one which has shaped his own highly sensitive response to executions and draws this back to stories about his father surviving possible execution three times and his grandmother having been executed.

I felt very passionate as a young man about anyone who would execute people. I found it very hard to watch executions. There was a beheading in one of the Arab states – [I] could not watch it. When I see movies, I can watch violence until the cows come home. When it comes to a reality, I cannot watch it ... I felt aware that I felt very disturbed by that and I understood why ... [it relates to my grandmother's execution and] my father facing execution. His version of how he escaped was that he talked his way through it ... I can now see that there was a defensiveness to it. He would say that the commander – one of them [an execution] was by the Germans – and he said, 'The commander recognized something in me and called me to do something' ... now what that means God only knows but he felt that it was because someone saw something special in him ... [facing execution occurred twice with the Germans and a third time with the *ardantes*]. He was gifted in terms of his speech ... and he always used that as the rationale for why he escaped and other people didn't.... This is what you grew up with. And they would get into that really profoundly melancholic space at the end of the story and my father would go incredibly silent.... He wanted to shake it off him and yet he would repeat the story at a future time. You could witness it – he was profoundly affected by it. But again would only talk about it as stories.

(Peter)

And yet the level of detail was limited and the specifics were vague. Overall, in the new home of Australia, his parents attempted to protect him and his younger brother from the 'contamination' of the past:

It was never telling the children.... When I was a young adult and I wanted him to tell me about the stories and he refused to tell me.... Because he felt his whole life was about protecting us and he didn't want us to be contaminated. In his mind that's how he organized it and he felt he didn't want us to be contaminated by the politics of the time. He said they were kind of things best left – left back there. He didn't want to carry it into this country. But it would come out in terms of he would say things like, 'Never speak your mind', 'Don't let anyone you know, let people know, what you actually believe'.

(Peter)

What sort of responsibility does he have as a parent and custodian of the family memory for passing on these stories to his own children?

I would tell them about Grandpa. But I wouldn't go into the horrible details about trauma, given what I know about trauma. You bet your life I won't ... I can see what trauma does. It can inform you and give you profound insight. But I don't think you necessary need that kind of [detail] ... I have done some very violent things in my life. Incredibly violent things. Punching the wall ... But I have also held a gun at someone's head. Now where did I get that shit from? It wasn't from the streets of Sydney. I didn't have that kind of background or that kind of peer group or whatever ... I know that they came from those stories.... Do I want to pass that onto my kids? Not in a million years. Am I proud of what I have done? The answer is no, but I know where it comes from – my uncles and whatever ... I have seen people do these things. I haven't [just] watched it on television. So how do you deal with difficult situations? You get a knife, you get a gun ... I was appalled afterwards ... I will let them understand in an academic way.

(Peter)

The reluctance to convey these war stories created a separation between history and life in his upbringing. The life in a new land was not to be contaminated by the bloody battles of the past and these were to be excluded in efforts to begin anew:

> You can see my parents almost protected me from any historical references.... My father did not want any of that to contaminate the path ... [He was] not unemotional ... [but] with the benefit of hindsight you can see it was quite a restricted existence. He has been traumatized.... He became quite religious but kept it very very privately...
>
> (Peter)

There was also no need for a witness in the children:

> He used the priest [to conduct] conversations about things he could not talk to about anything else. I suspect the priest was the person that heard the pain and the trauma and those stories. Bits that were quarantined from us. Because we were really protected from it. We were really protected from it.
>
> (Peter)

It was a conversation conducted among men, not women, and certainly not children.

> I know the atrocities were referred to in conversation with other men. The women were never included.... They would get into heated conversations about the politics. Then they would get to a certain point and they would stop. There was an end point. They were not going to go on with it. Am I curious? In an ideal world that would be one of the things I would do...
>
> (Peter)

The precise year his grandmother was killed, and by whom, remains unclear in the interview. But to seek these details would create more pain. Peter did not want to ask his mother for details which would 'stir it up' for her. 'When it was all said and done, I don't know whether it was war, trauma or sexual abuse.' It is 'obvious' he carried this experience:

> I deal with this [professionally] and I can recognize it at ten paces ... I became a health professional because of all that stuff ... without realizing it.... In that sense I was profoundly affected by it. I realize it. I was traumatized by it. I had no outlet because there was no way of talking about it at home. I made what I think were appropriate inquiries [but] they were

stymied. I think it was shut down. Shut down. Shut down. And ostensibly for my protection ... I mean, obviously now, from what I know, it was not for my protection. That was the overt reason. The covert stuff was that they were protecting themselves ... I don't think I was old enough to ask him that ... when he was alive to put that proposition to him. It is what it is, I suppose.[7]

(Peter)

Joanna's story

These themes of silence, talking, protection and bearing witness to war trauma within Greek immigrant families after the war point to the migrant's effort to relocate and to adjust in a new society. These themes also inform Joanna's testimony, but in different ways. Unlike Peter and Stephen, Joanna was born in Australia and in the early 1960s. Her parents arrived in Australia in the 1950s. Her uncle was killed in 1948 at the end of the Greek Civil War, an enduring shadow that was cast on her mother and which she has never properly mourned. In Joanna's upbringing, war stories were the central framing narrative of what was defined as Greek identity, of why the family had migrated and the reason for both separation and bonding to Greece and to Australia, which remain a current preoccupation in the journey of cultural adjustment:

> The experience of my parents during the Civil War and Second World War were stories which we grew up on. Far from being silent or reserved or reticent about sharing these memories, my mother would speak at length about her experiences – all tragic, melancholic and devastating – and there was no doubt these haunted us as children. The stories of Germans violently raiding villages for food, or of the devastating impact of bombings on families in the village or of the cruel starvation and hunger during these wars filled our childhood imagination. Clearly she felt the need to speak and continue to speak about these experiences.

(Joanna)

Why did she feel the need to share these with her children?

> It wasn't political. There were no slogans or a political programme associated with these stories, exalting us to take up some cause. Neither was it especially to preserve family history or memory. Many of these stories were of the experiences of other families, distant acquaintances, some of whom were unknown to us. It wasn't a history lesson either. My mother's historical knowledge of this period is rudimentary at best and she certainly didn't use this as an opportunity to encourage further reading or exploration of the topic. I would have to say that what drove this continued narration was twofold. First, what seemed to be a lifelong mourning of her brother, my uncle, as the stories would always come back to one point: her tragic painful

loss of a dearly loved sibling. Second, that this continuing, almost obsessive retelling was perhaps a justification to herself of why she agreed to migrate to Australia, which she never wanted to do, and at one level continues to resent even after living for over 50 years here.

(Joanna)

Another factor may be added and that is one of a form of survivor guilt. The term most commonly refers to victims of atrocities who manage to survive when others have perished. In this and other instances of parents discussing their experiences, Joanna's own feeling of guilt about survival had been passed on to her children (Wiseman *et al.* 2006: 177).

The ways in which this constant talking and referencing were a burden to her are revealing:

There is no question there is a kind of guilt here. The burden of succeeding is immense, even if it is not overt. The overachievement of first generation children of migrants is almost a cliché and I wonder if some of this does not derive from an overwhelming sense that their own sacrifices must be compensated in some way or justified through their children. But there is another dimension and that is bearing witness through these stories of their own trauma. In the safety of the home and familial setting these stories can circulate, find legitimacy, and be affirmed.

(Joanna)

Having been born in Australia, there is no question that Joanna considers herself an Australian, but this past and these war memories are certainly a part of her 'Greekness' in Australia. But the depth and nature of these memories have not found much recognition outside of the family and to this extent are not well integrated with cultural understandings of the experience of the immigrant. While there have been material achievements and accomplishments of migrants, these can often mask the subliminal issues which remain unresolved. 'It is a fine balance', she says, 'between keeping your history alive however brutal and painful, and yet recognizing that in order to integrate fully into a new society and contribute to it, such memories really have to be put aside.'[8]

Legacies of war and migration

Joanna tells a story of bearing witness to her mother's unresolved grief and perhaps survivor guilt, a presence that is overt in the family narratives about the distant land of Greece which fill her childhood and adolescence in the unlikely place of inner-city Melbourne. That the sacrifices of her mother and her unresolved grief must be compensated resonate as a theme in Joanna's story. This is inescapable, for her mother's obsessive retelling serves as a constant reminder and indirect transmission of her mother's haunting memories, defining family history and integral to Joanna's Greek-Australian identity.

Stephen and Peter are child witnesses to the grief of their parents, but, in contrast, they have to navigate a 'protective silence' imposed by their parents that is nonetheless just as powerful in its impact as the horrific details of tragedy conveyed by the incessant storytelling. For Peter, the shadow of the executioner looms psychologically large in his retelling. It is the haunting reminder of his grandmother's brutal and violent fate, a fate too devastating to contemplate even with the fading over time of scant yet highly dramatic details – 'up against the wall' – and which remains deeply unresolved in the collective family psyche. It reminds him of his father's near fate with the Germans who almost executed him. Stephen's driving quest to compensate for his parent's sacrifice for migrating to Australian and leaving a country that created the circumstances for the tragic and painful loss of family members provides a powerful paradigm for his life story. His sensitivity towards his parents' plight – 'they made the wrong decision' – leads to an embrace of an almost pure untainted Greek identity, as if an adoption of an Australian identity, of the place his mother detested and reluctantly migrated to after the war, would be disrespectful of their sacrifices and disloyal to their memories. These three narratives of the children of Greek immigrants reveal some similarities, but they also highlight differences in the process of negotiating indirect transmission of generational dislocation through traumas.

The two extremes of imparting family memories and history – obsessively repeating stories on the one hand and, on the other, refraining from telling children excessive details of the past so as not to 'contaminate' them – is a familiar tendency in several contexts of how stories of past wars have been related to children of survivors of those wars. Hadas Wiseman observes how 'survivors of trauma themselves live with the conflict between the wish to forget and the need to tell their stories'. This paradox provides at once both the 'silence and noise' experienced by those who are exposed to these stories (Wiseman *et al.* 2006: 183).

While the tension between silence and noise is a theme in the familial narratives, it is clear that the affect of their identity remains Greek. Peter reflects:

> If someone asked me what I am, I say I am Greek ... I *feel* myself to be Greek. [What makes you Greek?] My *feelings* ... I actually feel my way through things.... My primary organizing principle is feelings. I think part of my identity, I call it Greek, it is not recognized in this culture ... I feel it to be Greek.... So I still say I am Greek.
>
> (Peter)

In these interviews, the transnational self emerges as divided and the prevailing political culture of Australia in the 1950s and 1960s could not accommodate this division.

The transnational circulation of these stories is transmitted in ways which position the child as a witness to unresolved family trauma. For this generation of Greek-Australians, time and place have altered their life chances and their experience differs immeasurably from that of their parents. Theirs is a distinctive memory, however, one where the essence of the meaning of being Greek is intertwined with narratives of violence, trauma and war through indirect transmission of their parents' trauma. But their memories are also determined by imperatives of renewal and redemption. The repression of war stories in society at large reflects the wider absence of the enduring legacy of war experiences in Australian culture and society. And yet for migrants to be integrated, these experiences need to be culturally negotiated. These historical war stories return through the next generation – a legacy of the past which is forever present – and which serve as a reminder of the complexity of cultural dislocation and the elusiveness and challenges of social integration.

Notes

* I would like to thank the interviewees for kindly sharing their stories with me. I also wish to thank the editors for their extremely helpful feedback and Mary Tomsic for her valuable research assistance. I acknowledge funding from the Australian Research Council which made this research possible.
1 Interview with 'Peter', 18 March 2010, in possession of the author.
2 See, for instance, Roudometof and Karpathakis (2002); Miles and Thranhardt (1995).
3 For Holocaust studies, see Weiss and Weiss (2000); Yehuda *et al.* (1998); Wiseman *et al.* (2006); Soloman *et al.* (1988); Faye (2001); Mor (1990).
4 For a discussion of nation-state discourse and transnational migration, see Glick Schiller *et al.* 1995.
5 Interview with 'Stephen', 7 May 2010, in possession of the author.
6 For the process of indirect transmission of trauma, see Weiss and Weiss (2000: 374).
7 Interview with 'Peter', in possession of the author.
8 Interview with 'Joanna', 23 September 2010, in possession of the author.

Bibliography

Damousi, J. (2010) 'Ethnicity and emotions: psychic life in Greek communities', *Modern Greek Studies*, 14: 7–25.

Dimitreas, Y. (1998) *Transplanting the Agora: Hellenic Settlement in Australia*, Sydney: Allen and Unwin.

Doumanis, N. (1999) 'The Greeks in Australia', in R. Clogg (ed.) *The Greek Diaspora in the 20th Century*, St Antony's: Macmillan.

Faye, E. (2001) 'Missing the "real" trace of trauma: how the second generation remember the Holocaust', *American Imago*, 58(2): 525–44.

Glick Schiller, N., Basch, L. and Szanton Blanc, C. (1995) 'From immigrant to transmigrant: theorizing transnational migration', *Anthropological Quarterly*, 68(1), January: 51.

Hamilton, P. and Shopes, L. (eds) (2008) *Oral History and Public Memories*, Philadelphia: Temple University Press.

Iatrides, J.O. (1995) 'Greece at the crossroads, 1944–1950', in J.O. Iatrides and L. Wrigley (eds) *Greece at the Crossroads: The Civil War and Its Legacy*, Pennsylvania: Pennsylvania State University Press.

Mazower, M. (2000) 'Introduction' in M. Mazower (ed.) *After the War Was Over: Reconstructing the Family, Nation, and State in Greece, 1943–1960*, Princeton: Princeton University Press.

Miles, R. and Thranhardt, D. (eds) (1995) *Migration and European Integration: The Dynamics of Inclusion and Exclusion*, London: Fairleigh Dickinson University Press.

Mor, N. (1990) 'Holocaust messages for the past', *Contemporary Family Therapy*, 12(5), October: 371–9.

Portelli, A. (2003) *The Order Has Been Carried Out: History, Memory and Meaning of Nazi Massacre in Rome*, New York: Palgrave Macmillan.

Roudometof, V. and Karpathakis, A. (2002) 'Greek Americans and transnationalism: religion, class and community', in P. Kennedy and V. Roudometof (eds) *Communities Across Borders: New Immigrants and Transnational Cultures*, London: Routledge.

Smith, B. (2007) 'The state of the art in narrative inquiry', *Narrative Inquiry*, 17(2): 391–8.

Smith, B. and Sparkes, A.C. (2006) 'Narrative inquiry in psychology: exploring the tensions within', *Qualitative Research in Psychology*, 3: 169–92.

Soloman, Z., Kotler, M. and Mikulincer, M. (1988) 'Combat-related posttraumatic stress disorder among second-generation Holocaust survivors: preliminary findings', *American Journal of Psychiatry*, 145(7), July: 865–8.

Tamis, A. (2005) *The Greeks in Australia*, Melbourne: Cambridge University Press.

Weiss, M. and Weiss, S. (2000) 'Second generation to Holocaust survivors: enhanced differentiation of trauma transmission', *American Journal of Psychotherapy*, 54(3), Summer: 372–85.

Wiseman, H., Metzl, E. and Barber, J.P. (2006) 'Anger, guilt and intergenerational communication of trauma in the interpersonal narratives of second generation Holocaust survivors', *American Journal of Onthropsychiatry*, 76(2): 176–84.

Yehuda, R., Schmeidler, J., Wainberg, M., Binder-Brynes, K. and Duvdevani, T. (1998) 'Vulnerability of posttraumatic stress disorder in adult offspring of Holocaust survivors', *American Journal of Psychiatry*, 155(9), September: 1163–71.

4 An invitation to inclusion
Museums and migration

Kay Ferres

In North America, Australia and Europe, museums that document migrant histories, create new identities and imagine shared futures have emerged in response to a heightened awareness of migrant insecurity. Migrant museums acknowledge a duty to remember the past, to respect human rights and to contribute to public dialogue about how difference is recognized and integration is supported. The International Organization for Migration (IOM) and the United Nations Educational, Scientific and Cultural Organization (UNESCO), realizing that these museums offer an opportunity to promote public understanding of migrant experience, lower barriers to inclusion and build bridges across cultural and political differences, have sponsored an International Network of Migration Institutions. This partnership encourages the development of new museums to collect and safeguard objects and narratives relating to the history and culture of immigration and to the process of integration of migrant communities. Their ambition is to fashion the museum as a space for encounters between migrants and their host populations, in the hope that such encounters will foster empathy and reciprocity and reshape identities. The initiative also provides a forum for museum professionals to share expertise and more especially to understand their roles in promoting integration. So in addition to realizing new kinds of citizenship, these interventions also aim to develop a new kind of expert, a museum professional who interacts with policy makers and researchers as well as the broader public to build inclusive societies.

The Migration Institutions Initiative sets an agenda for museums: to deconstruct stereotypes, to enable migrant and host communities to find common ground, to foster a sense of belonging and to develop empathy. This sets aside some pressing questions about the terms of migrant integration. How is difference understood and welcomed into the larger polity? How are the rights of individuals within groups secured? What frameworks for understanding and managing diverse populations can these institutions draw upon? In Europe and elsewhere, liberal democracies are increasingly ambivalent about multiculturalism:

> retreating from it in certain policy respects and suspicious of the word, but, at the same time, institutionally and attitudinally reshaped by its commitments

and norms; reaching for a new idiom and a renewed emphasis on commonality, yet reluctant to quash diversity and reinscribe brute assimilationism.

(Levey 2009: 77)

Diversity can be troublesome for liberalism, especially when it makes unwelcome appearances in public space and when it is the basis of claims for special rights. It is being displaced by a new emphasis on social inclusion or social cohesion, but it is not clear that this vocabulary provides a sustainable 'new idiom' for citizenship. This chapter explores the museum as a site that animates democracy and activates citizenship, by describing how some Australian museums have addressed issues of inclusion and integration through their engagement with migration histories and migrant communities.

The museum's role in mediating diversity mobilizes its function as a forum. It is a site of cultural difference and manages that responsibility in a number of ways, often at the same time. It provides a space for cultural encounters and intercultural communication and potentially enables what Alain Touraine has called the 're-composition of the world' (Touraine 2000). Well designed exhibition spaces and associated public programs elicit particular ethical capacities: not merely tolerance, but mutuality and respect and a reflexivity that Touraine describes as 'remembrance and estrangement'. These capacities are critical to new forms of active citizenship, in a world where the compression of time and space allows and even demands that individuals maintain multiple allegiances. Migrant communities recognize cultural, economic and political obligations to their place of origin, even as they mobilize their rights in the host country. Tolerance, indifference to difference, is no longer all that is required if we are to find ways to live together, according to Touraine. Tolerance leaves things as they are: recognition accommodates difference with common systems of law and justice; while remembrance and estrangement shifts boundaries, remaps social relations and 'recomposes' the world.

Touraine's recognition of the importance of intercultural exchange chimes with Iris Marion Young's account of communicative ethics (Young 1997, 2000). Young describes how public spaces of deliberation might be more genuinely inclusive by adopting new norms of conduct. Her focus is on 'internal exclusion', identifying the practices and norms that impede full participation by marginalized groups. Young claims that 'a theory of democratic inclusion requires an expanded conception of political communication' if participants in political discussion are to achieve understanding, to resolve problems and ultimately to make proposals that shape new agendas (Young 2000: 56). She builds on a feminist critique of public reason to elaborate practices of greeting, rhetoric and narrative that would give substance to formal equality and promote respect. These practices recognize social difference as a resource for democratic communication, increasing the store of social knowledge and creating new solidarities. This chapter's discussion of the museum as a forum demonstrates how it offers a space for such communication to occur. It focuses on museum practice and on the ways museum professionals have gone beyond their traditional roles as conservators and curators to develop new expertise as cultural interpreters and community mediators.

While the role of print culture in constructing the 'imagined community' is prominent in discussions of nations and nationalism and political scientists have noticed the role of stories in securing political membership (Smith 2003), attention has more recently turned to the role of museums in constructing narratives of peoples and nations and to the social purposes that museums serve (Gurian 2006; Sandell 2006; Janes 2009; Silverman 2010; Black 2011). Museums internationally have extended their brief to conserve and interpret the past and have embraced a responsibility to imagine the future. They have extended their ambit from objects to ideas. Through their collections, exhibitions, educational services and public programs, museums have enhanced the public realm and encouraged democratic participation. They are 'reaching for a new idiom' that recognizes commonality and difference.

The social purpose of museums

The nineteenth century museum developed as an adjunct to the rise of the human and natural sciences and illustrated debates about human evolution. The generation of new knowledge drove its impetus for collection and classification. The narrative of the natural history museum was a story of human progress from primitive to modern; its displays emphasized the development of technologies, the subordination of nature to culture and the triumph of rationality. At the same time, the popularity of collecting and widespread interest in ruins and antiquities manifested this narrative in everyday life. As Tony Bennett (1995) has shown, the museum as an institution also had a critical role in the management of populations. It was an exclusive institution, defining 'civilization' in European terms and civilizing urban populations by regulating access and applying the techniques of rational recreation to the visitor experience.

In the late twentieth century the museum faced a crisis. The decline of empire, the emergence of postcolonial nations and the collapse of totalitarian regimes called its mission into question. Formerly colonized peoples made claims for the repatriation of objects, including human remains from existing European collections. National museums in immigrant societies like Canada, Australia and New Zealand reconfigured national narratives to give prominence to indigenous peoples and cultures and to recalibrate time and space. The museum's dual role as a temple and a forum was reconfigured in response to these new realities and to a new awareness of the visitor's role in producing meaning. In response to expressed visitor preferences, exhibition design and public programs are increasingly attentive to the dynamics of dialogue between visitor and display and among visitors. The 'resonance and wonder' generated by objects and exhibits are enhanced by opportunities for social interaction and civic dialogue (McLean 1999).

This new interest in the social purpose of museums and their role in civil society has taken hold in an increasingly troubled world (Janes 2009). After the devastation of civilian populations and the ruin of cities in twentieth century wars, memory and commemoration of the past were a powerful impetus for the creation of new museums. Histories of conflict, narratives of displacement and atonement for injustice have driven the development of memory museums and sites of conscience. In this context, it is not surprising that museums have come to be regarded as palliatives for all kinds of social problems (Prior 2011) and the target of heightened expectations: 'The most important and essential work museums do is to use their unique resources to benefit human relationships and, ultimately, repair the world' (Silverman 2010).

While these symbolic purposes are both important and contentious, museums also provide a public space for what Elaine Heumann Gurian has called 'peaceable congregant behaviour', the 'going to be with others' that underpins collective life. She has called for museums to be 'sites of reconciliation between strangers who are wary of, but curious about, each other'. Drawing on her work at the Boston Children's Museum, the National Museum of the American Indian and the United States Holocaust Memorial Museum, Gurian's ideas and practice are directed towards making the museum 'a fitting safe place for the discussion of unsafe ideas', whose public programs might turn 'strangers into acquaintances' (Gurian 2006). These ideas have taken hold and have the institutional support of the American Association of Museums (AAM). In partnership with the philanthropist organization Americans for the Arts, AAM has assisted museum professionals in identifying their civic mission and has provided toolkits and other resources to enable them to conduct civic dialogue.

This embrace of museums' social purpose and public value has its critics. Within the sector, those who value the museum as a research institution with a focus on natural history are not comfortable with this new orientation; from outside, there are those who see the museum as irredeemably elitist, exclusionary and, worse, irrelevant. These changes are better understood as part of a broader concern with the cultural sector's contribution to social policy and community development. Internationally, the cultural sector (comprising individual artists, arts organizations and cultural institutions) has been prominent in social inclusion strategies for some time. In the US, cultural vitality has been seen as central to urban regeneration, crime prevention and public safety. Local initiatives have sought to replace old industries with a creative economy; to repair the urban fabric; to engage with marginalized communities; to drive neighbourhood renewal and to revitalize public space. Many of these initiatives involve the development of new networked institutions, such as museums, arts centres and libraries.

In Canada, the cultural sector has had a key role in the management of cultural diversity and the recognition and maintenance of cultural rights. In Europe, the European Union has used the cultural sector to support integration, directing funding to 'cities of culture' for projects that embrace urban renewal and community cultural development. In the UK, the social exclusion agenda has been linked to government initiatives to address unemployment and disadvantage and to the revival of the civic realm. The local cultural sector (museums, libraries and archives) has played a significant role in this 'civic localism'. In his discussion of the sector's role, Kevin Harris conceptualizes museums, libraries and archives as community resources that support political participation. These institutions symbolize civic values, provide resources and expertise to inform citizenship and promote a sense of belonging and inclusion in a particular place (Harris 2006). With their growing understanding of their role in the public realm, museums' use of their exhibition and meeting spaces can contribute to the enlarged understanding and reciprocity that animates citizenship (Young 1997).

In Australia, the government has lately reaffirmed its 'unwavering support for a culturally diverse and socially cohesive nation' and restated its commitment to multiculturalism: 'a truly robust society *is* a multicultural society' (Bowen 2011). Migrants are offered 'an invitation to inclusion' that requires their commitment to Australian democratic values and that emphasizes individual freedoms:

> Multiculturalism is about involving every individual member of society to be everything they can be and supporting each new arrival in overcoming whatever obstacles they face as they adjust to a new country and society and allowing them to flourish as individuals. It is a matter of liberalism.
>
> (Bowen 2011)

Migrants' rate of take-up of Australian citizenship is one of the highest among Organisation for Economic Co-operation and Development (OECD) countries. Citizenship confers national membership: political, legal, social and civil rights that secure and protect the individual and shape Australia's democratic institutions. While research commissioned by the Department of Immigration and Citizenship (DIMAC) demonstrates high levels of employment among migrants who have taken up citizenship (Smith *et al.* 2010), the Australian Multicultural Advisory Council (AMAC) has expressed concern that some cultural and migrant groups exhibit low rates of social participation. The Council, who advises on issues relating to social cohesion and migrants' social and civic participation, has recommended that the government's social inclusion agenda, which emphasizes access to education, economic participation and welfare services, should also recognize and address the particular needs of vulnerable migrants and refugees. AMAC's emphasis on the value of 'overlapping social participation' underlines its approach to integration and provides an opportunity for the cultural sector to play a part in social inclusion. Community arts organizations have been the focus of projects and events that celebrate diversity and promote harmony and belonging. Museums at the local and state level have acknowledged Australia's migrant history, represented the experience of different cultural groups and increasingly provided resources to support intercultural communication.

Museums and citizenship

Lois Silverman brings social work perspectives to the museum's work as an agent of social change and well being. She describes it as a communicative institution:

Fundamentally, museums offer interactive social experiences of communication in which relationships are activated and people make meaning of objects. This communication yields beneficial consequences: people may meet fundamental human needs like the need for self-esteem and self-actualization; achieve change in essential areas such as knowledge, skills, values and behaviour; build and strengthen social connections and relationships, including social capital; address social problems; and promote social justice and equality. The consequences may involve and/or benefit individuals, groups and society at large. In effect, through museum communication people enact, share, and alter key elements of *culture* that shape the very operation, quality and experience of social life. This includes not only our selves, relationships, social problems and social structure, but also the understandings, solutions, and broader vision that inform our daily lives as well as our individual and shared futures.

(Silverman 2010: 21)

While Silverman makes large claims for the museum here, she also expresses an aspiration that guides contemporary museum practice, especially in social history museums and museums of memory. These museums value social justice and inclusiveness and see themselves as agents of social regeneration and change (Sandell 1998). Responding to the growing global influence of human rights discourses, the proliferation of previously marginalized voices and the impact on Western societies of increased global mobility, museums have reoriented their role and purpose as 'agencies with the potential to promote cross-cultural understanding and respect' (Sandell 2006). In the Australian context, immigrants and the migrant experience are a focus of that aspiration. Migration museums are supported by state and local governments to engage with local populations and visitors. Their strategies emphasize voice and representation, offering migrants and community groups a means to tell their stories and share their cultures.

The case studies discussed here show how, in their separate locations, each of these museums engages with the tensions between identity and difference, offering a space for individuals to negotiate their individual identities, social ties and civic responsibilities. The museums play a role in linking personal and collective narratives, promote a sense of belonging and reflect the changing social realities of community life. Exhibitions and public programs provide a space of dialogue where differences can be expressed and potentially understood. 'By listening to the different stories others tell, and giving their own in exchange, [people] come to see their common and interwoven histories together form a multiplicity of paths' (Tully 1995: 26).

Public memory: the Immigration Museum, Melbourne

The Immigration Museum's purpose is to connect and collaborate with culturally and linguistically diverse communities in the state of Victoria to create exhibitions and cultural festivals. The museum curates its own exhibitions, hosts travelling exhibitions, screens films and provides individuals with databases and other resources to trace and record their own histories. The permanent exhibitions explore aspects of migrant experience (*Leaving Home*; *Journeys of a Lifetime*), document changes in migration policy (*Getting In*) and address issues of belonging (*Identity: Yours, Mine, Ours*). The museum's partnerships with communities, as much as the exhibitions and events, promote mutual respect, open dialogue and collaboration. Community members are involved in planning projects, research and development of collections and in evaluation of outcomes.

The museum has access to resources provided by Museums Victoria and acts as a portal to those resources. Most significant of these is *Origins*, a web-based resource accessed through touch screens in the museum. It brings together historical statistics, documents and photographs that provide information about the history of migration to Victoria since 1854. The communities it identifies are constituted by population size at the 2006 census: data is available for groups of 1,100 or more born in the country of origin. It includes demographic data (such as age, gender, faith, employment) represented numerically and graphically and in official languages of the country of origin, as well as English. This resource provides a 'bigger picture' context for exhibitions and confirms Australia's status as a nation of immigrants. Almost half the population is overseas-born or has one parent who was born overseas.

The museum's activities reflect that reality. They also create a context where official and vernacular narratives and memories come into contact and potentially conflict (Rowe *et al.* 2002). The official narrative acknowledges migrant histories, incorporates migrants into the larger Australian narrative of settlement and offers a positive view of diversity. Its orientation to voice and representation opens a space for vernacular narratives that challenge accepted views and offer new perspectives. This unsettles the authority of the institutional voice and provides an entry point for dialogue.

Temporary exhibitions have highlighted particular communities. A travelling exhibition from the Migration Museum in Adelaide, *Australia's Muslim Cameleers*, documents Australia's 'first Muslim community', the cameleers who came from India and Afghanistan to support exploration and to provide transport links in central Australia from the 1860s. The exhibition establishes a longer history of Muslims in Australia and incorporates them into Australian settler history as pioneers and part of the enterprise of opening up the outback. *Survival of a Culture: Kurds in Australia* presents a narrative of cultural survival, focused on practices such as tattooing, carpet making, music, dance and textiles. Objects represent the resilience of the Kurds in the face of the partition of traditional lands, conflict and violence. The arrival of refugees since the 1980s – from the Middle East, Armenia and Georgia – and their cultural adaptation provides the main thread of the narrative.

A continuing collaboration with multimedia students from Victoria University of Technology, whose campuses are located in suburbs with concentrated migrant populations, has produced a series of short films *Narratives Across Cultures*. These films explore common refugee experiences: deportation, resettlement, the impacts of displacement and loss of homelands. While this project represents a migrant experience, it also required the filmmakers to come to their own informed understanding of the issues and to think about their role as intermediaries of that experience for visitors. Individuals and groups also generate their own histories through everyday objects. *Small Object Big Story* is an online resource that provides a model of research practice, gives guidance in research skills (interviewing, oral history methods, establishing the provenance of objects) and encourages the wider dissemination of stories through advice on publication and exhibition making. Apart from individuals, the resources are used by schools, community groups and adult learners.

The notion of contested narrative has altered the practice of social historians, who have exploited new methods and genres to include and legitimate marginal people and their experience. The expansion of museum practice to incorporate other voices has drawn on these methodologies, but additionally reproduces elements of the public square. However, voices are not heard simultaneously, but are orchestrated through the design of physical and virtual spaces and the sensitive use of interpretive text. The role of the professional curator is to contextualize migrant experience so that the museum visitor is able to mediate vernacular and official narratives.

A city museum: Museum of Brisbane

Museums have long been embedded in local communities, interpreting place, its natural history and the modes of human habitation it has supported. The Museum of Brisbane (MoB) was conceived as a city museum, to engage local communities with 'ideas and stories that illuminate Brisbane's past and present and help us to imagine our future'. MoB's mission is to promote community well being and social cohesion and to be a vital part of city life. Its exhibitions and public programs have represented the diversity of the city's population, recovered histories of marginalized people, documented political dissent, examined city architecture and planning, and celebrated everyday life.

The museum actively involves members of the community in developing exhibitions. Like other local government services, MoB's focus is community engagement. Its inner city location, in a City Hall that has traditionally been a meeting place, is supplemented by access to the suburban network of Brisbane City Council libraries, which runs its own series of public programs. The museum is a community resource, creating a sense of place and belonging and contributing to quality of life for local residents, as well as providing a destination where visitors can experience the social history of Brisbane. This engagement brings publics into being, encouraging participation in an expanded community of memory, spirit and ideas (Kotler and Kotler 2000: 277).

Brisbane City Council is responsible for the largest local government area in Australia and one whose migrant population is rapidly growing and diversifying. The history of migration and the contribution of migrants to Brisbane life has been a recurrent theme of MoB's exhibitions. They have focused on the continuing transformation of the city by successive waves of migrants from Europe, Asia, the Middle East and Africa and on the shared destiny of established residents and recent arrivals. They have explored migrants' adaptation to their new location, the importance of faith in the community and the entrepreneurial spirit of migrant communities.

Moorooka Encounters documented a suburban shopping strip, profiling the shopkeepers who work there. The diversity of their origins – Italian, Ethiopian, Eritrean, Sudanese – is reflected in the businesses they run, from cafes to credit unions. Their 'unique and personal stories' reveal the circumstances that brought them here, their hopes for the future and their varied contributions to the local economy. *Communities of Faith Walking Together* responded to community interest in a project to encourage intercultural understanding of ethical pluralism. Its intention was 'to increase understanding and respect between faith communities and foster awareness within the wider community'. Its evolution over several years involved representatives of nine religious groups, their leaders and communities, including the Ba'hai, Buddhist, Christian, Hindu, Jewish, Muslim, Sikh and Taoist faiths and Aboriginal spirituality. The groups themselves sourced materials for the exhibition, arranged photography and contributed to all dimensions of the displays. The exhibition was designed to provoke questions about belief and the place of faith in contemporary society. The process of its development also brought questions of authority and community to the fore. Determining who could speak for a community and how that community constituted itself was a confronting experience for both museum staff and the groups themselves.

Walking Together might describe the ways MoB contributes to more engaged citizenship. The communities who contribute ideas, objects and civic spirit to exhibitions also actively deliberate about shared values, collective identities and commitments. This process also exposes differences and presents practical problems to be resolved within the group: who speaks for the community, how their lives should be represented and how objects and narratives are to be interpreted. Museum professionals act as civic intermediaries, providing resources and enabling connections. These practices give meaning to diversity in the local context and help foster new solidarities.

A community museum: the Jewish Museum of Australia, Melbourne

The Jewish Museum of Australia has been in existence since 1982, initially located in the synagogue of the Melbourne Hebrew Congregation, but since 1993 in its own building in St Kilda. While this move affirmed its purpose as a cultural, not a religious institution, it remains embedded in the Melbourne Jewish community. Its purpose is to 'explore and share the Jewish experience in Australia and benefit Australia's diverse society'. The design of the exhibition spaces reflects that purpose.

The permanent exhibition represents facets of Jewish life and tradition. To enter the space, the visitor passes a small painting representing the horror of the

Holocaust, a reminder of the shared history and suffering of Jewish people. Within, the exhibition reflects the flourishing of Jewish life in a pluralist society. Jewish people have settled in Melbourne since the late nineteenth century and in larger numbers after World War II. Their successful integration has secured the future of new generations but threatens the continuity of identity. As its director has observed, museums have become important institutions in the Diaspora, exploring the 'question of minority identity within the multicultural mosaic'. They are a community resource, enabling individuals to enrich their own identity and understanding of what it means to be Jewish, while supporting and revitalizing collective identity (Light 2005). The Australian museum's links to an international network of similar museums promotes transnational cooperation and sharing of expertise.

Like the Immigration Museum and the MoB, the Jewish Museum engages directly with individuals wishing to explore their migrant experience. The Babel Project extends the museum's reach beyond St Kilda. This community arts project provides free cameras and photography workshops in outer suburban locations from industrial Broadmeadows to rural Packenham. Professional photographers share expertise and skills to enable participants to document experiences of diversity and multiculturalism.

The permanent exhibition establishes the museum's interpretive horizon, while its occasional exhibitions and programs typically connect with larger public issues. That connection is made through the theme, 'Justice and Law'. In 2010 and 2011, the museum focused its attention on refugees and irregular migrations, a contentious question in Australia as elsewhere. Here, the treatment of 'illegal arrivals' and 'queue jumpers' has polarized public opinion. The museum has opened a space for discussion of these issues. It participated in public commemoration of the arrival of HMT *Dunera* in Australia during World War II, with a lecture by the distinguished historian Ken Inglis on the internment of 'enemy aliens'. An exhibition, *Children in Detention*, comprising drawings by children held in the Woomera and Maribyrnong Detention Centres, engaged with the obligation to protect children in the wake of the political scandal surrounding the Federal Government's response to the sinking of refugee boats. A public program on 'people smugglers' exposes failures of leadership on these issues.

The practices of these museums demonstrate their aspiration to provide a forum for community debate and to be a repository of objects and stories. Their engagement with cultural diversity and ethical pluralism is underpinned by a commitment to democratic values of equality, fairness and justice. While their exhibitions and public programs accord recognition to migrants, they also understand the migrant experience as a process of negotiating a life with others. Their public spaces offer opportunities for the kinds of encounter that turn strangers into acquaintances.

Communication and inclusion

Iris Marion Young's work offers a way of conceptualizing the contribution of the museum to the project of democratic inclusion. Like Seyla Benhabib (1992, 2004) and Nancy Fraser (1992), Young has examined how formal equality is reinforced or undermined by norms of democratic communication and the organization of the public sphere as a realm of rationality. Policy interventions aimed at including minorities and the marginalized have often and too apparently failed to make a difference in organizations and the broader public sphere. While members of these groups have a presence, their influence is diminished by norms and protocols that have an exclusionary effect. Young has developed an analysis of alternative modes of communication that have enabled more voices to be heard in the public sphere, have promoted better understanding across socially structured groups and support the emergence of new solidarities or 'local publics'.

The alternative modes of communication that she identifies are greeting (or public acknowledgment), rhetoric and narrative. They do not replace the kind of argument that is necessary to address disagreement and competing claims for justice, but they build the capacity of all participants in debate. Together, these modes can enable argument, by promoting respect and trust, and extend argument, by motivating action.

> Inclusive democratic communication assumes that all participants have something to teach the public about the society in which they dwell together and its problems. It assumes as well that all participants are ignorant of some aspects of the social or natural world, and that everyone comes to a political conflict with some biases, prejudices, blind spots or stereotypes. Frequently in situations of political disagreement, one faction assumes that they know what it is like for others, or that they can put themselves in the place of others, or that they are really just like the others. Especially in mass society, where knowledge of others may be largely mediated by statistical generalities, there may be little understanding of lived need or interest across groups. A norm of political communication under these conditions is that everyone should aim to enlarge their social understanding by learning about the specific experience and meanings attending other social locations. Narratives make this easier and sometimes an adventure.
>
> (Young 2000: 77)

Meaningful political discussion requires shared understandings: of what the dimensions of a problem are, of normative principles that apply and a shared idiom in which alternatives might be expressed.

Narrative, according to Young, can sometimes speak more effectively across differences to establish these shared understandings. She identifies five ways that storytelling can foster participation and motivate collective action across structurally differentiated social groups. Storytelling can express the experience of being wronged and help to translate mute suffering into a claim for justice. It can articulate collective affinities and facilitate the formation of a local public. Members of that local public can use narrative to politicize their situation. Their stories in turn can counter prejudice and lack of understanding in the wider community. Stories also reveal the source of values, priorities and cultural meanings which underpin the normative principles of particular groups. Perhaps most importantly, narrative enlarges thought:

> By means of narratives expressed in public with others differently situated who also tell their stories, speakers and listeners can develop the 'enlarged thought' that transforms their thinking about issues from being narrowly self interested or self-regarding about an issue, to thinking about an issue in a way that takes account of the perspectives of others.
> (Young 2000: 76)

Difference does not disappear in Young's conception of the public realm. She follows Hannah Arendt in 'understanding plurality rather than unity as a defining characteristic of a public' (Young 2000: 111). The public is a space of conflict, not comfort, and difference is not an obstacle to be overcome or set aside in the pursuit of an identity in common. For her, difference is a resource that can be drawn on in the formation of social groups, collectives of individuals defined through their actions and interactions with each other, and through the actions and interactions of individuals outside the group (Young 2000: 89). Unlike associations, social groups are not formed around a common objective or agenda of action. Nor do they have identities, though individuals' identities and statuses are formed through their positioning within such groups. They may build on or overlap with cultural groups, but it is their positioning within the social structure that is critical: 'a structural social group is a collection of persons who are similarly positioned in interactive and institutional relations that condition their opportunities and life prospects' (Young 2000: 97). Relations of inequality, of domination and subordination are the basis of public political claims, rather than assertions of identity or distinctiveness.

A world of strangers

In *The Fall of Public Man* (1977) Richard Sennett traced the emergence of 'the intimate society' beginning in the rapid urbanization of the nineteenth century and culminating in the obsession with personality and celebrity of the late twentieth century. This concern has driven Sennett's continuing interest in the shifting balance of private and public life in the information age. His theme is the importance of impersonal social relationships in creating a just society. His work acknowledges a debt to Alexis de Tocqueville, who voiced a similar anxiety:

> Each person, withdrawn into himself, behaves as though he is a stranger to the destiny of all the others. His children and his good friends constitute for him the whole of the human species. As for his transactions with his fellow

citizens, he may mix among them, but he sees them not; he touches them, but does not feel them; he exists only in himself and for himself alone. And if on these terms there remains in his mind a sense of family, there no longer remains a sense of society.

(de Toqueville, cited in Sennett 1977)

The intensification of private life has come to pass, in a globalizing world where boundaries separating private and public space have been permeated by electronic media. 'Home' is now a threshold onto a world of abstraction (flows of money, information, people), a site of impersonal transactions with corporations and government, and extended, intensified and inescapable contact with the workplace. It is also regarded as a safe haven, a focus of personal networks with family and friends, close at hand and distant. Individuals invest considerable time and resources in maintaining this personal space.

Alain Touraine has characterized this world as one of 'multi-communitarianism'. In the Global North, individuals are positioned at the juncture of an extroverted desocialized world of instrumental relationships and an introverted private world of ethical formation where we pursue our personal projects (Touraine 2000). At the same time, the global movement of people and the expansion of communication networks have given ethical pluralism a new visibility. Political borders and social categories are more permeable, but some categorical (cultural, ethnic) identities have solidified. In the midst of this mobility, we can no longer behave as strangers to the destiny of others. But new kinds of public space and new forms of communication and engagement are required to effect this change.

In the industrializing world of modernity, urban and communicative spaces were compartmentalized and specialized. Institutions loomed large and played a critical role in separating social identities. The crowd was encountered face to face on the streets. In the contemporary mass-mediated age, institutions have become more permeable and accessible through their web presences; their physical locations are dispersed. Communities of interaction are transportable, through mobile devices and connections. Mobility means taking your familiars with you, across cities and continents. As our relocation to the 'virtual' world of electronic communication takes hold, web-enabled life also hosts shifting worlds of strangers.

Joshua Meyrowitz has described the changing relations of inclusion and exclusion, familiarity and strangeness. In traditional societies, a relatively thick boundary separates insiders and outsiders: 'Each oral society is a small world of "familiars" separated from a vast and mysterious world of strangers.' In modern societies, brought into being through the technology of print and the expansion of mass literacy, the larger boundary of the nation-state is a permeable but regulated border. Within it, hierarchies of class, gender, ethnicity and age create internal and shifting boundaries. 'Members of the modern nation-state move in and out of the internal boundaries on a regular basis, and the encountering of strangers within the boundaries of the nation is a frequent occurrence' (Meyrowitz 1997: 69). Now, according to Alain Touraine, the boundaries take a new form. 'Global' citizens live their instrumental lives in a borderless world of markets and communication, while their cocooned private lives are centred on producing themselves as subjects.

While privileged groups are the beneficiaries of this world of possibilities, vulnerable groups of migrants and refugees seek the protection of solidarities. In Australia, migrants from troubled places have taken out citizenship, to be afforded the security of an Australian passport and to formalize social and political membership. Their inclusion as citizens and their claims to equality, however, require the kind of expanded political communication that Young describes. Museums have an important role to play as sites of that communication and as places of belonging.

The International Network of Migration Institutions may prove to be one of UNESCO's most important contributions to international cooperation and security. The emergence of the civic museum in Europe is symbolized by the opening of a new museum of immigration in Paris in 2007. The *Cité Nationale de l'Histoire de l'Immigration* gives a new legitimacy to migrant experience in France. Since the emergence of *les Beurs* through the protest march of 1983, rising racial tension in *les banlieues* and the '*affaires des foulards*' have exposed the vulnerability of the Republic's commitment to secularism. The structures, rules and manners denoted by *laïcité* limit access to the public sphere. While cultural and religious difference is sequestered in the private sphere and characterized as traditional and backward looking, the actually existing inequalities of the dominant culture are screened from view. Instead of a retreat from multiculturalism, the state needs to find new ways to be inclusive (Scott 2007).

Theorists of the public sphere argue that the French commitment to secularism constrains the range of identities that can be visible and active in the civic realm. The logic of identity is deployed in a way that turns difference into absolute otherness (Young 2000). Secularism conceals a profound antipathy to difference and the insistence on a unique 'French' identity closes off the possibilities of politics (Scott 2007; Volpp 2007).

The new Immigration Museum, located in the former Palace of the Colonies, will provide a forum where such issues can be explored and policy changes advocated. Replacing the word '*musée*' with '*cité*' in the museum's name, highlights the new role that is being created for this cultural institution, which is determined to 'shed light on what it means to be French in a world in which the issue of identity causes tension and denial' and to acknowledge the contribution that 'foreigners' have made (Vinson 2007: 2). Perhaps one of the museum's achievements will be to develop a new idiom for republican citizenship that consigns the term 'foreigner' to the archive.

Bibliography

Australian Multicultural Advisory Council (2010) *The People of Australia: The Australian Multicultural Advisory Council's statement on cultural diversity and recommendationstogovernment.* Availableat:www.immi.gov.au/about/stakeholder-engagement/_pdf/people-of-australia.pdf. (accessed 6 April 2011).

Bennett, T. (1995) *The Birth of the Museum: History, Theory, Politics*, London and New York: Routledge.
Benhabib, S. (1992) *Situating the Self: Gender, Community and Postmodernism in Contemporary Ethics*, New York: Routledge.
Benhabib, S. (2004) *The Rights of Others: Aliens, Residents and Citizens*, Cambridge: Cambridge University Press.
Black, G. (2011) 'Museums, memory and history', *Cultural and Social History*, 8(3): 415–27.
Bowen, C. (2011) 'Multiculturalism in the Australian context', *The Sydney Institute Papers Online*, Issue 10.
Fraser, N. (1992) 'Rethinking the public sphere: a contribution to the critique of actually existing democracy', in C. Calhoun (ed.) *Habermas and the Public Sphere*. Cambridge: MIT Press.
Gurian, E.H. (2006) *Civilizing the Museum: The Collected Writings of Elaine Heumann Gurian*, London and New York: Routledge.
Harris, K. (2006) *Localism, Governance and the Public Realm: Issues for the Local Cultural Sector*, London: Museums, Libraries and Archives Council.
Janes, R. (2009) *Museums in a Troubled World: Renewal, Irrelevance or Collapse?*, London and New York: Routledge.
Kotler, N. and Kotler, P. (2000) 'Can museums be all things to all people?: missions, goals and marketing's role', *Museum Management and Curatorship*, 18(3): 271–87.
Levey, G.B. (2009) 'Review article: what is living and what is dead in multiculturalism', *Ethnicities*, 9(1): 75–93.
Light, H. (2005) 'Changing headsets: the impact of museums on social thinking', 2005 Australia–Israel Hawke Lecture, The Bob Hawke Prime Ministerial Centre, University of South Australia.
McLean, K. (1999) 'Museum exhibitions and the dynamics of dialogue', *Daedalus*, 128(3): 83–107.
Meyrowitz, J. (1997) 'Shifting worlds of strangers: medium theory and changes in "them" versus "us"', *Sociological Inquiry*, 67(1): 59–71.
Prior, N. (2011) 'Speed, rhythm and time-space: museums and cities', *Space and Culture*, 14(2): 197–213.
Rowe, S.M., Wertsch, J.V. and Kosyaeva, T.Y. (2002) 'Linking little narratives to big ones: narrative and public memory in history museums', *Culture and Psychology*, 8(1): 96–112.
Sandell, R. (1998) 'Museums as agents of social inclusion', *Museum Management and Curatorship*, 17(4): 401–18.
Sandell, R. (2006) *Museums, Prejudice and the Reframing of Difference*, New York: Routledge.
Scott, J. W. (2007) *The Politics of the Veil*, Princeton: Princeton University Press.
Sennett, R. (1977) *The Fall of Public Man*, London: Penguin.
Silverman, L.H. (2010) *The Social Work of Museums*, New York: Routledge.
Smith, D., Wykes, J., Jayarajah, S. and Fabijanic, T. (2010) *Citizenship in Australia*, Canberra: Department of Immigration and Citizenship.
Smith, R.M. (2003) *Stories of Peoplehood: The Politics and Morals of Political Membership*, Cambridge: Cambridge University Press.
Touraine, A. (2000) *Can We Live Together? Equality and Difference*, Cambridge: Polity Press.
Tully, J. (1995) *Strange Multiplicity*, Cambridge: Cambridge University Press.

Vinson, I. (2007) 'Editorial: the legacy of migrants', *Museum International*, 233–34: 1–4.
Volpp, L. (2007) 'The culture of citizenship', *Theoretical Inquiries in Law*, 8: 571–601.
Young, I.M. (1997) 'Asymmetrical reciprocity: on moral respect, wonder and enlarged thought', *Constellations*, 3(3): 341–63.
Young, I.M. (2000) *Inclusion and Democracy*, Oxford: Oxford University Press.

Websites

Immigration Museum: www.museumvictoria.com.au/immigrationmuseum
Jewish Museum of Australia: www.jewishmuseum.com.au
Museum of Brisbane: www.museumofbrisbane.com.au
Social Inclusion: www.socialinclusion.gov.au
United Nations Educational, Scientific and Cultural Organization (UNESCO), International Organization for Migration, Migration Museums Initiative: www.migrationmuseums.org

5 Negotiating migration, sentiment, and insecurity
Encounters with sadness and shame in Australia

Sara Wills

In 2005, Australians were witness to revelations about the treatment of two women caught up in the 'border disorder' around refugees and migrants, security and insecurity, citizenship and social inclusion in Australia. Receiving prominent coverage in the media, these are cases that alert us in particularly stark form to the existence of insecure migrant belonging in Australia, and the partiality and differential quality of integration for some, especially at a time of heightened 'national security'. Specifically, I draw attention here to the manner in which facing up to these women's stories provides insight into processes of national remembering and forgetting – revelation and concealment – of the 'public secret' of migrant melancholy in Australia. Having first assembled an 'archive of feeling' and considered how forms of migrant sadness may question integration and security, I address the circumstances of these women's cases and highlight findings of two major inquiries in order to introduce questions of culture and sadness. I then examine how representations of these two women (de)faced the nation and performed but also masked shameful (auto)biographies. By coming face-to-face with sadness, however masked or concealed, considerable meaning emerges, as well as new ethical possibilities for migrant hospitality and belonging in Australia. These are in part contingent on the embodied presence of a melancholic migrant subject in Australia and the capacity to be touched by the memories that could thread us together to form new and affective communities.

(Dis)integration: an archive of migrant feeling

1 Cornelia, May 2005

A German-born woman resident in Australia is released from a psychiatric hospital in South Australia; she had previously spent ten months in various forms of immigration detention. She faces the press to tell her story: 'I was locked up like a caged animal', she says, 'this isn't supposed to happen to people like me in Australia'. Defiant. Indignant. Brave. Mad? At one moment her face drops, her skin reddens, and I am touched by her sadness; the flush of her face becomes:

a sort of superabundance of connectedness when the face has to hyper-mask, or as a giveaway sign of shame, reveal to the world that one has given away something secret, imposed on secret terrain, or had one's secret revealed.
(Taussig 1999: 38)

2 Vivian, May 2005

Rumours that a Filipino-born woman with Australian citizenship had been deported four years ago emerge in the Australian press. She is then discovered 'ailing but alive' in a hospice in Olongapo, north-west of Manila. Following a front-page story revealing 'the face unacceptable to Australia', another smaller article features a photo of a worried Vivian turning in a wheelchair to ask: 'Are you going to look after me, really?' Later a Commonwealth Ombudsman's report finds this to be a 'shameful episode' in the history of Australia, and I continue to worry about the possibilities for Vivian being looked after 'really'.

The pain of such women ... not evoked or sentimentalised as the true burden of community, but mov[ing] the story on, as a sign of the persistence of a connection, a thread between others, in the face of separation.
(Ahmed 2004: 39)

3 Me, December 2005

A British-born woman with Australian citizenship tells the story of Cornelia and Vivian at a conference on Australia's 'faces and interfaces' in Paris. As she leaves the conference, an Australian-born anthropologist resident in France catches her in the street and says: 'Do you know how much your face mirrors that of the women you are describing?' She reaches out to touch my arm and says: 'This migrant sadness is almost unbearable'.

It is by means of this contingency that I am alerted to the tenderness of face and of faces facing each other, tense with the expectation of secrets as fathomless as they seem worthy of unmasking.
(Taussig 1999: 3)

4 Mammad, January 2006

Following anti-immigrant riots at Cronulla Beach in Sydney and related attacks on Australians 'of Middle Eastern appearance', an Iranian-born writer now resident in Australia speaks to me about phenomenology, sadness, the destruction and loss of 'home', and the gaps in authentic dialogue between migrants in Australia. He tells me that after 20 years he is still encountered as 'other' in Australia and we speak about the possibilities for 'co-authentic' experiences of belonging with other migrants. He reminds me that sadness is the beginning of philosophy and, not for the first time, we consider that sadness may be productive of authentic and hospitable community in Australia.

> I think it is possible to say that this kind of sadness can also be creative if you know you're fooling yourself into some kind of aesthetic posture. There is a normative element in this [but] ... the solitude of creative sadness organises a community of feeling which knows how to read between the lines.... Without being confessive, a writer adopts a voice. Without seeking self-reference, a reader puts on a mask of curiosity.
>
> (Castro 2007: 4)

Questioning integration and migrant security through sadness

Like any archive, an archive of feeling is a mark of particular (and not disinterested) curiosity in gathering information that 'belongs' together. The 'contact zone' assembled above, for example, takes shape because of how I have moved towards 'others' and been touched: because of threads that run between the personal and the public, the individual and the social, and between a reader and her chosen texts.[1] It marks, therefore, the performance of an affection, but also of an attempt at integration: a bringing together of moments when migrant insecurity in Australia is sharply encountered. In such moments, I argue, it is possible to appreciate how the experience and mediation of insecure belonging effects the circulation of sentiment between migrant bodies, and how these sentiments may be productive of a semi-permanent community and culture premised on non-integration and sadness. However unwanted, damaging, and destructive, such public and personal moments of lost cohesion and sadness enable, I argue, the recognition of more complex forms of belonging in Australia and offer also an alternative, non-instrumental mode of valuing forms of differential integration and migrant community.

In particular, I am concerned in this chapter to 'organize a community of feeling' to examine the cases of two women much more than sadly – more like catastrophically – (mis)understood and (mis)treated by Australian immigration authorities between 2001 and 2005. I want to explore the possibilities and meanings generated by thinking about the mediation of these cases, both in a public realm and at a national level, but also through my reading of a more intimate everyday encounter still formative of social space. Drawing on Sara Ahmed's discussion of 'strange encounters' and the cultural politics of emotion, I am drawn to understand such mediations as always 'partial' but still productive of meaning and forms of sociality. I am interested, like Ahmed, in 'how [the stranger] is put to work, and made to work in particular times and places' (including in my own labours), by acknowledging the 'modes of encounter' through which others are faced (Ahmed 2000: 15, 144–5). Facing these women in sadness is one way that I hope to hold open a space that is 'receptive to the trace ... of the self in the other and the other in the self' (Scott 2005: 14).

Migration, sentiment, and insecurity 67

The women in question are Cornelia Rau and Vivian Alvarez Solon, whose cases became well-known in Australia in 2005. Reading the newspaper articles and reports generated by the Rau and Alvarez Solon cases began, for me, as part of an ongoing effort to understand the representations and dissimulations, public presences and absences, and social and cultural memories and forgettings of migrancy – of the experience and position of the migrant and migrant consciousness – in Australia. This inquiry took on a more urgent and critical form as increased numbers of asylum seekers reached Australia's shores from the late 1990s and were 'detained, deterred and denied' in ways that pointed to an almost utter abjection of memory in a migrant nation: of an inability to 're-member' sadness and loss (Wills 2004: 50–65). Subsequently, watching the emergence of the stories of Rau and Alvarez Solon, and particularly the striking presence of their faces across the Australian news media, I felt these traces invoked both their individual sorrows and pain and a collective form. Through processes of revelation and concealment, individual and collective sadness came to be held in tension.

So I want to consider questions of sadness, community and culture here to contribute to an archive of migrant feeling that I find lacking or insufficiently articulated in Australia, and which speaks to new conditions for the experience of security in Australia. Focusing particularly on feelings of loss and sadness, I draw on those who argue for the 'capaciousness of meaning in relation to losses encompassing the individual and the collective' (Eng and Kazanjian 2003: 3) and contend that a focus on migrant sadness may create new representations of the nation and alternative possibilities for community and belonging. I am motivated in part by the call to recognize sadness as a 'militant affect' – as formative of an active, abundant, social, and 'prescient space of socialized becoming' – and as a 'crucial touchstone for social and subjective formations' (Eng and Kazanjian 2003: 10, 14, 23). I wish to create an opportunity to rethink national belonging in Australia in terms of affective encounters with migrant sadness.

It is not a totalizing claim; but in drawing attention to the 'melancholic agency' released by Australia's coming face-to-face with Cornelia Rau and Vivian Alvarez Solon – alongside their very specific histories – I respond also to larger questions about memory and melancholic community in Australia. These are questions that others in Australia have asked in relation to histories of colonialism and Indigenous dispossession, but may (somewhat problematically) apply also to questions of migrancy: the condition of being a migrant and the ongoing senses of place, space, and belonging formed in histories of interaction and (un)settlement. How is it that migrancy – and particularly a sad and unsettled migrancy – seems to appear and then (much more readily) disappear in public culture and history in Australia? As Chris Healy has argued, one of the ways such patterns occur is through some strangely repetitive forms of remembering and forgetting in Australia (Healy 2008: 8–10). We might think of these in this instance as forgetting the fact that Australia is a migrant nation and then 'uncovering' that history; forgetting what is left behind through migration and exile and then recalling it later; forgetting the incarceration of asylum seekers and then remembering their stories; forgetting Vivian and Cornelia and then facing up to these 'shameful episodes' in the media.

This is also to underline the ethics of such memory and identity formations 'as a question concerning politics' (Scott 2005: 13). Such ethics become vulnerable at times when a community or nation feels itself under threat. Yet, as Judith Butler has argued, '[i]f we are interested in arresting cycles of violence to produce less violent outcomes, it is important to ask what, politically, might be made of grief besides a cry for war' (Butler 2004: xii). Addressing the 'precarious life' in a migrant nation of subjects, such as Alvarez Solon and Rau, is to draw attention to the way that personal and national identity formations are not 'fixed and permanent ... through time but an always unfinished suturing together of fragments' (Scott 2005: 14). It is to argue for the necessity in Australia of:

> an ethics of the self and other [and hence forms of security and social inclusion] attuned precisely to the edges, the margins, where 'identity' [and 'security'] ceases to hold with certainty and where ambiguity, otherness, finitude, the outside, begin to decentre and undermine its fables of stable self-presence.
>
> (Scott 2005: 15)

Strange stories and sad cultures: the 'conundrum' of Cornelia and the 'matter' of Vivian

That the stories of Cornelia Rau and Vivian Alvarez Solon amounted to a 'conundrum' for the Australian Government is obvious not only because of the disastrous and criminal mishandling of their cases, but also through the details revealed and language utilized in subsequent official inquiries. The government's difficulty in handling what are identified by these inquiries as 'complex cases' and 'odd' and 'collateral histor[ies]' brings questions of culture, community, and sadness into particular focus. This is apparent from page one of the Inquiry into the Circumstances of the Immigration Detention of Cornelia Rau ('the Rau Inquiry') (Department of Immigration and Multiculturalism and Indigenous Affairs, DIMIA, 2005), which headed its introductory chapter with an outline of 'The Conundrum' in terms that appear simple if not stark:

> How could an Australian resident of German origin be detained in prison in Queensland for six months and at the Baxter Immigration Detention Facility for four months and not be identified for all that time? How could this person's long-standing medical condition remain undiagnosed? How could she undergo a six-day in-patient psychiatric assessment at Princess Alexandria Hospital and be diagnosed as not suffering from a mental illness? Why did it take so long to have her re-assessed in a dedicated psychiatric facility at the Glenside Campus of the Royal Adelaide Hospital, despite a continuing record of 'odd' and 'bizarre' behaviour?
>
> (DIMIA 2005: 1)

The 208 page report then outlines 'the sequence of events', laying out the journey of Cornelia Rau ('Cornelia') from March 2004, when she was first detained under the Migration Act on suspicion of being an unlawful non-citizen. The report highlights that DIMIA focused on establishing Cornelia's identity 'for the purpose of enabling her removal from the country' (DIMIA 2005: viii), rather than fully investigating the possibility that she might be an Australian resident. Owing in part to Cornelia's unwillingness and incapacity to reveal her identity – but also the failure of police and DIMIA officials to identify her through other means and to properly assess the nature and extent of her illness – serious questions are asked in the report about the circumstances, policies, and procedures of immigration detention in Australia. It is concluded that 'the "system" failed Cornelia Rau' (DIMIA 2005: 107), with processes and policies that 'defied commonsense' and indicated: a 'disconnect' between DIMIA detention policy and the realities of operational requirements, including 'glacial' responses from DIMIA management to urgent operational concerns; an 'absence of any meaningful monitoring by DIMIA staff'; and an 'assumption culture' that limited the efforts made to provide an adequate standard of care (DIMIA 2005: 81, 43, 120).

As a consequence of its investigations, the report made 49 recommendations about policy and operational procedures. Yet the most significant outcomes were those outlined in a considerable number of the 34 'main findings' pertaining to 'deep-seated cultural and attitudinal problems within DIMIA' (DIMIA 2005: xi): 'a culture that is overly self-protective and defensive, a culture largely unwilling to challenge organisational norms or to engage in genuine self-criticism or analysis' (DIMIA 2005: ix). These findings about 'culture' need to be read in a wider context and considered as a feature of government and nation more broadly rather than the sole provenance of DIMIA. The Rau Inquiry's acknowledgment of this is only partial and implicit: when, for example, it gestures to 'lively debate in many quarters ... as a result of the influx of "boat people"', and that an understanding of 'past stories' or a 'melting pot of stories' was 'important in establishing context for the Inquiry' (DIMIA 2005: 7).

Here we sense that these are 'questions of culture' that circulate more broadly within Australia and indeed contribute to the 'considerable gap[s] in understanding' that the Inquiry finds within DIMIA (DIMIA 2005: 81). The Rau Inquiry outlines that 'fundamental cultural change' is required in the handling of complex cases, because '[t]he present culture seems to have operated to stifle original thought, inhibit individual action and discourage wider consultation or referral' (DIMIA 2005: 54). The 'prevailing culture' needs to be addressed (DIMIA 2005: 119), the Inquiry finds, in order to trace 'the footprints in the sand' left by those who have trouble establishing their identity (DIMIA 2005: 97): an ability to follow these traces needs to replace 'a culture of denial and self-justification' in face of the depression of many detainees and an inability to heed criticism of the system (DIMIA 2005: 168). Summarizing the need for cultural change, the report highlighted that an emphasis on 'quantitative yardsticks' rather than 'qualitative measures' had failed 'to deliver the outcomes required by government in a way that ... respects human dignity' (DIMIA 2005: 171). Outlining its concern that a 'control-minded culture ... might now be dominant' (DIMIA 2005: 173), it speaks most urgently of its concern about the need for broader 'cultural change and attitude realignment':

> The deficiencies in practices and procedures can be remedied, and many instructions are being amended. But the attitudes of the people who have responsibility for managing these instructions will take much longer to change. Old values and attitudes must be removed, and a new, enabling culture must be fostered...
>
> [T]he extensive reforms that are needed cannot come solely from within. The answer is not to be found in creating yet more structure: that itself sends the wrong message.
>
> (DIMIA 2005: 171–2)

The urgency of identifying, developing, and conveying the right message became only more tragically apparent with the release of findings into the case of Vivian Alvarez Solon.

Vivian Alvarez Solon ('Vivian') became an Australian citizen in March 1986, two years after her marriage to Robert William Young and her initial arrival in Australia from the Philippines. The 'Main Findings' of the Commonwealth Ombudsman's Inquiry into the Circumstances of the Vivian Alvarez Matter ('the Alvarez Inquiry') (Commonwealth Ombudsman 2005) state that she came to the attention of DIMIA following events in early March 2001 when she was found injured in a park in Lismore, New South Wales, having fallen into a deep drain. Vivian was admitted subsequently as an involuntary patient to a psychiatric unit. The Alvarez Inquiry states that a social worker at the unit advised local DIMIA officers that Vivian might be an illegal immigrant, but notes that her case was not actively pursued by DIMIA for over a month. The Inquiry states:

> DIMIA officers first interviewed Vivian on 3 May 2001, at Lismore Base Hospital. On the basis of information Vivian gave them, the officers involved assumed she was an unlawful non-citizen, and it is this assumption that appears to have been the catalyst for much of the subsequent response by DIMIA.
>
> (Commonwealth Ombudsman 2005: ix)

This began a 12-week period that saw a physically and mentally vulnerable woman shuffled between various forms of detention in Australia until she could be removed from the country. During the management of her case, which the Inquiry states 'can only be described as catastrophic', DIMIA officers failed to pursue and thus successfully establish Vivian's identity; they reneged on their responsibility to take action when opportunities to establish her identity arose and they compromised Vivian's privacy, dignity, and welfare. While the case was difficult and various misrepresentations were made by Vivian herself and while some DIMIA officers were found to have pursued their role with conscience and integrity, what emerges most clearly from the report are concerns about the 'negative culture' of DIMIA, the 'limited connectivity' not only between DIMIA's own divisions but also between DIMIA and other government agencies and the operation of immigration procedures in Australia.

This resulted in Vivian's eventual unlawful removal from Australia to the Philippines on 20 July 2005 in the most abject circumstances. A week prior to her removal in July 2001, Vivian was placed under 24-hour guard at a Brisbane motel, and the details of her last days in Australia are indicative of the failures of DIMIA to provide appropriate care. Notes in a log maintained during this period by the Australasian Correctional Management (ACM) staff responsible for guarding Vivian indicate that she was 'basically immobile/she requires assistance for walking, dressing and all basic hygiene needs' (Commonwealth Ombudsman 2005: 15). During this period, a DIMIA officer contacted a colleague in Manila to advise that Vivian is 'a very frail, tiny woman' and (erroneously) that she has 'no family in the Philippines to assist her' (Commonwealth Ombudsman 2005: 15). The Inquiry notes that on the same day a note was placed on DIMIA's Alvarez file that stated: 'Smuggled into Australia as a sex slave. Wants to return to the Philippines. Has been physically abused' (Commonwealth Ombudsman 2005: 15). None of these details were ever substantiated by the Inquiry. A memorandum was also sent on this day from the Philippines Embassy to the Philippines Honorary Consulate General in Brisbane asking the Consulate to:

> make representations with DIMIA for therapeutic counselling for Ms Alvarez before she is sent home ... [She] is obviously a trauma victim and would require necessary treatment.... Please impress upon DIMIA authorities that the Australian Government is currently collaborating with the Philippine Government on several initiatives to address the plight of women migrants in distressful conditions.... As such, DIMIA should be more compassionate to her plight and true to their commitment to help by being able to provide assistance beyond their traditional response of deportation.
> (Commonwealth Ombudsman 2005: 16)

Two days later a Filipino community representative visited Vivian and later gave evidence that she had seen her having a seizure. The Philippines Embassy contacted DIMIA to express concern about Vivian's ability to travel. DIMIA contacted ACM and asked them to arrange for a doctor to assess Vivian, but ACM arranged only for a locum medical practitioner, with no access to a medical history that had been established through considerable periods of hospitalization and assessment over the last three months. Vivian was certified 'medically fit' and on the following day was removed from Australia, escorted by a Senior Constable from the Queensland Police Service (Commonwealth Ombudsman 2005: 15–16).

While the exact course of events remain unclear, it seems that, on arrival in Manila, this officer left the wheelchair-bound Vivian in the care of a nun, whom the officer mistakenly assumed was at the airport to meet Vivian. After both the officer and the nun had departed, Qantas ground staff took Vivian to the counter of the Overseas Workers Welfare Association (OWWA) and OWWA personnel took Vivian to a nearby hospital for medical examination. Vivian was subsequently transferred to the OWWA Halfway Home for two days and then to the care of the Daughters of Charity at Olangapo. It emerged later that DIMIA had not made arrangements for Vivian's reception in Manila (Commonwealth Ombudsman 2005: 62). It was not until 12 May 2005 – almost four years later – that Vivian was 'discovered' by Australian authorities at this hospice. The Alvarez Inquiry found that it was only due to the persistence of Vivian's former husband, Robert Young, that this occurred.

While it is difficult to weigh or compare the degrees of dereliction of duty in this case – 'morally, professionally and legally' as the Inquiry found (Commonwealth Ombudsman 2005: 77) – possibly the most disturbing outcome of the Inquiry was the fact that Vivian's unlawful removal from Australia was discovered by several DIMIA officers at a number of stages throughout 2003. This included one occasion in August 2003 when, after a screening of the US drama *Without a Trace* on commercial television, a short profile was given of Vivian as a missing person. Although several senior DIMIA officers were notified of the unlawful removal of an Australian citizen, none took any action (Commonwealth Ombudsman 2005: xiv). During interviews with officers involved, the Inquiry found that one response from a Deputy State Director of DIMIA to the revelation of Vivian's removal was: 'This is terrible. Let's not spread it any wider than it has – than it has to be' (Commonwealth Ombudsman 2005: 81). Thus, even though Vivian had not disappeared 'without a trace', no serious attempt was made to face up to the matter. DIMIA staff also revealed to the Inquiry that they were concerned they would be 'criticised for pursuing welfare-related matters instead of focusing on the key performance indicators for removal' (Commonwealth Ombudsman 2005: 31). In a section outlining systemic problems with 'DIMIA culture', the Alvarez Inquiry stated that it had found substantial evidence to support the Inquiry into Cornelia Rau's case, and that 'the culture of DIMIA was so motivated by imperatives associated with the removal of unlawful non-citizens that officers failed to take into account basic human rights obligations' (Commonwealth Ombudsman 2005: 31). Perhaps symptomatic of the 'culture' at DIMIA is a statement made by one DIMIA officer during the Inquiry that '[t]here was a lot worse things going on than this particular case...'

> We were trying to deal with a huge amount of complex and difficult removal cases at the time ... [and I thought] that's not an issue I can resolve. This is bigger than me. This is huge ... I couldn't even think of a way out of it, insofar as how you could even begin to resolve it.
> (DIMIA Officer, quoted in Commonwealth Ombudsman 2005: 81)

Shameful (auto)biographies: women (de)facing the nation

The DIMIA officer was right: the issue was substantially bigger. And while it was and remains crucial that both inquiries' recommendations addressing policy and procedure were and continue to be pursued (and that Rau and Alvarez Solon were both eventually able to achieve degrees of rehabilitation), I want to argue here that it is much more than the culture of the Department of Immigration that needs addressing; it is also broader questions pertaining to migration and social inclusion – an (in)ability to narrate trauma and sadness as part of the nation-self (Bhabha 1990) and go beyond forms of 'stranger fetishism' and shame that fail to shift the boundaries of inclusion (Ahmed 2000: 7, 14).

The publication of both the Rau and Alvarez Solon inquiries was accompanied by a wide raft of telling press coverage, with the faces of these two women featuring prominently throughout the Australian media during May to September 2005 and their stories often circulating together. In the case of Rau, headlines included: 'Anna's journey in detention's living hell' (Roberts and Sproull 2005); 'Passport to madness' (Marr 2005); 'Rau's odyssey' (Topsfield 2005a); and 'Revealed: how nation failed Rau' (Roberts and Bockmann 2005). The Alvarez Solon case attracted similarly striking coverage: 'We threw out an Aussie' (Moncrief 2005); 'No one wanted to know her story, now everyone does' (Levett 2005a); 'Deported Australian left son behind' (Jackson 2005); 'Wrongly deported woman thought she was being helped' (Levett 2005b); and perhaps most memorably 'The face unacceptable to Australia' (Gordon and Gratton 2005). As these titles and captions indicate, in many cases these stories were reported and represented ultimately as a basis for a form of national shame in the face of 'catastrophic' mismanagement by the government. In the wake of further revelations about the government's (mis)handling of a variety of refugee and asylum seeker issues, including the detention of thousands of asylum seekers during this period (and later other botched or questionable deportations), the Rau and Alvarez Solon cases facilitated a considerable outpouring of emotion.

Highlighted in red bold print across the front pages of Melbourne's *The Age* broadsheet newspaper, for example, was a rendering of the verdict of the Alvarez Inquiry as a 'damning judgement against the Immigration Department':

> It is a shameful episode in the history of immigration to Australia. The management of Solon was 'catastrophic'. The unlawful removal of one of our citizens is 'almost unthinkable'.
>
> (Topsfield 2005b)

Much of the journalism was of a high calibre and my intention is not to question the reportage of individual writers or media outlets. Yet while these cases are described as 'almost unthinkable', clearly they are not quite. And what was also made 'thinkable' by the Rau and Alvarez Solon cases prompted other questions about forms of sociality, subjectivity, and belonging in Australia. Like others in Australia, I found myself comparing the exposure and degree of sympathy extended to these women with the fate of others caught in what has been described as the 'Kafkaesque' nightmare of Australia's immigration detention system since the 1990s. Asylum seekers from Central Asia or the Middle East, who were far less familiar to most in Australia during this period, remained faceless due in part to government directives not to publish 'humanizing' images of detainees and those seeking asylum. As some observed, the amount of exposure granted to the cases of Rau and Solon had something to do with the sense that they were, to a greater or lesser extent, 'one of us' rather than 'one of them'; that they were Australian citizens or residents rather than 'illegals', asylum seekers, or 'unlawful non-citizens'. Human rights lawyer and advocate Julian Burnside stated bluntly:

> The treatment received by Cornelia Rau is commonplace in Australia's detention centres. The only novel feature of the Rau case is that she is uncomfortably like us. She looks like a typical Aussie girl. We are shocked at her treatment.... Why is it acceptable to treat asylum seekers this way, but shocking when it is done to one of us? ... The answer to that question lies at the heart of the moral problems surrounding Australia's treatment of asylum seekers. It is an alarming possibility that the careless indifference of the department is simply a reflection of a society that is also indifferent to the fate of those of us who are not like us.
>
> (Burnside 2005)

On this basis, we might understand that Alvarez Solon suffered more because she was less 'like us' – because she had a face that was for some 'unthinkable' as Australian. Yet her case was not 'unthinkable' for those who saw the case as 'a warning for us all'. Reflecting on a 'culture of official racism' in Australia, *Age* journalist Jacqueline Hewitt was prompted by the Alvarez Solon case to recount her own racial profiling at customs 'every time I enter the country ... because I look oriental'. 'It's always a wonderful welcome back for people like me', she notes wryly. Hewitt was one of the few journalists to note that she also felt 'saddened, as the apparently safe nation that I live in is not so safe for my family, simply because my mother was born in another country' (Hewitt 2005).

Yet before we consider sadness as a response to the stories of Rau and Alvarez Solon, it is worth dwelling on the much more prevalent response of shame in the face of such stories. It has been argued that shame is a 'recurring element in Australian social history', relating 'not only to racism, but also to displacement, religion, war and migration' (Dalziell 1999: 4). More specifically, Rosamund Dalziell has considered the role of 'shameful autobiographies' in Australia and found them 'deeply embedded' in Australian culture. In particular, Dalziell argues, 'the emotion of shame threatens the self's sense of its own solidity', and thus generates a desire 'to affirm the existence of the self in the face of threats of dissolution'. 'The autobiography', Dalziell argues, 'can be read as an affirmation of the autonomy of the narrating self's memory' (Dalziell 1999: 11–16).

It is tempting to read both the inquiries and newspaper coverage of the Rau and Alverez Solon cases as a form of 'shameful autobiography', an 'emotion of self attention' that has a strong bearing on our sense of identity as it is intended for the gaze of others (Dalziell 1999: 253–4). As it is '[r]evealed: how nation failed Rau' (Roberts and Bockmann 2005), or when '[t]he Alvarez case [becomes] a warning for us all' (Hewitt 2005), the nation seems to waver on the brink of a response characterized by initial shock, sometimes sadness, but mostly by shame: how could this have happened in Australia? How shameful.

And yet this occurred during a decade in our history when we impounded thousands of asylum seekers, some of whom resorted to hunger strikes and stapling or stitching their lips together to claim our attention. And while some in Australia responded with sympathy, if polls are to be believed, many more took their cues from a government and Immigration Minister concerned to deny the validity of any sympathetic response or connection:

> Lip-sewing is a practice that is unknown in our culture.... It is something that offends the sensitivities of Australians, and asylum-seekers believe it might influence the way in which we would respond.... It can't and it won't.
>
> (Minister for Immigration, Philip Ruddock, cited in West 2002)

Of critical importance also was the fact that these statements came soon after the end of a year of Centenary of Federation celebrations – 100 years since the Australian states had federated to become a nation – when it was argued that our migration program has been 'the great Australian success story' (Hirst 2001: 115–16). While the Australian Government introduced legislation to restrict the definition of 'persecution' in determination of refugee cases, argued that measures were necessary to 'reduce Australia's attractiveness' to those seeking asylum, and migration legislation was amended to attempt to make the country literally a 'never never land' for many seeking asylum,[2] we were told that 'Australia has a very proud record ... of assisting people in great humanitarian need', and that it is 'vital that unfounded and patently incorrect claims are not used to form judgments that erode the pride we as a nation are entitled to feel about the hand we extend to those in such great need' (Ruddock, cited in West 2002).

In this respect I think that the moment of these cases was an exposure of what Michael Taussig has called 'public secrets'. When quarter-page images appear of Vivian as the 'face unacceptable to Australia', for example, we may recall Taussig's observation that:

> When the human body, a nation's flag, money, or a public statue is defaced, a strange surplus of negative energy is likely to be aroused from within the defaced thing itself.
>
> (Taussig 1999: 1)

Taussig describes how 'the English language brings together as montage the face and sacrilege under the rubric defacement' and states that this contingency alerts us 'to the tenderness of face and of faces facing each other, tense with the expectation of secrets as fathomless as they seem worthy of unmasking'. Taussig argues, however, that while defacement may be 'like Enlightenment', 'bring[ing] inside outside, unearthing knowledge, and revealing mystery', in the process it 'may also animate the thing defaced and the mystery revealed may become more mysterious' (Taussig 1999: 3). What we become aware of in the Rau and Alvarez Solon cases is the public secret that migration to Australia can be a history of sadness and shame seared into the bodies, into the skin, of some migrants, but is a melancholy the nation refuses. As Taussig argues:

> knowing what not to know lies at the heart of a vast range of social powers ... [the fact] being not that knowledge is power but rather that active not-knowing makes it so. So we fall silent when faced with such a massive sociological phenomenon, aghast at such complicities and ours with it...
> (Taussig 1999: 6–7)

For all the outpourings of shame and disbelief, for all the supposed revelations about the nation, what I see in the end in much Australian press coverage of these cases is precisely coverage, a 'reconfiguration of repression in which depth becomes surface so as to remain depth' (Taussig 1999: 5). The Alvarez Inquiry re-covers as it reveals this is 'a shameful episode'. The inquiries are 'shameful autobiographies' of the nation, but of the kind Paul de Man described as the 'autobiography of defacement': an '[a]utobiography that veils a defacement of the mind of which it is itself the cause' (de Man 1979: 930). It is a defacement that seeks to conceal as much as reveal the nation and points to the contradictory politics of shame that convert it back into pride. As Ahmed has argued, a sense of shame 'exposes the nation, and what it has covered over and covered up in its pride in itself, but at the same time it involves a narrative of recovery as the recovering of the nation' – a familiar trajectory of national shame in Australia in recent decades (Ahmed 2004: 112). While Ahmed's subject has been shame and sorrow expressed in relation to injustices perpetrated against Indigenous Australians and the discourse of reconciliation in Australia, her observations are salutary here. 'What is striking', she argues, 'is how shame becomes not only a mode of recognition of injustices committed against others, but also a form of nation building': a process in which 'shame becomes a "passing phase" in the passage towards being-as-nation' (Ahmed 2004: 102–3, 113).

Yet as Ahmed also notes, '[s]uch optimism does not originate from a subject, but is generated through promises made to the subject, which circulate as "truths" within public culture' (Ahmed 2004: 196). Cornelia is released and 'treated'; Vivian may return and be 'looked after'. Even as early as the end of May 2005, an editorial in the national *Weekend Australian* insisted that 'it must be said' that 'the behaviour of the two women made them partly the architects of their misfortune'. 'Perhaps the law was applied too harshly ... but Alvarez was only inadvertently denied her rights as an Australian citizen', the editor stated (Topsfield 2005a).

Face-to-face in sadness and loss

What else might emerge from the captured biographies of these women other than the alienation of their sadness for the sake of national recovery? I am struck still by looking at their faces in clippings I collected from the press: by a level of defiance – even in the 'frail' Vivian, although more obviously in the 'disruptive' Cornelia. How else to face up to Cornelia and Vivian as they stare back at us? In some of these images I feel there is more of a 'face off' than a 'face up': the face that says 'I am unfathomable to you'. Gail Weiss has explored relationships between body images that stress Merleau-Ponty's notion of 'intercorporeality': that 'the experience of being embodied is never a private affair, but is always mediated by our continual interactions with other human and non-human bodies' (Weiss 1999: 5). For Merleau-Ponty, it has been noted, the very experiences which make the body ' "my body" ... are the very same experiences which open "my body" to "other bodies", in the simultaneous mutuality of being touched, and seeing and being seen' (Ahmed and Stacey 2001: 5). What might happen if we faced up to the unfathomable sadness of others and developed a sociality based on such a mode of being with others in sadness?

This is the difficult territory explored perceptively by a number of scholars recently in Australia, further outlined below. Particularly pertinent to this discussion is Ahmed's caution that, in attempting to be touched or moved by another's pain, we must be careful of 'flattening out the differences [between us] ... or turning the sociality of pain into a new form of universalism'. Pain, Ahmed argues, produces 'uneven effects' and the fetishization of pain or its transformation into an identity 'cuts the wound off from a history of "getting hurt" or injured'; it turns pain and the wound that caused it into something that is, rather than something that has happened, that has a history (Ahmed 2004: 31–2). And, as we have seen with the cases of Vivian and Cornelia, harm has very specific histories made up of traumatic elements that did not happen to us all and are not available as a totality, that cannot be appropriated to form a singular identity for a migrant nation (Ahmed 2004: 33–5). I may be moved and respond with emotion to their stories, but theirs is not my pain or sadness. I have not been deported or detained; Vivian and Cornelia are not asylum seekers from Afghanistan or Iraq. Not all migrants suffer in the same way as Vivian and Cornelia; Australia's history and immigration policies have never acted on all migrants in the same way. Needless to say, the wound of migration and its associated pain and sadness provide not only a highly ambivalent but also a highly problematic identity for a migrant nation.

And yet, as Ahmed argues, 'pain is not simply an effect of a history of harm; it is the bodily life of that history', and bodies can face and even touch each other when brought together in an encounter. Drawing on Levinas and his insistence on the asymmetrical co-presence of the face-to-face encounter, Ahmed argues that pain surfaces in relationship to others, who can bear witness, authenticate, and sometimes take some responsibility for it (Ahmed 2004: 30–1). Thinking and feeling my way through readings and re-readings of the Rau and Alvarez inquiries, and the sense of sadness I find that they evoke in me, I apprehend this, paraphrasing Ahmed, not so much as a feeling that brings us together, but at least one that does not keep us apart (Ahmed 2004: 38). It is a connection, but one forged through loss, 'the loss of a "we", the loss of a community based on everyday connections', where we are forced to confront the 'conundrums' of bodies that get hurt by the kind of nation we inhabit. Out of the presence of the injured body, and what we see that it means for the migrant 'community' of the nation, Ahmed continues to argue:

> surfaces a different body, forged as it is by the intensity of pain. The language of pain aligns this body with other bodies; the surface of the community comes to be inhabited differently in the event of being touched by such loss.
>
> (Ahmed 2004: 39)

It is also perhaps an 'outside belonging' of the kind addressed by Elspeth Probyn (1996), but certainly the loss of one kind of togetherness, and a call not to 'feel' another's pain 'but for a different kind of inhabitance' and politics.

This is not to make martyrs of Vivian and Cornelia, whose suffering is unwanted. It is simply to note how sadness might be 'a crucial touchstone for social and subjective formations' (Eng and Kazanjian 2003: 23) (and to note also women's role in its embodiment, which is beyond the scope of this chapter).[3] Face-to-face with Vivian and Cornelia, we are recalled to emotions that 'show how histories stay alive, even when they are not consciously remembered; how histories of ... violence shape lives and worlds in the present', and how 'emotions open up futures, in the ways they involve different orientations to others' (Ahmed 2004: 203). As Eng and Han have argued, drawing on Ann Cvetkovich's work, only with a fuller sense of the affective life of politics 'can we avoid too easy assertions of a "political" solution to the affective consequences of trauma' (Eng and Kazanjian 2003: 15). Only then can the question of national belonging be rethought in terms of an affective history that might usefully describe the insecure immigration and incomplete integration of many into the national fabric.

A thread between others in the face of separation

Vivian and Cornelia slip from view and their faces disappear from the daily news. Are their stories lost? How to configure our connection, our debt, to them?

What if we saw migrant sadness not as pathology, but as an integral part of life in Australia (along with other forms of melancholy also)? What if we could remember the way that what is lost is internalized or, more accurately and crucially, how this 'insideness' could also be an 'outside belonging', which involves the process of being affected by others: how 'we are "with others" before we are defined as "apart from" others'? Ahmed writes:

> To preserve an attachment is not to make an external other internal, but to keep one's impressions alive, as aspects of one's self that are both oneself and more than oneself, as a sign of one's debt to others.
>
> (Ahmed 2004: 160)

I find this sense of one's 'debt to others' perhaps the most convincing premise for conceiving a semi-permanent community of feeling in Australia that might produce new modes of social inclusion – even if only temporary and partial. Writing about what happens 'after loss' and attempting to bring theory to bear on the analysis of social and political life, Butler has suggested that this could be:

> a place where belonging now takes place in and through a common sense of loss (which does not mean that all these losses are the same). Loss becomes condition and necessity for a certain sense of community, where community does not overcome the loss, where community cannot overcome the loss without losing the very sense of itself as community.
>
> (Butler 2003: 468)

In a similar vein, but different context, Gilbert Caluya has asked:

> If cultural critics have written about strategic alliances formed from separate grievances, what about the possibilities for affective alliances formed from separate losses? If we begin to build affective alliances, is there the possibility of forging connections with those who do not share a particular grievance?
>
> (Caluya 2006: 98)

Can we come together as communities of sadness? What are the possibilities for this in Australia and thus of making a place in the act of reaching out to the out-of-place-ness of some migrant others? What of the desire for a community reached across and towards the faces of other bodies that might pull us together, but 'move the story on, as the sign of a persistence of a connection, a thread between others, in the face of separation'? (Ahmed 2004: 39).

Staging some of his recent 'impressions' of Australia, Brian Castro has read Australia as profoundly lacking a kind of creative sadness that is at once 'a form of posturing, but ... also a civic disposition ... a hermeneutic mode of relating to the world' which offers an alternative to the tools of 'instrumental reason'. Castro bemoans the lack of a complex civility in Australia, 'a semi-permanent community of understanding' (Castro 2007: 4). Instead he finds Australia opting for 'the unbearable lightness of global cynicism' that reduces questions of loss, and enforces a 'cheerfulness [that] is historically and culturally driven':

> Since Australia is unable to mourn for the past, for in mourning the past it automatically erases its distinctive premise of occupation, its distinction and its own raison d'etre as an occupying and paternalistic nation, it employs postmodern, globalised rationales to exculpate guilt through parody and celebration. It is all about having a good time at the expense of meaning; not anticipating the shudder of meaninglessness, but producing a never-ending series of empty signs. No imagined catastrophe would ever be large enough to produce self-reproach in such lucky country.
>
> (Castro 2007: 7)

Because meaning is too difficult to confront, we are faced with what Amartya Sen has called the 'conceptual disarray' of much identity politics and national aspirations that are, Castro argues, 'reductive and singular', producing in turn a country that is 'punitive' against its others: 'asylum seekers, indigenous Australians and down-at-heel immigrants'. Most powerfully, Castro underlines:

> If it is negative, then it cannot be productive for the nation. The gesture of Australian culture has always been to wipe off the muddy footprints on the white linoleum floor. But culture is in effect, a muddy footprint in itself. It leaves a guilty white stain if it is forever sanitised. Australian pragmatism has historically assumed the function of the sanitising cloth: the clean and wipe. But the residue of empty sadness remains.
>
> (Castro 2007: 8)

For Castro, an answer to this dilemma is provided through the 'insubordination of art' that refuses happy endings and produces vision through a 'future mourning' that communicates something of the 'insecure sadness of inhabiting lost worlds' (Castro 2007: 8).

This is not an option open to everyone and I am not arguing here that some form of recovery from sadness is not desirable or necessary in most cases. But we should listen to the communities of sadness that remind us that such recoveries come at the cost of turning away from skin memories that will always be with us. Sites of migrant melancholy are spaces of possibility; semi-permanent communities of sadness that dwell with the meaning, the marks, and impressions of 'shameful episodes' and catastrophe.

Lasting impressions

> If catastrophe is not representable according to the narrative explanations that would 'make sense' of history, then making sense of ourselves and charting the future are not impossible. But we are, as it were, marked for life, and that mark is insuperable, irrecoverable. It becomes the condition by which life is risked, by which the questions of whether one can move, and with whom, and in what way are framed and incited by the irreversibility of loss itself.
>
> (Butler 2003: 472)

In May 2005, as noted above, the *Weekend Australian* concluded that Vivian and Cornelia's behaviour made them 'the architects of their own misfortune' and that they had 'nothing to do with the Government's border protection policy'. 'Despite all the strident rhetoric that Ms Alvarez is a victim of the hard line the Howard government has adopted since the Tampa asylum seekers affair, the truth is that she, as well as Ms Rau, appears to be the victim of official apathy [and] bureaucratic bungling'. 'This will disappoint intellectual opportunists', the author continued, 'who will want to exploit these two dreadful incidents as examples of a racist Government's racist policies'. We are told: 'They are nothing of the sort ... [O]ne ill Australian was locked up and left to rot, and another was banished overseas'. 'There can be no more cases of this kind' was the rather ambiguous final sentence (Topsfield 2005a).

Such statements risk nothing, venture nothing, gain nothing. They open no space for thinking about the ongoing ethics and politics of identity formations in Australia, let alone for considering more carefully the impact and affects of the response of the Global North to millions of others around the world who confront control and 'securitization' of movement. Feminist geographers in particular have noted how 'the material conditions and depictions' of those who wait in limbo without any permanent legal status have produced 'a feminization of asylum' and a 'shifting, not a sharing' of global responsibility (Hyndman and Giles 2011: 361–79). Indeed, Australia's treatment of Cornelia and Vivian reminds us how 'sedentarism' is valorized over movement in the Global North: 'a way of thinking', Tim Cresswell notes, 'that sees mobility as suspicious, as threatening, and as a problem'. 'The mobility of others is captured, ordered, and emplaced', Cresswell argues, 'in order to make it legible in a modern society' (Cresswell 2006: 55). In this respect, one might argue, Vivian and Cornelia were caught up in processes of ordering people supposedly 'out of place' that are central to an immigration policy characterized, as Peter Mares has recently argued, by 'fear and instrumentalism'. As their 'legibility' was enforced, we lost what Mares has outlined as 'a broader conception of migration [that] would take into account the potential developmental benefits of human movement for some nations and for migrants themselves' (Mares 2011: 407–22).

But unfortunately, the 'cases of this kind' do continue:[4] the impressions of Vivian and Cornelia, and others, mark us for life 'and that mark is insuperable, irrecoverable' for any notion of national pride. Instead we might consider putting on a 'mask of curiosity' about such sadness.

Notes

1 I draw here on Mary Louise Pratt's idea of the contact zone as 'an attempt to involve the spatial and temporal co-presence of subjects previously separated by geographic and historical disjunctures' (Pratt 1992: 7).
2 Referring to the MV *Tampa* on 28 August 2001, Prime Minister John Howard stated 'that boat will never land in our waters, never'. For example of the reports of this, see Price and Garran (2001).
3 See Nira Yuval-Davis (1997); and for an interesting recent discussion of women's and

feminized places in such transnational ruptures, see the special issue of *Gender, Place & Culture*, 18(3), 2011.
4 See, for example, the series of Commonwealth Ombudsman's reports detailed under Immigration Detention Review Reports, available at: www.ombudsman.gov.au/reports/immigration-detention-review.

Bibliography

Ahmed, S. (2004) *The Cultural Politics of Emotions*, New York: Routledge.
Ahmed, S. (2000) *Strange Encounters: Embodied Others in Postcoloniality*, London: Routledge.
Ahmed, S. and Stacey, J. (2001) 'Dermographics', in S. Ahmed and J. Stacey (eds), *Thinking Through the Skin*, London: Routledge.
Bhabha, H.K. (1990) 'Introduction' in H.K. Bhabha (ed.), *Nation and Narration*, London: Routledge.
Burnside, J. (2005) 'The abuse of one exposes what we're doing to them', *The Age*, 7 July.
Butler, J. (2004) *Precarious Life: The Powers of Mourning and Violence*, London: Verso.
Butler, J. (2003) 'Afterword: after loss, what then?' in D.L. Eng and D. Kazanjian (eds), *Loss: The Politics of Mourning*, Berkeley: University of California Press.
Caluya, G. (2006) 'The Aesthetics of Simplicity: Yang's *Sadness* and the Melancholic Community', *Journal of Intercultural Studies*, 27(01–02): 83–100.
Castro, B. (2007) 'Impressions and impersonations: reading Australia after Howard', public lecture delivered at the University of Melbourne, 18 October (typescript provided by the author), amended version published as Castro, B. (2009) 'Arrested motion and future-mourning: hybridity and creativity', *Cultures in Transit, Transtext(e)s/Transcultures*, 4: 83–99.
Commonwealth Ombudsman (2005) *Commonwealth Ombudsman's Inquiry into the Circumstances of the Vivian Alvarez Matter: Report under the Ombudsman Act 1976 by the Commonwealth Ombudsman, Prof. John McMillan, of an inquiry undertaken by Mr Neil Comrie AO*, APM, Canberra.
Cresswell, T. (2006) *On the Move: Mobility in the Modern Western World*, London: Routledge.
Dalziell, R. (1999) *Shameful Autobiographies: Shame in Contemporary Australian Autobiographies and Culture*, Carlton: Melbourne University Press.
de Man, P. (1979) 'Autobiography as de-facement', *Modern Language Notes, Comparative Literature*, 94(5), December: 930.
Department of Immigration and Multiculturalism and Indigenous Affairs (DIMIA) (2005) *Inquiry into the Circumstances of the Immigration Detention of Cornelia Rau: Report undertaken by Mick Palmer*, Canberra: Commonwealth of Australia.
Eng, D.L. and Kazanjian, D. (2003) 'Mourning remains', in D.L. Eng and D. Kazanjian (eds) *Loss: The Politics of Mourning*, Berkeley: University of California Press.
Gordon, M. and Gratton, M. (2005) 'The face unacceptable to Australia', *The Age*, 14 May.
Healy, C. (2008) *Forgetting Aborigines*, Sydney: UNSW Press.
Hewitt, J. (2005) 'The Alvarez case: a warning for us all', *The Age*, 14 May.
Hirst, J. 'More or less diverse' in H. Irving (ed.) (2001) *Unity and Diversity: A National Conversation. The Barton Lectures*, Sydney: ABC Books.
Hyndman, J. and Giles, W. (2011) 'Waiting for what? The feminization of asylum in protracted situations', *Gender, Place & Culture*, 18(3): 361–79.

Jackson, A. (2005) 'Deported Australian left son behind', *The Age*, 7 May.
Levett, C. (2005a) 'No one wanted to know her story – now everyone does', *The Age*, 14 May.
Levett, C. (2005b) 'Wrongly deported woman thought she was being helped', *The Age*, 14 May.
Mares, P. (2011) 'Fear and instrumentalism: Australian policy responses to migration from the Global South', *The Round Table*, 100(415): 407–22.
Marr, D. (2005) 'Passport to madness', *The Age*, 18 July.
Moncrief, M. (2005) 'We threw out an Aussie: Minister', *Sunday Age*, 1 May.
Pratt, M.L. (1992) *Imperial Eyes: Travel Writing and Transculturation*, London: Routledge.
Price, M. and Garran, R. (2001) 'PM weighs his anger in stormy seas – Howard weighs his anger in the stormy seas of global censure', *Australian*, 1 September.
Probyn, E. (1996) *Outside Belongings*, New York: Routledge.
Roberts, J. and Bockmann, M. (2005) 'Revealed: how nation failed Rau', *The Australian*, 29 June.
Roberts, J. and Sproull, R. (2005) 'Anna's journey in detention's living hell', *The Australian*, 29 June.
Scott, D. (2005) 'Stuart Hall's ethics', *Small Axe*, 17, March: 14.
Taussig, M. (1999) *Defacement: Public Secrecy and the Labour of the Negative*, Stanford: Stanford University Press.
Topsfield, J. (2005a) 'Rau's odyssey', *The Age*, 6 July.
Topsfield, J. (2005b) 'It is a "shameful episode" in the history of immigration in Australia. The management of Solon was "catastrophic". The unlawful removal of one of our citizens is "almost unthinkable"', *The Age*, 7 October.
Yuval-Davis, N. (1997) *Gender and Narration*, London: Sage.
Weiss, G. (1999) *Body Images: Embodiment as Intercorporeality*, New York: Routledge.
West, A. (2002) 'Asylum-seeker teenagers join lip sewing protest', *Herald-Sun*, 20 January.
Wills, S. (2004) 'Losing the right to country: the memory of loss and the loss of memory in claiming the nation as space', *New Formations*, 51: 50–65.

Negotiating integration

6 Would-be citizens and 'strong states'

Circles of security and insecurity

Paul James and Anne McNevin

One of the taken-for-granted frameworks of contemporary political theory and practice is that states provide security for their citizens. Going back to Max Weber's classical definition of states as holding the legitimate monopoly over the means of violence within a given territory, states have been seen as the protectors of the people who reside within their territorial boundaries. More recently, and in line with this definition, there has been serious concern expressed about weak or failing states contributing to foundational issues of human insecurity. Thus, regular calls go out for the necessity of state building support for weak states (Fukuyama 2004). The other side of this process, one less often directly discussed, is that strong states are part of the problem. Strong states contribute to foundational issues of human insecurity through wars of 'humanitarian' or pre-emptive intervention, support for corrupt regimes, hardline negotiation over resources and insufficient action on existential issues such as climate change.

The fallout from a world-in-tension is that states, in attempting to secure the lives of their citizens, effect contradictory outcomes. The overall argument of this chapter is that attempts by strong states to resecure aspects of their sovereignty are currently either making things worse or flattening out the possibilities of a more complex negotiated human security. One group of people who suffer the brunt of the unintended effects of securing the sovereignty of citizens are those who move across state borders without legally-protected status. In the face of heightened security measures against certain kinds of cross-border movement, asylum seekers and others sometimes turn to 'people smugglers' to navigate their passage. In doing so, they confront a circle of insecurity. Citizens who read in newspapers of these transnational markets in human traffic feel increasingly insecure and governments respond, in turn, with ever more restrictive one-dimensional security management against unwanted flows. Closing the circle, thus, for an increasing number of asylum seekers makes people smugglers a necessary conduit to movement.

This circle is related to two current trends. First, there is an inverse relationship between the material abstraction of the processes of movement and the way in which those processes are regulated in relation to state boundaries. The more embodied the process of movement, the more intense the regulation of boundary crossing. Across the world, state regulation of the movement of people (embodied globalization) has intensified over the past few decades. This has corresponded with a negotiated deregulation of traded objects and an ever-increasing flow of materially more abstract processes such as electronic financial transactions or cultural expressions (James 2006). These parallel regulatory extremes are qualified by a second trend in relation to those persons who move across borders. State responses to border-crossers vary in line with broader processes whereby market values are embedded in notions of national interest and techniques of risk-assessment are refined. States differentiate between those who bring capital or capital relations – tourists, students and business people – and those who bring risk or unspecifiable outcomes: 'dangerous' aliens or strangers 'undeserving' of support. In short, border control is now given effect by a mode of organization framed by instrumental rationality and commodification. This does not, of course, equate with public rhetoric. Securing the national lifeworld is subjectively voiced through rhapsodies of welcome for tourists, laments of humanitarian concern for refugees and screeds of security-talk in relation to terrorists and queue jumpers. At the same time, the objective reception for all people – welcome or otherwise – is objectively instrumentalizing and coldly calculating. The overall affect is intended to be comforting – at least to those citizens 'safely' at home inside the managed borders – while the effect is ever more brutalizing.[1]

Thus, governments across the world are enacting increasingly stringent border security in relation to embodied movement and, at the same time, continue to deregulate financial and cultural information flows. They rally against outsiders in defence of the cultural realm, while positively extending opportunities for economic exchange to all-comers who are measured as meeting the national interest. States across the world – whether liberal democracies, federated or single-party republics, constitutional monarchies or authoritarian dictatorships – are becoming increasingly defensive about what the national interest entails and what security forces defend. In a minimal conventional sense, all states are nation-states, but the integrating relations between communities (including nations) and polities (states) are becoming more brittle.[2] This is the case for weak states as much as for strong states like Canada, China, the United States or the United Arab Emirates, where a comparable spectrum of tension holds. If citizenship is defined as recognized membership of the political community of a state, then, by virtue of being citizens, all persons are inevitably caught in these tensions. All citizens are also subject to heightened surveillance and screening for the 'right' kind of citizenship. States project commitment to dialogical political participation while inexorably centralizing the levers of instrumental power. They legislate to protect citizens, while that same legislation makes anybody suspected of crossing the line as 'an enemy of the state' increasingly vulnerable in legal terms. And they defend local jobs markets as a national shibboleth, even as those same leaders know that globalizing capitalism does not work that way and most governments are acting globally to negotiate away important areas of state control over such matters.[3]

These trends contribute to the complex mix of processes that challenge the security of would-be citizens as they move between states of recognition and alienation. For many who have been displaced by localized transnational violence and geopolitical upheaval, the insecurity of displacement and irregular status has become a way of life. Uneven development within and between states, the environmental degradation of regions and localized effects of climate change and the consequences of neoliberal restructuring on a global scale are powerful incentives for individuals, families and communities to seek a better life elsewhere, regardless of the dangers involved in border transgressions. For some, migration is an urgent necessity. For others, living and working away from the locality of their birth for extended periods is part of a long-established and sometimes state-sponsored means of financially supporting families and communities at home through remittances.

In view of these migration pressures, there are four overlapping categories of people who find themselves in a particularly vexatious position – asylum seekers, refugees, internally displaced persons and the more generic category of irregular migrants. Asylum seekers, as the prevailing definition would have it, are persons seeking refuge but not yet accepted by another nation-state as being 'genuine refugees'. To be an asylum seeker is thus to be in-between and in-waiting, suspended in space and time. It is to be subject, for example, to a tautologous logic which gives legal credence to the bizarre designation by the Australian government that persons arriving at excised off-shore places (places which for all purposes other than migration are part of the state territory) need not be dealt with as even potential refugees. These 'off-shore entry persons', legally created in relation to the 'non-territory' in which they arrive, can simply be sent away.

Refugees, by comparison and for all their vulnerabilities, enjoy recognition as forced migrants who are outside their original state of citizenship and deserving of protection (at least by signatory states to the relevant conventions). They are persons who now have a legally recognized place in a new state, or at least a right to have such a status. In legal terms they have a right to reside, however difficult that residence might be. In social terms this could, of course, mean being located in concentrated camps of semi-organized squalor, but in colloquial terms they are, at the same time, people at a distance for whom we should feel sympathy (Malkki 2002). 'Internally displaced persons', by distinction, have not crossed their state border and are in the invidious position of retaining their citizenship status in states that can no longer afford them secure protection. They currently number a staggering 27 million people, a figure that has doubled over the last decade and a half (Birkeland *et al.* 2010).

The fourth category of persons relevant here are 'irregular migrants'. This category is now widely used within academic literature and policy circles. The term has emerged in the context of what bureaucrats call 'mixed flows' of political and economic migrants and growing recognition that reasons for crossing borders cannot be neatly pigeon-holed into one-dimensional categories (either political persecution or economic self-interest). As such it refers to all those who cross borders without prior authorization, regardless of their reason, and encompasses asylum seekers as well as undocumented labour migrants. The term is often used in a self-conscious effort to avoid pejorative and inaccurate references to 'illegal' migrants, especially when applied to asylum seekers and refugees. Yet the discourse of 'irregularity' is implicated in a broader culture of governance with respect to the movement of people that generates administrative categories to document and manage mobility in line with broader ideological imperatives.

Far from neutral, the term 'irregular migrant' carries the spectre of not being 'regular' and therefore attracting appropriate controls – border controls – that impose order on disorderly movements of people. The whole enterprise of border control (and it is an increasingly marketized enterprise) is now the focus of global governance. Intergovernmental security and migration agencies work in tandem with bilateral and regional consultations to instruct and 'build capacity' in relevant state agencies in order to combat 'irregular' flows. 'Best practice' models represent border control as a technical rather than political exercise and one that, when mastered and implemented, demonstrates weak states' entré into 'good' governing international society (Andrijasevic and Walters 2010). As the target of intervention, 'irregular migration' is not the merely 'technical' category it is often claimed to be. Rather, 'irregular migrants' are constructed within hierarchies of mobility as a generic class of illegitimate traveller. To this extent it is possible to talk about 'irregular migrants' less in terms of a clear cut administrative category and more in terms of those who, for a variety of reasons, are demonized, criminalized and subject to increasing insecurity.

What is the effect of state securitization on irregular migrants?

One arc of our argument is that strong states, in acting to protect the security of their recognized citizens, are making the lives of irregular migrants increasing insecure. Some 50 million people are currently estimated to be living and working outside their countries of origin, with irregular status (Koser 2010). Strong states host several million of these migrants – some 11 million reside in the United States alone (Passel and Cohn 2011: 1). A familiar narrative accounts for the rising numbers of irregular migrants as a relatively recent phenomenon and a consequence of the geopolitical fallout from the end of the Cold War, when Europe, in particular, confronted the potential for mass movements of people from former Eastern bloc states on its doorstep. The numbers of people crossing borders spontaneously and seeking asylum in industrialized countries rose in the early 1990s, catapulting the issue of human smuggling onto intergovernmental agendas as part of a focus on transnational and globalized crime. As some borders came down (notably those internal to Europe), others became increasingly militarized (especially the US–Mexico border and the European frontier). Resources devoted to preventing unauthorized flows of people were massively expanded and increasingly incorporated into the general security apparatus of the state. All this in the name of defending sovereign territory from unregulated access, maintaining security standards against unchecked and suspect flows and protecting fragile welfare states and labour markets from unsustainable pressure that would accompany 'floods' of desperate, poor people.

Growth in irregular migration, however, should be read alongside an increasingly restrictive immigration environment from the 1980s onward. Circumscribed avenues for licit migration mean that many migrants who in previous eras might have travelled as guest workers now cross borders without official sanction to fill similar jobs. Stricter border-policing and the dangers of illicit border-crossings mean that many who might otherwise have been seasonal workers, returning to their homelands regularly, now stay on indefinitely because they cannot guarantee subsequent re-entry. Douglas Massey has shown how this counterproductive aspect of border-policing has characterized the recent experience of the United States in particular (Massey 2005).

Tightened criteria for refugee status have had a similar effect. Governments defending such moves hold that migrants increasingly make specious asylum claims in order to circumvent mainstream migration procedures. Rising numbers of rejected asylum seekers accordingly support the notion that the majority are disingenuous and justify ever tighter restrictions.[4] Critics of this viewpoint, ourselves included, hold that the proportion of claims rejected is more indicative of unrealistically high burdens of proof resting with the claimant and that many people suffering from genuine political persecution no longer have access to a fair asylum procedure. As a consequence, some prefer to risk an illicit border-crossing or to overstay short-term visas rather than return to the places from which they have fled (Sirtori and Coelho 2007; Gibney 2000; Reynolds and Muggeridge 2008; Dauvergne 2008).

In an effort to avoid the administrative hurdles attached to deciphering 'mixed flows' of 'political' and 'economic' migrants, policing against unwanted migrants is increasingly conducted well before they reach the border in question. Italy and Spain, for example, work with Moroccan and Libyan authorities to intercept would-be migrants from other parts of Africa as they move towards European destinations. In 2003, British Prime Minister Tony Blair suggested to the European Council that transit processing centres be established outside European territory for irregular migrants seeking entry to Europe. In 2005, Otto Schily, German minister of the interior, advanced variations on this idea. In 2011, Julia Guillard, Australia's prime minister, effected a similar policy in an agreement with Malaysia (Blair 2003; Schily 2005).[5] Although these proposals remain controversial as official policy options, they reflect the growing phenomenon of informal camps and detention centres funded by strong states within the territories of weaker states such as Morocco, Libya and Ukraine, places where irregular migrants congregate en route to Europe and to which they are deported if they are intercepted (Schuster 2005; Kasparek 2008; Amnesty International 2005; Andrijasevic 2009). When the European or Australian borders are externalized in this way, irregular migrants are prevented from entering territories where states are obliged under international law to examine claims to asylum.

In states that are not party to the United Nations Convention Relating to the Status of Refugees (Libya, for example), status categories such as 'asylum seeker' and 'refugee' have few means of being realized. Authorities simply distinguish between 'legal' and 'illegal' migrants, and those without a valid visa become 'illegal' by default. It is at this point that the 'technical' exercise of border control begins against a generic class of illegal bodies whose exclusion from destination states appears a matter of common sense. This kind of policing is exacerbated by the post-September 11 2001 security environment. If not directly linked to the threat of terrorism, irregular migrants are invoked as part of a general state of insecurity that requires a hardline response (Huysmans and Buonfino 2008; Bigo 2002). Thus, in 2009, Italy affirmed 'illegal immigration' as a new criminal (rather than administrative) offence, authorized detention of 'illegal' immigrants for up to 18 months and sanctioned the use of citizen patrols to assist the police in identifying criminal migrant targets.

The more general result of this ever more restrictive environment is a process of 'illegalization' and therefore intensifying insecurity of both the means of transit available to people on the move and of irregular migrants themselves. This is another of the circles of insecurity. The securitization of migration involves a circular process of responding to threats that are, in large part, generated and exacerbated by the criminalizing framework applied. Migration becomes an issue of law and order – at worst of societal breakdown – rather than prompting political questions of just distribution in an age of intensifying globalization. For Nicholas De Genova, this situation necessitates that the study of illegality become the focus of scholarly attention rather than 'illegal' migrants per se. This shift, he contends, is essential if studies are to avoid reproducing the very same discursive tools and administrative categories through which people's movements and entitlements are unjustly constrained (De Genova 2002). From this perspective, we might also question the discursive shift to 'irregularity'. As a governmental technique, the shift creates the appearance of standing firm against misleading populist efforts to characterize a complex spectrum of migration in black and white terms of legality and illegality. Yet in reality, undertaking border control against irregular migrants remains at the forefront of contemporary efforts to 'manage migration' and does little to mitigate its brutalizing effects on those who find themselves on the wrong side of the border.

Acknowledging a circular process of intensifying insecurity for irregular migrants is not to dismiss the very real dilemmas that arise for states on the question of migration in general. There are no easy ways of balancing the rights of political communities to regulate entry and limit group membership with the many compelling reasons for seeking through migration a safer, more decent and prosperous life beyond what is offered in that place to which one is tied by an accident of birth.[6] The point is not to minimize these complex and enduring questions, but to move beyond the scapegoating and crisis mentalities that shape much of the discourse and practice of border control.

Does the global movement of people create its own insecurities?

The movement of people from one part of the world to another raises questions in relation to the intersection of insecurity and material inequities, whether in relation to economics, food, health, environment or politics. These inequities are starkly revealed in the context of conflict zones frequently experiencing mass population displacements. The departure of a large number of working people from a region produces a strong economic impact, both at national and local levels, and all the more so when displacement is produced by globally- or regionally-framed civil conflict (Weiner 1996). The interim placement of refugees in mass camps is a setting for another kind of institutionalized constitution of long-term inequalities and insecurities. When conflicts and refugee movements are associated with differences across ethnic–racial–religious lines, access to services and employment in host states as much as origin states are further compromised by the transfer of ethnic–racial–religious tensions. Over the long-term, continuing structural inequities and uncertainties compound the dissension, conflict and violence associated with the causes of human displacement.

While the stark insecurity of those who move across borders without legal protection is apparent, what does this mean for the security of the places to which they move? And how can we address the potential for this kind of insecurity without buying into populist efforts to simplistically equate the irregular movement of people with sovereign and existential threat? Two examples illustrate the kind of insecurities that are apparent in the wake of recent patterns of migration and their longer-term historical contexts. The first involves tensions arising from migration flows to Europe from former colonies and elsewhere. On 27 October 2005 riots began following an incident in Clichy-sous-Bois, an immigrant suburb of Paris with high unemployment and uneven poverty. Teenagers running from the police climbed a wall to hide in a power substation; two of the boys, one of Malian background and another of Tunisian, were electrocuted; a third boy, whose parents are Turkish Kurd, was injured and hospitalized. Subsequently 9,000 vehicles were torched in Paris across 20 days of rioting. Across late October and into early November, this initially very local incident spread across France and Europe as related fire-bombings and violence occurred in Belgium, Denmark, Germany, Greece, Netherlands and Spain. By the beginning of December, typing 'Zyed Benna', the name of one of the teenagers who died, into the Google Internet search engine, brought forth 22,800 sources listed from across the web-connected globe. Here face-to-face relations – the grieving pain of family and friends – are overlaid with disembodied processes of global extension as 'Zyed Benna' became an iconic reference for patterns of grievance. The local had 'become' global, carried by an unprecedented intersection between embodied globalization and disembodied communication systems.

If the riots in Paris became an example of local insecurities escalating to global proportions, then we can also identify social relations that are global in scope but take on decidedly local security dimensions. There are several well-documented instances of globalized diasporic communities playing a significant role in precipitating violence and conflict in localities a world away. Crucial support is extended in various guises and forms. These include financial support, networking at international fora, delivering arms and ammunition to diaspora-connected ethno-religious groups and insurgents, as well as in some cases sending individuals to fight as combatants. While there are several such cases of diasporic support for localized transnational wars in South, Southeast and Central Asia, one obvious example was the Tamil diasporic community of Sri Lanka, spread across Asia, Australasia and North America. The diaspora extended generous support, both financial and ideological – through the World Wide Web – to the Liberation Tigers of Tamil Eelam for three decades until they were finally defeated in 2009 (Ranganathan 2010; Kapferer 2001).

Domestic politics within the 'kin states' profoundly affects the political articulations of the diasporic communities. However, the institutional strength of diaspora communities to intervene in the politics of kin states depends to a great extent on their internal organization, the level of economic-financial resources and their capacity for transnational communication of ethno-national identity (in other words, the capacity of diasporas formed in ties of embodied subjectivity to reach out beyond their immediate connections through relations of institutional and disembodied extension, including the web as a means of extended communication). Those who have these capacities are far more effective in 'challenging the leading role of indigenous elite within the homeland and becoming powerful independent actors both within the kin state and in the international arena' (Weiner 1996: 10). In summary, the existence of transborder ethnic groups or diasporas, themselves often formed by globalizing violence, represent a potential, but only potential, source of conflict. While emerging global diasporas are likely to be significant policy targets both for the kin states as well as the host states, the pattern of violence depends on the wider social context.

In response to these patterns there has been an unhelpful bifurcation in the literature between those who celebrate the movement of refugees and migrants for bringing hybrid differences and those who accentuate the increasing possibilities of violence. Concerns about diasporic violence are not confined to the extreme Right. Mary Kaldor, for example, a left-wing critic of nationalism, believes that although there can be positive forms of identity politics that come out of the global movement of people, the new diasporic nationalism is exclusivist, closer to religious fundamentalism and will contribute to 'a wild anarchic form of globalisation' (Kaldor 2004: 162). On the other side, Arjun Appadurai, although still a left-cosmopolitan critic of the old nationalism, looks to post-national extensions of culture as carrying a deterritorialized identity that will help to resolve increasing levels of institutionalized violence in the world today. Supposedly, post-nationalism will usher in the end of the territorial nation-state and rid us of one of the main sources of violence (Appadurai 1996). Neither position is satisfactory.

Both writers are right to accentuate that new diasporic movements include post-national sensibilities that stretch across local and global. And both writers are right that the new identity groups are able to garner support from various elements across the diaspora, from individuals to non-governmental organizations and religious schools. It is here that the role of identity politics and embodied subjectivities come to the fore as a factor in local and global (in)securities, even while communicated across long distances of spatial extension by such means as the World Wide Web. This means that we need to begin by saying that globalization has ignited identity as a motif of both conflict and interconnection.

How then do we come to terms with mobile diasporas and their politics? There is no doubt that diaspora politics play a significant role in global affairs. Myriad ethnic groups are now spread across transnational frontiers and their worldviews and practices play a special role in several areas of national and global interest. However, the general perception among scholars that transborder ethnic ties are loci of violence needs substantial qualification. Robert Harkavy and Stephanie Neuman, for example, quite unselfconsciously use the term 'ethnic conflict' as almost a synonym for localized transnational conflict (Harkavy and Neuman 2001). Such terms normalize the generalized conclusion that diasporas per se are an abiding source of insecurity in the places to which they come. To the contrary, ethnic difference is rarely a direct basis for militarized or institutionalized violence, at least not by itself. Rather, ethnic identity, like religious observance, tends to become an embodied or symbolic marker of grievance located within circles of lifeworld disruption, criminalization of cross-border movement and mutually reinforcing discourses of xenophobia (held by some citizens) and resentment (held by some migrants and refugees). In short, while there is a strong argument to suggest that diasporic cultural politics are not innocent of chauvinist agendas and rhetorical excesses, the link between those tendencies and sources of violence still needs to be debated. As James Clifford argues, while:

> some of the most violent articulations of purity and racial exclusivism came from diaspora populations ... such discourses are usually weapons of the (relatively) weak.... Whatever their ideologies of purity, diasporic cultural forms can never, in practice be exclusively nationalist. They are deployed in transnational networks built from multiple attachments, and they encode practices of accommodation with, as well as resistance to, host countries and their norms.
>
> (Clifford 1994: 307)

Can irregular migrants generate a politics of localized security?

The other side of these patterns of violence are stories of the self-creation of localized security. For all the dramatic renditions of horror, there are also quiet moments of positive politics. The City of Los Angeles, currently home to an estimated 1 million undocumented migrants (Pastor and Ortiz 2009: 36), provides a place to consider these possibilities. In recent decades the city has been the focus of gradual coalition building between immigrant organizations and the wider labour movement. In the 1990s, for example, the innovative 'Justice for Janitors' Campaign played a pioneering role in mobilizing undocumented service workers and transforming labour organizing strategies accordingly (Savage 2006; Narro 2005–2006). The specific conditions faced by low-wage immigrant workers in Los Angeles' prototypical post-Fordist urban economy galvanized progressive social movements to bridge historic divides and work for mainstream political change. By the mid-2000s, a surging Latino vote had transformed the political landscape such that immigrant rights (regardless of citizenship status) became a central concern. Momentum peaked most dramatically in 2006 when hundreds of thousands of people took to the streets of Los Angeles in the largest of nation-wide demonstrations opposing legislation that aimed to criminalize undocumented people.

In light of this momentum, much has changed in the tone of public debate concerning the city's undocumented residents. Commenting nearly two decades ago, Stephanie Pincetl observed that 'Los Angeles is fighting the presence of non-Anglo nonwhite undocumented immigrants rather than developing ways to validate the dynamism of such communities, their imagination, and entrepreneurial spirit' (Pincetl 1994: 914). Her comments continue to resonate with trends in a number of cities across the United States in which local police forces and local administrative ordinances (relating to business licences and property leasing permits) are increasingly deployed to make work and housing more difficult for undocumented people and thereby to drive them away. Today, however, numerous examples exist in which Los Angeles is pragmatically and inclusively disposed towards undocumented migrants. The Los Angeles City Council, for instance, has introduced initiatives that integrate services for undocumented day labourers into regulatory arrangements for formal businesses (home improvement centres) on whose premises day labourers trade. The council has opened avenues for undocumented people to train in water-efficient gardening techniques and to supply a ready workforce for the city's long-term plan to maintain drought-tolerant green city spaces. The council also runs workshops for undocumented students to inform them about their eligibility for higher education in the state of California and the Los Angeles Police Department continues to operate a 'don't ask, don't tell' policy that limits cooperation with federal immigration enforcement agencies and works on the principle of better policing through community relationship building (Los Angeles City Council 2008; Villaraigosa 2009; Haas 2010; Los Angeles Police Department 2011).

Given Los Angeles' nodal position in a global division of labour, it seems reasonable to suggest that quasi-forms of recognition for undocumented people simply provide more effective ways of sustaining the cheap and flexible workers that capital requires. From this perspective, it is no surprise that elected officials and local business leaders have come together in opposition to federal immigration workplace raids, or that advocates for migrants encourage local authorities to view undocumented residents proactively as an 'emerging market' worthy of economic and community development investments – a view that ties pragmatically with the drive towards competitive advantage in a context of regional competition (Pastor and Ortiz 2009: 34). For Nicola Philips, such gestures are part of an unspoken strategy to entrench existing divisions of labour, albeit with minor modifications to wages and working conditions (Phillips 2009). Accordingly, we might question whether public recognition of undocumented migrants adds a misleading gloss to what remains an instrumental and market driven mutation of citizenship into neoliberal forms.

Yet, even a pragmatically-driven approach to undocumented residents provides enabling conditions for more profound challenges to citizenship norms that arise from the actions of undocumented people themselves. By claiming certain kinds of rights and recognition, undocumented migrants engage in subject-producing practices with political effects that go beyond the success or failure of the immediate issue at hand (wage claims or legalization, for example). Their struggles are at once reactions to their marginalized condition and productive of new forms of citizenship. Council initiatives simultaneously generate an atmosphere of ambiguity in which it is possible to push at the limits of citizenship in new and unpredictable ways. The following three cases are examples of this kind of migrant-driven activity that initiates new modes of political belonging. The cases are based on a series of informal conversations and interviews conducted in Los Angeles in 2009.

Underground undergrads

In April 2009, in the lead up to university exams, about 20 students held a mock graduation ceremony in the grounds of University of California, Los Angeles (UCLA). The event was the culmination of a series of actions over the course of a week that had drawn attention to undocumented students on campus. Many of the students participating were soon to graduate and faced the prospect of being unable to use their qualifications or to work at all on account of their immigration status. Most of these students had grown up in the US, had attended Californian high schools and did not necessarily have other countries to which they could say they unambiguously belonged. Some were the children of visa overstayers, some had more complex forms of status, caught in the gaps of administration systems which rendered them undeportable. Various flags pinned to their backs – Mexican, Korean, US and others – reflected this ambiguity as well as the multiple homelands and transnational affiliations that shaped the students' identities. Dressed in graduation robes, they held mock certificates that simply read, 'What Now?'

The event constituted a public outing of undocumented status. Students openly declared their legitimate right to be present, to be students, to work and to contribute to the places they called home. They also sought recognition as full and active members of society – literally as citizens, regardless of their formal status. After the event, students explained that it had taken several years to reach the kind of collective confidence it took to speak out so openly. Their activism came with considerable risks to themselves and to their families. One former student recalled a number of cases where students who spoke up about their status were harassed by anti-immigrant groups in emails and phone calls. When a UCLA student testified before Congress with regard to her situation, her family was subsequently arrested by federal immigration agents, detained overnight and released subject to electronic monitoring (Madera *et al.* 2008). Countering the fear inspired by the potential for seizure and sanction was one of the main tasks of a support group founded in 2003 on UCLA campus: Improving Dreams, Equality, Access and Success (IDEAS). IDEAS is now one of 29 such groups operating throughout California. The group aimed to overcome the isolation that many undocumented students felt, unaware that others like them were on campus. More concretely, the students aimed to disseminate information about college eligibility to undocumented high school students, to fund raise for college expenses in lieu of the formal right to work and to advocate for state and federal legislation (DREAM Acts) that would open pathways to formal citizenship for undocumented students. Bina, a student involved in IDEAS, explains the affirming and radicalizing effect of joining the association:

> Oh, it was so good. It's like any feeling that an outcast has when she realizes that there are other people like him or her. It's ecstatic. But I do confess, the best thing was realizing that if these people could be politically active and nothing bad was happening to them, then I could do it too … [U]ntil I started going to IDEAS … I had no idea that we actually did have a political avenue that we could travel to become active, and that we could do things, and could talk about it [our status] in certain ways and that there were people who wanted to listen. I thought it was some sort of alien situation. Like now if I don't have to I don't say 'illegal alien', I don't say 'illegal immigrant' so my whole terminology has changed … I say 'undocumented'.
>
> (Bina, interview 12 May 2009)

For Bina, joining IDEAS not only gave her the confidence and strategic direction to focus her political energies, but changed the terms of reference through which she framed her sense of belonging and entitlement. In the shifting of her language from 'illegal' to 'undocumented', the narrative that explained her status also transformed from a story of illicit border-crossings to one of bureaucratic fallibility. This shift in subjectivity profoundly affects the strategies employed by undocumented students to advocate for their rights. Specifically, it provides the grounding to move from an underground presence to a publicly open one.

Magic Cleaners

The Magic Cleaners business cooperative operates from a small office in the northern suburbs of Los Angeles. The cooperative is a limited liability company formed under Californian law and an economic development project of the community organization *Instituto de Educacion Popular del Sur de California* (Institute for Popular Education of Southern California, IDEPSCA). Magic Cleaners' members are equal owners in the business and income earned is split after operating costs have been covered. Members thus avoid paying high commissions for agency placements; they can independently negotiate the clients they do business with and the conditions under which they work. The business takes seriously the harsh effects of cleaning substances on the health of its members. Those involved had previously suffered from repeated exposure to toxic chemicals. Using only environmentally-friendly products, Magic Cleaners have created a targeted niche as a green cleaning service.

This legal business entity, owned and run by undocumented women, generates a space of employment that is difficult to categorize according to prevailing assumptions about formal and informal economies and who does what work where. Magic Cleaners' owner-members cannot be legally employed by others but there is nothing to stop them from starting a business under Californian law which does not require a social security number in order for them to do so.[7] Clients engage the business rather than the workers directly and the exchange takes place entirely within the formal economy. The cooperative generates an avenue of social recognition that bridges the divide between legitimate and illegitimate status. 'Being in the cooperative', one member explains, 'clients have learnt to respect us, because the company is backing us up'. In discussion, members express pride in their work and in their status as business owners. They now feel more secure in their work and can plan with more certainty for the future (interview 6 May 2009). As Magic Cleaners, moreover, undocumented women are integrated into administrative systems in a cultural and ideological context that rewards entrepreneurs as model civic subjects.

Inspired by the model set by Magic Cleaners, staff at the Pilipino Workers Center in downtown Los Angeles are investigating options for a care-givers' cooperative and working to build a client base that would support such an endeavour. For staff involved in establishing these projects, worker cooperatives are also part of a broader community development strategy. From this perspective, the businesses represent local people investing in their own communities, generating profits which are reinvested locally and creating terms of employment that restore dignity to the client – worker exchange. The process, in other words, lends itself to building social and political ties in distinctly local forms that cross-cut divides between citizens and non-citizens.

Parents mobilizing for educational justice

Asociación de Padres de Pasadena Luchando por la Educación (Pasadena Parent Association Advocating for Equitable Education, APPLE) is a parent-led organization that pushes for reform in public education in the Pasadena Unified School District. Parents established APPLE when they noticed that schools were failing to respond to the needs of their majority Spanish-speaking students and when they witnessed their children ignored and belittled by their teachers on account of poor English language skills. Parents, many of whom were undocumented, worked with several community organizations to overcome their fears about speaking out, to mobilize as a community and to approach authorities with a case for reform. Thanks to the efforts of APPLE, the District Board now recognizes English learners as one of its key priorities and is obligated to translate official school documents into languages other than English so that non-English speaking parents can participate in the educational life of their children. Parents are now positioned in key decision-making bodies where they can exert real influence on school programs and administration.

Some members of APPLE are now attempting to bring the Pasadena model to other areas of Los Angeles. Mario is working to organize parents in the downtown Pico Union neighbourhood, which is a low-income gateway for recently arrived and undocumented migrants. In broadening the struggle, Mario is linked to other initiatives, prompted when service-sector unions realized that their membership was comprised of parents with children in some of the lowest performing schools in the city. Union staff wondered whether the numbers of parents within their membership might be strong enough to build a potentially powerful base from which to campaign. For Mario, the task is uppermost about building a sense of attachment, investment and community among the parent population:

> We are going to start working with parents trying to define what is a community, what is the role of the parents in the school, what kind of power do we need to be there and to advocate for the students. Because a community doesn't exist until you build it ... we can talk about neighbourhood but not a community ... a community needs to mean something.
> (Mario, interview 22 May 2009)

Mario's emphasis on community building reflects the interplay between neighbourhood places, cultural ties, associational networks and the 'work' that it takes for marginalized groups to enter into the public. While 'the public' may be imagined and discursively created, membership within it nevertheless brings a degree of legitimacy to struggles for social change. Building community (in the sense of harnessing pre-existing ties, proximity and shared interests) is a crucial stepping stone for 'outsider' groups to generate resources with which to confront relative strangers and 'insider' groups with a counter-public presence. In the case of APPLE, undocumented parents established themselves as equal parties to negotiations on public education and compelled 'insiders' to adapt to the cultural and linguistic differences of parents and children alike. In the classroom as in the boardroom, parents compelled authorities to recognize Spanish speakers, to listen to broken English with patience, purpose and respect and to find a more equal medium of communication. All parties are transformed by this experience. Encounters of this kind destabilize prevailing categories – citizen/non-citizen, legal/illegal – that shape the uncertain terrain of political belonging in Los Angeles and beyond.

Shifting grounds of security

What can be said in general of these three examples and localized forms of security? The first thing to notice is a politics of presence – an embodied taking-up of public space. The students provide the most dramatic example in this regard by openly outing themselves. Like other public outings in other social movements, the students invite public scrutiny precisely on account of the status that marks them as outsiders. In doing so, they contest processes of illegalization and generate their own security by drawing attention to that which makes them insecure. While parents do not raise their immigration status in the course of their educational activism, they also insist on taking up public space. A central part of their strategy is simply to be there, at the table, in school committee meetings and in representations to the School District Board, declaring by their presence their legitimate role as parties to negotiation regardless of immigration status. Magic Cleaners too have carved out a space for themselves in the formal economy. While this is a much more abstracted place than school meeting rooms or university campuses, it nevertheless (and increasingly) shapes norms of civic engagement.

If seizing public space is an embodied process, it is also place specific. It sends a message that we are here, as we are, in this place – this campus, this school, this workplace and this city – which we mark, however subtly or dramatically, as our own. Public space, and a space in the public, is enacted through face-to-face exchanges between students and academics, business owners and clients, workers and union officials, parents and school board members, residents and councillors. Across this array of exchanges, a common sense takes shape about who has a stake in local communities and who contributes positively to them. Undocumented people shift from association with sources of insecurity to association with a shared and mutually constituted future. Through expressions of belonging to local communities as parents, workers, students and so on, a 'becoming' of the citizen takes place. When actions that ritualize community and belonging are incorporated into daily routines (working, studying, parenting) in shared institutions (businesses, schools, universities, assemblies) and backed by support from local officials, business leaders and community sectors, a cumulative momentum is generated that transforms what it means to be part of a civic life. This momentum suggests that new modes of citizenship are enacted in places that capture at once the significance of embodied encounters and their positioning within complex trans-local geographies.

The tension between mobility and being-in-place that infuses the three examples above suggests that a kind of shifting ground is in play in relation to contemporary forms of citizenship. By this, we mean more than the fact that citizenship is dynamic and constantly remade by those who contest it. We also mean more than the fact that citizenship is being enacted in places (cities for instance) that challenge 'national' and 'territorial' frames of reference for political membership. Nor are we merely emphasizing that people, including undocumented people, move in and out of different forms of (non)citizenship status (from 'citizen' to 'illegal migrant' and 'resident') as they move between different places and jurisdictions (from Mexico to Arizona and Los Angeles, for instance). The shifting grounds we have in mind are of a more layered nature. They are mobilized if and when certain acts (even as apparently simple as building a community of parents or operating a business) bring them into being by bringing together the old and new worlds of the people concerned. Such acts both contract and expand the spatial and temporal horizons of citizenship in ways that subvert modern Cartesian reference points for political belonging. They challenge us to radically reconceptualize political space in ways that do not simply map onto subject or status coherence, that is, with that which can be included or excluded in socio-spatial terms in the first place.

A different way of saying this is to imagine a political terrain that leaves open the possibility, at one level and for certain times, of opting out of modern state citizenship altogether. What would it mean, for example, if the ontologies of traditional religions – from syncretic Mexican Catholicism to orthodox Islam – were lived as countervailing spaces of meaning rather than confined to tolerated semi-private spaces, framed by modern ontologies of time and space? How might such alternatives expose the limits of modern liberal democratic socio-spatial vocabularies and concepts to reflect the range of political subjectivities and practices that are possible and/or desirable? Could different and plural ontologies challenge the conceptual routing of citizenship in a progressive modern notion of time, whereby enactments of citizenship necessarily move in a linear direction towards fuller modes of inclusion, however spatially grounded they might be? Such a challenge would entail renegotiating the meaning of inclusion and exclusion.

The questions we are posing here relate to the limits of the conventional definition of human security, understood in terms of inequalities, deprivations and material denial of resources. This definition has taken us a considerable way towards understanding the conditions of insecurity in the world today. However, we want to insist that security also exists across layers of ontological practice and meaning – an intersection of layers that is both challenged and enlivened by changing and globalizing modes of communication and organization. It is certainly the case that the material insecurity that fixes the attention of conventional approaches is ontologically foundational. But it is also worth considering the existential aspects of ontological insecurity from a less one-dimensional perspective.

Here the final step in our argument is to claim that insecurity is caught in the intensifying tensions of intersecting social formations as processes of globalization have thrown together practices and sensibilities associated with different life-worlds. This might be called a 'clash of ontologies'. The reference here to Samuel Huntington's *Clash of Civilizations* is as critique rather than as an extension of his approach (Huntington 1998).[8] The clash that we are referring to is not between ill-defined 'civilizations', nor is it a dubious variation on the 'ethnic differences cause violence' argument discussed above. Rather, the clash refers to tensions that arise at the intersection of different ways of being in the world –

customary tribal, traditional, modern and postmodern ways of living temporally, spatially and corporeally. These are not understood as separate domains but as layers of meaning and practice, criss-crossing the world and often held together at the same time in the bodies and minds of people who find themselves moving across different lifeworlds. When, for example, asylum seekers at the Broadmeadows Detention Centre in Melbourne sew their lips together in an act of desperation and post the photos on Facebook,[9] they are at once enacting a modern process of political mimicry and (intentionally or unintentionally) drawing on much older traditions of scarification, body-piercing, shamanistic silence and death-mask suturing that the rest of us find incomprehensible.

One crucial aspect of the clash of ontologies is that globalizing modern practices and meanings – including modern politics of resistance – are caught in tension with the continuity of traditionalism and customary relations, which themselves have been stretched globally in new ways. Traditional religions provide a good example of this process. They are at once carried across the globe by modern processes of organization and communication and they increasingly give rise to a modern politics of ethnic–cultural identification, but they remain grounded in traditional truths and authority claims that are anathema to modern rights. Claims to the eternal meaning of subjectivity given by God or Allah are in direct tension with modern practices of abstract citizenry and individual autonomy. This means that the pretensions of postmodern cosmopolitanisms to sweep away these kinds of tensions – for example, by arguing for a borderless world or becoming strangers to ourselves (Kristeva 1991) – have little traction in practice. It means that, to the extent that cosmopolitanism remains unreflexive about the tensions that we are describing, it cannot provide a grounded answer to the insecurities of our time.

Embodied globalization engenders responses which take the form of what Roland Robertson calls a 'localizing dialectic' (Robertson 1992). This dialectic takes shape across locales criss-crossed by layers of different ontologies of temporality, spatiality, embodiment and epistemology. Responses to embodied globalization include defiance, resignation, self-help, conflict, violent armed action and so on – sometimes enacted as simple modern resistance; sometimes articulated in confrontation with the hegemony and the false universality of modern culture; sometimes themselves modernist reclamations of traditional verities. At the edge of this process we get extreme orthodoxies from Christian fundamentalism to Islamic jihadism. More often, people struggle to make sense of the discrepancies that occur in the intersection of layers of globalizing modern practices and continuing local and regional cultural traditions of integration and differentiation.

One outcome, to re-traverse ground covered earlier, has been a renewal and revival of cultural–political expressions of identity, lifted in many cases to reflexive defensiveness: neo-traditional religious loyalties, ethnic and racial identities, genealogical and linguistic differences (Mittleman 1994). This 'looking back' draws together people who feel the tension without having moved and those persons, lifted out of place, who look back upon their old identities from the distance of being refugees, migrants, guest workers or exiles somewhere else. In most circumstances these are the bases of deep insecurities.

However, what we are suggesting is that in this reflexive 'looking back' there is also the possibility of finding contingent and creative ways of positively living with such insecurity. When Magic Cleaners in Los Angeles display ambivalence towards citizenship in its conventional form while enacting new modes of belonging, they also enliven the possibility of forms of human security that can be positively negotiated at a local level across difference and division. Such examples suggest that material insecurities can begin to be addressed by people-in-place working together. The answer to the clash of ontologies is more difficult. It can only partly be handled locally. And it will require much more, we would argue, than the assurance of the strong security state as it frames a self-serving sovereignty dominated by a modern singularity. Unfortunately, that seems to be the best that is on offer at the moment. An alternative, still on the horizon, will be achieved at the global level by reflexive negotiation over regimes of care and hospitality across the continuing boundaries of social difference. In the meantime, local processes of reconciliation, recognition and mutual support offer significant steps forward.

Notes

1 Some of the concepts here such as the 'rationalization of the lifeworld' are associated with the work of Jürgen Habermas (1987); however, the methodological framing for understanding the two trends comes from the constitutive abstraction argument associated with *Arena Journal*.
2 This is not to suggest that the global consolidation of the nation-state as the dominant and generalized formation of the present is likely to break up in the foreseeable future. Nevertheless, the tensions between community formation and statehood are considerable.
3 The contradictory complexity of what we are describing goes against such authors as Philip Bobbit (2002), who suggest that the market-state has replaced the nation-state. To be sure, market relations dominate the contemporary politics of the nation-state, but this is a different issue.
4 See, for example, Department of Immigration and Multicultural and Indigenous Affairs (2002). For evidence of this logic in official French discourse, see also Freedman (2009).
5 The text of the agreement between the Australian and Malaysian governments can be accessed from the Press Office of the Prime Minister of Australia at www.pm.gov.au/press-office/australia-and-malaysia-sign-transfer-deal (accessed 24 April 2012).
6 For discussions on these dilemmas, see Carens (2008) and Shachar (2007).
7 The documentation required was two forms of identification (a passport and IDEPSCA's organizational ID card) and an Individual Taxpayer Identification number. The latter is issued by the Internal Revenue Service to those ineligible for a social security number, regardless of immigration status.
8 See the critique by Senghaas (2002).
9 See www.crikey.com.au/2011/07/25/broadmeadows-asylum-seekers-sew-lips-together-post-pics-on-facebook (accessed 24 April 2012).

Bibliography

Andrijasevic, R. (2009) 'Deported: the right to asylum at EU's external border of Italy and Libya', *International Migration*, 48(1): 154.

Andrijasevic, R. and Walters, W. (2010) 'The International Organization for Migration and the international government of borders', *Environment and Planning D: Society and Space*, 28(6): 977–99.

Amnesty International (European Union Office) (2005) 'Immigration Co-operation with Libya: The Human Rights Perspective', briefing ahead of the Justice and Home Affairs Council meeting, Brussels, 14 April.

Appadurai, A. (1996) *Modernity at Large: Cultural Dimensions of Globalization*, Minneapolis: University of Minnesota Press.

Bigo, D. (2002) 'Security and immigration: toward a critique of the governmentality of unease', *Alternatives*, 27 (special issue): 65–73.

Birkeland, N.M., Halff, K. and Jennings, E. (eds) (2010) *Internal Displacement: Global Overview of Trends and Developments in 2009*, Geneva: Internal Displacement Monitoring Centre and the Norwegian Refugee Council.

Blair, T. (2003) 'New international approaches to asylum processing and protection', paper submitted for discussion at the European Council, Brussels, 20–21 March.

Bobbit, P. (2002) *The Shield of Achilles: War, Peace and the Course of History*, New York: Alfred A. Knopf.

Carens, J.H. (2008) 'The Rights of Irregular Migrants', *Ethics and International Relations*, 22 (special issue).

Clifford, J. (1994) 'Diasporas', *Cultural Anthropology*, 9(3): 316–17.

Dauvergne, C. (2008) *Making People Illegal: What Globalization Means for Migration and Law*, Cambridge: Cambridge University Press.

De Genova, N. (2002) 'Migrant "illegality" and deportability in everyday life', *Annual Review of Anthropology*, 31: 422–3.

Department of Immigration and Multicultural and Indigenous Affairs (2002) *Refugee and Humanitarian Issues: Australia's Response*, Canberra: Commonwealth of Australia.

Freedman, J. (2009) 'Mobilising against detention and deportation: collective actions against the detention and deportation of "failed" asylum seekers in France', *French Politics*, 7(3–4): 345–6.

Fukuyama, F. (2004) *State Building: Governance and World Order in the Twenty-First Century*, London: Profile Books.

Gibney, M.J. (2000) *Outside the Protection of the Law: The Situation of Irregular Migrants in Europe*, Working Paper no. 6, Refugee Studies Centre, Oxford: University of Oxford.

Haas, G. (2010) 'Native green gardening co-op', 5 June. Available at: http://drpop.org/2010/06/native-green-gardening-co-op/ (last accessed 16 August 2011).

Habermas, J. (1987) *The Theory of Communicative Action: Volume Two, Lifeworld and System*, Cambridge: Polity Press.

Harkavy, R.E. and Neuman, S.G. (2001) *Warfare and the Third World*, New York: Palgrave.

Huntington, S. (1998) *The Clash of Civilizations and the Remaking of the World Order*, London: Simon Schuster.

Huysmans, J. and Buonfino, A. (2008) 'Politics of exception and unease: immigration, asylum, and terrorism in parliamentary debates in the UK', *Political Studies*, 56: 782–3.

James, P. (2006) *Globalism, Nationalism, Tribalism*, London: Sage Publications.
Kaldor, M. (2004) 'Nationalism and globalization', *Nations and Nationalism*, 10(1–2): 162.
Kapferer, B. (2001) 'Ethnic nationalism and the discourses of violence in Sri Lanka', *Communal/Plural*, 9(1): 33–67.
Kasparek, B. (2008) 'Frontex und die Europäische Außengrenze', in *Was ist Frontex? Aufgaben und Strukturen der Europäischen Agentur für die Operative Zusammenarbeit an den Außengrenzen, Materialien gegen Krieg, Repression und für andere Verhältnisse*, no. 4 (brochure by order of Tobias Pflüger, Member of European Parliament, 2008).
Koser, K. (2010) 'International migration and global governance', *Global Governance*, 16(3): 301–15.
Kristeva, J. (1991) *Strangers to Ourselves*, New York: Harvester Wheatsheaf.
Los Angeles City Council (2008) Permit Process/Day Laborer Operating Standards/Home Improvement Stores, Ordinance No. 180174, introduced 23 June 2008.
Los Angeles Police Department (2011) 'Understanding Special Order 40', 11 January. Available at: http://lapdblog.typepad.com/lapd_blog/2011/01/understanding-special-order-40.html (accessed 24 April 2012).
Madera, G., Mathay, A.A., Najafi, A.M., Saldívar, H.H., Solis, S., Titony, A.J.M., Rivera-Salgado, G., Shadduck-Hernández, J., Wong, K., Frazier, R. and Monroe, J. (eds) (2008) *Underground Undergrads: UCLA Undocumented Immigrant Students Speak Out*, Los Angeles: UCLA Center for Labor Research and Education.
Malkki, L.H. (2002) 'News from nowhere: mass displacement and globalized "problems of organization"', *Ethnography*, 3(3): 351–60.
Massey, D.S. (2005) 'Backfire at the border: why enforcement without legalization cannot stop illegal immigration', *Trade Policy Analysis*, 29, Washington: Centre for Trade Policy Studies.
Mittleman, J. (1994) 'The globalization challenge: surviving at margins', *Third World Quarterly*, 15(3): 427–43.
Narro, V. (2005–2006) 'Impacting next wave organizing: creative campaign strategies of the Los Angeles Worker Centers', *New York Law School Law Review*, 50(2): 465–513.
Passel, J.S. and Cohn, D. (2011) *Unauthorized Immigrant Population: National and State Trends, 2010*. Washington: Pew Hispanic Centre.
Pastor, M. and Ortiz, R. (2009) *Immigrant Integration in Los Angeles: Strategic Directions for Funders*, Program for Environmental and Regional Equity and Center for the Study of Immigrant Integration, Los Angeles: University of Southern California.
Phillips, N. (2009) 'Migration as Development Strategy? The New Political Economy of Dispossession and Inequality in the Americas', *Review of International Political Economy*, 16: 231–59.
Pincetl, S. (1994) 'Challenges to citizenship: Latino immigrants and political organizing in the Los Angeles area', *Environment and Planning A*, 26: 914.
Ranganathan, M. (2010) *Eelam on Line: The Tamil Diaspora and War in Sri Lanka*, Newcastle: Cambridge Scholars Publishing.
Reynolds, S. and Muggeridge, H. (2008) *Remote Controls: How UK Border Controls Are Endangering the Lives of Refugees*, London: Refugee Council.
Robertson, R. (1992) *Globalization: Social Theory and Global Culture*, London: Sage Publications.
Savage, L. (2006) 'Justice for janitors: scales of organizing and representing workers', *Antipode*, 38(3): 645–66.

Schily, O. (2005) 'Effecktiver Schutz für Flüchtlinge, Wrikungsvolle Bekämpfung illegaler Migration', press statement, 9 September. Available at: www.bmi.bund.de/cln_012/nn_662928/Internet/Content/Nachrichten/Archiv/Pressemitteilungen/2005/09/Fluechtlingsschutz.html (last accessed 26 August 2011).

Schuster, L. (2005) *The Realities of a New Asylum Paradigm*, Working Paper no. 20, Centre on Migration, Policy, and Society, Oxford: University of Oxford.

Senghaas, D. (2002) *The Clash within Civilizations: Coming to Terms with Cultural Conflicts*, London: Routledge.

Shachar, A. (2007) 'Against birthright privilege: redefining citizenship as property', in S. Benhabib, I. Shapiro and D. Petranovic (eds), *Identities, Affiliations, and Allegiances*, Cambridge: Cambridge University Press.

Sirtori, S. and Coelho, P. (2007) *Defending Refugees' Access to Protection in Europe*, Brussels: European Council of Refugees and Exiles.

Villaraigosa, A.R. (2009) 'Mayor Villaraigosa announces opening of over 40 "cash for college" financial aid workshops throughout Los Angeles', press release, Office of the Mayor, City of Los Angeles, 2 February.

Weiner, M. (1996) 'Bad neighbours, bad neighbourhood: an enquiry into the causes of refugee flows', *International Security*, 21(1): 5–42.

7 Negotiating integration
Refugees and asylum seekers in Australia and the UK

Susanne Schech and Sophia Rainbird

Introduction

In the first decade of the new century, refugees and asylum seekers in the Global North have faced a challenging environment in which to negotiate their rights to asylum, integration and citizenship. In the recipient communities, the new arrivals are increasingly associated with negative concepts such as welfare dependency, social disharmony and terrorism and are viewed as people who should be kept at a safe distance if not actively expelled. These associations are shaped and reinforced through government and media discourses which focus on the deviancy of asylum seekers and the dependency of refugees. At the same time, there is ever greater insistence on the rapid and successful integration of immigrants as productive, self-sufficient and responsible members of the wider community. In this chapter we explore two aspects of the contemporary environment – the fragmentation and racialization of the refugee label and the shift from multiculturalism to integration as the preferred mode of incorporating newcomers, associated with integration being contrasted with segregation as its opposite.

First, the label 'refugee' no longer designates a respectable identity location. It has been torn from its moorings in humanitarian discourse and become politicized through the proliferation of bureaucratic categories that are designed to manage the growing number of displaced people, including 'asylum seekers', 'temporary' and 'humanitarian' protection and country specific labels (Zetter 2007). In this 'fragmentation of the refugee label', each label carries a different package of rights, entitlements and resources, which refugees and asylum seekers can only claim by adopting their label but, in doing so, they risk exclusion from host communities that are increasingly preoccupied with social cohesion and cultural homogeneity (Zetter 2007). Being positioned between a rock and a hard place, between refugee identity and fitting in, evokes a range of responses ranging from denying one's refugee identity (Kumsa 2006) and evading questions about one's refugee status, to retreating into refugeeness and diaspora communities.

Second, the past decade has seen a backlash against multiculturalism which has been accused of fostering segregation among ethnic minorities and growing ethnic tensions. Although there is debate as to the extent and causes of this backlash (Banting and Kymlicka 2010; Vertovec and Wessendorf 2009), commentators agree that there has been a discursive shift towards citizenship and social cohesion associated with a 'more assimilationist and mono-cultural model of integration' (Zetter 2007: 187) and at times 'fairly harsh and coercive "civic integration" policies' (Banting and Kymlicka 2010: 44). These policy shifts have been observed in many countries of the Global North to a greater or lesser extent. However, the concept of integration remains vague both in terms of the length of time and the goals to be achieved and imbued with a range of contested meanings (for example, Castles *et al.* 2001; Robinson 1998; Schneider and Crul 2010).

These aspects of the current debate on refugee integration will be explored in the next section, which is followed by an analysis of integration challenges facing refugees and asylum seekers. The empirical material is drawn from two separate studies conducted in the early to mid-2000s, one with refugees in South Australia and the other with asylum seekers in East Anglia in the UK. There are undoubtedly differences in the asylum legislations and practices of Australia and the UK and in the legal position of refugees and asylum seekers which shape their responses to assimilation pressures. The room for manoeuvre is greater for refugees in Australia than for asylum seekers in the UK. However, we argue that the experiences of both groups show some similarities. This is due on one hand to the fragmentation of the refugee label, mentioned above, and the trend towards ever-tighter asylum policies which is accompanied by a growing international convergence in policy and practice. On the other hand, asylum seekers in the UK still face the imperative to integrate despite their uncertain status. Although the UK refugee integration policy only applies to refugees and explicitly excludes asylum seekers (UK Border Agency 2009), those who arrive as asylum seekers live in the country for years and many end up settling long term.

Placing the East Anglia and the South Australia case studies side by side offers insights into how refugees and asylum seekers position themselves in relation to the imperative to integrate. What do refugees and asylum seekers perceive themselves integrating into and how do they go about achieving it? What do they see as preventing or facilitating their integration? How do they read the community's responses to their presence and how does this reading affect their strategies of engagement with their new environment? The UK case study is drawn from a doctoral research project on asylum seekers conducted in the UK in 2002 and 2003.[1] It focused on dispersed 'asylum seekers' and their struggles with labelling, which they see as standing in the way of their integration. These and other issues are also raised by the Australian case study which interprets data collected in 2006 and 2007 for a research project on refugee settlement and citizen making processes.[2] This project focused on a heterogeneous group of 'refugees', of whom some arrived as 'Convention refugees' from 'off-shore' camps or as sponsored 'humanitarian entrants' or family members, while others entered Australia as asylum seekers and were granted first temporary then permanent residence after a period in immigration detention. We have selected the most poignant sections from a database of 37 interviews conducted with asylum seekers in the UK project and 42 interviews with individuals of refugee background collected for the Australian project. Together these two case studies shed light on the challenges that refugees and asylum seekers face with the imperative to integrate.

Both research projects involved a narrative interview strategy and excerpts from interviews are identified by the adopted name of research participants and the date of their interview. Both projects were conducted in locations considered less multicultural than the main immigrant magnets in Australia (Sydney and Melbourne (Hugo 2008: 558)) and the UK (London), but which had in recent years received more refugees and asylum seekers than in the past as a result of government migrant distribution policies. Since the majority of refugees and asylum seekers come from Africa, Asia and the Middle East, they are more readily identified as refugees and asylum seekers in places with a more limited range and size of visibly different populations, and thus may find blending into the mainstream a greater challenge here than in hyper-diverse mega-cities like Sydney and London. On the other hand, the opportunities for social connection between refugees and asylum seekers and the long-term resident population may also be greater because the former are compelled to rely on mainstream support and resources in places where ethnic and refugee organizations are less developed or altogether absent. However, the ways in which refugees and asylum seekers position and represent themselves and how they engage with their social environment at the local level are shaped by broader national and international public and policy discourses which in recent years have been dominated by hostility and fear, as will be discussed below.

Refugee integration in a post-multicultural era

There is little doubt that a hostile view of refugees and asylum seekers has taken hold across countries of asylum in the Global North since the early 1990s. This is expressed in ever more restrictive asylum policies spreading like a highly infectious contagion across Europe, North America and Australia (Bloch and Schuster 2005; Briskman *et al.* 2008; Marfleet 2006) and in media discourses that paint asylum seekers as cheats and criminals, a socio-economic burden, a security risk and a threat to the nation's identity and cohesion (Leudar *et al.* 2008; Pickering 2001). While refugees have always occupied a vulnerable position in a world that considers them as outside the realm of 'normal' rooted citizens in a system of nation-states (Haddad 2008), contemporary concerns over security and terrorism have eroded the humanitarian argument which has been their main support. Even before the terrorist attacks in the US on September 11 2001, international migration became increasingly seen as a security issue and immigrants as a source of insecurity which grows when their movements are seemingly illegal or out of control (Haddad 2008: 194). Today, second and third generation immigrants are believed to still retain a threatening potential, as seen in the media portrayal of the 2005 London bombers as '"inadequately integrated"' (Brighton 2007: 2). In response to the securitization of migration, governments have modified their asylum policies to restrict access and have in the process 'fractioned' the label of the refugee (Zetter 2007). In contrast to 'genuine' refugees with the UNHCR identity card, 'asylum seekers' are often labeled 'illegal' or 'unauthorized' if they arrive without valid immigration documents. Asylum seekers are subject to mandatory detention if they arrive unauthorized on Australian shores and are either turned back or processed in off-shore detention centres if intercepted on their way to Australia. Between 1999 and 2008, such asylum seekers were only eligible for temporary protection visas if they were granted refugee status. This Australian government policy encouraged an 'unhelpful rhetoric about "good" (off-shore) and "bad" (on-shore) refugees' (Crock et al. 2006: 18) and hampered the ability of refugees on temporary protection visas to settle into a new life in Australia (Leach and Mansouri 2004; Marston 2003).

In the UK, a key plank in the government's response to the rise of asylum applications is the dispersal policy instituted by the Immigration and Asylum Act 1999. It aims to spread the burden that asylum seekers are deemed to place on receiving communities and ease inter-ethnic tensions (Boswell 2001; Robinson 2003). A deterrence effect has also been attributed to the dispersal policy as asylum seekers are no longer able to obtain accommodation support if they decline their assigned settlement location and choose to settle close to family or friends (Bloch and Schuster 2005). Integration has not been a significant consideration in the making or implementation of the dispersal policy, leading to claims that dispersal 'marginalizes the refugee from his/her social and cultural milieu, alienates him/her from local hosts who understandably resent impoverished migrants forcibly dispersed to their already deprived communities, and compels the claimants to live in controlled poverty' (Zetter 2007: 182).

While the fractioning of the refugee label creates several groups of refugees and asylum seekers who are portrayed as more or less deserving of refugee status, it also demarcates asylum seekers and refugees as a homogeneous group positioned vis-à-vis the 'host' or long-term resident community. According to Zetter (2007: 185), refugees and asylum seekers have become the focus of anxieties about strangers that reflect 'a growing preoccupation with culturalism' in Northern countries of asylum concerned about the perceived erosion of national identities. The multiplication of refugee labels, which are indistinguishable to the wider population, undermines the legitimacy of seeking refuge of those 'who flew here' at the same time as reinforcing the boundaries of British and Australian identity of those 'who grew here' (Due and Riggs 2008). This construction of the stranger has elements of the 'new racism', which has no overt reference to biological notions of 'race' but instead relies on notions of 'culture' and 'community' (see also Barker 1981; Gilroy 1992: 53; Taguieff 1999). The term 'new racism' is controversial as it assumes that racial prejudice remains central to the issue of cross-cultural exchanges, rather than the self-definition of the broader community. Nonetheless, aspects of the new racism are useful in situating the current context in which refugees and asylum seekers position themselves in relation to mainstream society. In her study of young Oromos in Canada, Kumsa found a widespread rejection of the refugee label among her research subjects, who regarded it as a racialized label of exclusion, of not belonging to the nation. Canadians saw no difference between a refugee with an entry permit and a 'stupid, misfits, ignorant, poor, and uncivilized FOB [Fresh Off the Boat]' (Kumsa 2006: 242) if both shared external markers of difference. Kumsa's respondents pointed out that, unlike them, white refugees can fit in and evade the refugee label.

The retreat from multiculturalism has contributed to the shrinking space for the stranger within societies of the Global North. In Australia, multiculturalism has been pursued since the early 1970s as 'a pragmatic and modest policy approach' based on 'a broad philosophy that carefully chosen human beings could be settled within a stable and prosperous society' whatever their race or culture (Jupp 2007: 17–18). Designed to manage the relationships between settlers and new immigrants, Australia's state sponsored multiculturalism has different points of origin from British multiculturalism, which has been more concerned with racial equality between immigrants from the former colonies and the native population (Hewitt 2005: 132). Both countries have in recent years experienced a backlash against multiculturalism, fed on the one hand by critics that see 'the multiculturalism based in exclusive, essentialist communitarianism as an obstacle to the achievement of equity' (Hewitt 2005: 145; see also Viviani 1996), and on the other by a concern about 'cultural extinction' (Hage 2003: 61) or 'cultural invisibility' (Hewitt 2005: 126) among white citizens of British or Anglo descent. This popular backlash was supported by a growing scholarly interest in ethnic concentration, segregation and enclaves and the real or possible consequences for race relations (Finney and Simpson 2009).

The retreat from multiculturalism in Australia was cemented in the 2000s when the term was dropped from the name of the ministry that had carried it for over 20 years. Although recently the Labor Government has signalled a return to multiculturalism (Bowen 2011), for much of the 2000s the Australian government's emphasis was on citizenship, social cohesion and integration focused around an assumed core culture that it saw as binding the nation together – western civilization, English language and Anglo-Saxon cultural roots (Tate 2009). While there has been a marked shift in government rhetoric, some have argued that the claim of a backlash against multiculturalism is overdrawn (Banting and Kymlicka 2010). Even at the height of integrationism, multicultural policies were still implemented and funded by Australian governments. Acceptance of 'everyday multiculturalism', as Stratton (1998: 206) terms 'the lived experience of cultural diversity', appears to be widespread (Moran 2005; Vertovec and Wessendorf 2009) even though it continues to coexist with racism, xenophobia and antagonism towards some cultural groups (Forrest and Dunn 2007: 700). The coexistence of multicultural, integration and xenophobic discourses creates a complex environment for refugees rebuilding their lives and identities in Australia. As part of the resettlement process, they are encouraged and assisted in forming community organizations based around national and ethnic identities, while also being expected to know and embrace Australian values and to do much of the work of building bridges across cultural boundaries. Although integration is frequently used in government documents related to immigration and citizenship, Australia does not have an official refugee integration policy (Department of Immigration and Citizenship 2007).

In the UK, multiculturalism was blamed for encouraging ethnic segregation which in turn was perceived to be a root cause in the 'racial' disturbances that spread across some northern English towns in 2001 (Phillips 2006). In the wake of these disturbances and the 9/11 attacks in the US, the Blair government's (1997–2007) early embrace of social inclusion was modified by a growing focus on community cohesion (aimed at established ethnic minorities) and integration (aimed at refugees) (Robinson 2005). The UK's integration strategy (Home Office 2005) identifies language and economic mobility, fair representation and access to mainstream services as the keys to refugee integration, which is measured by indicators drawn from Ager and Strang's integration model discussed below (Ager and Strang 2008). This policy has been criticized for paying insufficient attention to civic participation and equity in comparison with the host community (Phillimore and Goodson 2008), failing to clarify what refugees are expected to integrate into, and excluding asylum seekers from its application (Threadgold and Court 2005). More broadly, integration is increasingly seen to stand for the opposite of segregation in government discourses about community cohesion. As Kalra and Kapoor (2009: 1398) point out, '[t]he re-packaging of segregation as "parallel lives" and of integration as "community cohesion" has enabled a shift away from the progressive elements of these discourses that were related to material inequalities and political exclusion'.

Evidently, integration is difficult to define and takes on different meanings according to the environment in which it is used. It has rapidly become almost as hotly debated as multiculturalism, and there is at times a narrow line between integration and assimilation. Both rely on normative values, including loyalty to the nation, shared language and other resources, and a focus on adaptation which involves abandoning cultural practices that do not fit, at least on the part of the minority ethnic individual (Schneider and Crul 2010). To more clearly define integration, Ager and Strang (2008: 170) identify ten dimensions of integration grouped within four main areas: markers and means, social connection, facilitators and foundation. In this chapter we focus on social connection which, according to Ager and Strang, is inspired by social capital theory. They borrow from Putnam's (1993) and Woolcock's (1998) conceptualization of social capital three concepts – bonds, bridges and links – to describe different modes of social connection. Bonds refer to the connection with like-ethnic groups which provides a voice, contact point, expertise and sensitive response, as well as cultural and social activities which offer refugees a chance to maintain their own customs (Ager and Strang 2008: 178). Bridges and links refer to refugee participation in host society (for example, being recognized and greeted by neighbours) and to connection with the structures of the state (for example, local services that are capable of responding to refugee needs). Integration is more successful where migrants have access to and can participate in social networks while being most elusive for those who are most at risk of being socially isolated, such as women with young children or the unemployed (Hugo 2003; Khawaja *et al.* 2008; Zetter *et al.* 2006). Numerous studies have shown that refugees whose usual social networks were disrupted by persecution and flight seek to build alternative social connections, even if this requires secondary migration to towns and countries where like-ethnic networks and resources are available (Fuglerud and Engebrigtsen 2006; Hardwick and Meacham 2005; Harte *et al.* 2009; Simich *et al.* 2002; Valentine *et al.* 2009; Williams 2006). In the following sections we hope to show how refugees and asylum seekers tread the fine line of integration in different political environments, first in East Anglia, then in South Australia.

East Anglia

While British governments and local authorities have made several attempts in the past to influence the settlement of refugee populations, it was not until the 2000s that a comprehensive asylum seeker dispersal policy was put in place. The aim is to direct the growing flows of asylum seekers to regions outside London where accommodation and access to services were more readily available (Bloch and Schuster 2005; Boswell 2001; Griffiths *et al.* 2006; Robinson 2003; Zetter *et al.* 2005). The policy was implemented at a time of heightened insecurity among the wider British population around the war in Iraq and fear of terrorism and cultural, ethnic and religious difference. Asylum seekers dispersed to East Anglia were highly visible in an overwhelmingly white British population of 95.6 per cent (compared with 71.2 per cent white British in London) (National Statistics 2003).[3] A key issue for them was how to avoid racialized reprisals from local residents.

Insecurity

These concerns were evident during interviews with asylum seekers from Great Yarmouth, Norwich and Peterborough and participant observation at drop-in centres for asylum seekers. These centres were run by a small number of concerned local residents who provided a safe space, social support and advocacy, but the widespread fear of asylum seekers made bridging and linking between asylum seekers and the local community very difficult. Ahmad, a Kurdish Iraqi, had been walking out on the street in Great Yarmouth when three people punched him, knocked him to the ground, and then kicked him because, as he perceived it, he looked like a 'foreigner' (Ahmad, 28 May 2003). Consequently, he avoided public places for fear of being attacked again. At the same time he positioned locals as misinformed:

> A few weeks ago in all the newspapers and TV news it was about asylum seekers and how they could be terrorists. People believe this and then it creates problems. I have experience of this felt from local people who are

very careful of me. I will not go [...] anywhere at night because people may get violent because they are afraid of who I might be. I feel this every day.

(Ahmad, 28 May 2003)

Eduardo, a Congolese asylum seeker, observed that local people considered some differences as a greater threat than others. It was newcomers like his Kurdish Iraqi friend Hawar who bore the brunt of local perceptions of danger:

I mean, they [the locals] see the faces, you see? [...] When they don't feel like you're different, they treat you alright. But where I was living, I was living with Iraqis. And when they see the Iraqis, they know that they are asylum seekers. For them, Iraqis just means straight asylum seekers. So, they just do their best to get the Iraqis in trouble. Or, to make their life harder, you see [...] And I feel sorry for the guy because I know [...] how difficult it is.

(Eduardo, 13 August 2003)

Eduardo was also concerned about his own safety and avoided certain places in the town, aware that the police would be unlikely to assist in the event that an attack took place:

There are areas in Peterborough where you don't go because you will be attacked. I am always aware that I might be attacked.

(Eduardo, 13 August 2003)

These comments highlight the rupture asylum seekers feel between their identity as people seeking safety and an imposed identity of 'foreigner' or 'asylum seeker' as a potential threat. Both asylum seekers and local residents are distanced from what they may have in common and retreat to their respective communities in response to alienation and fear.

Blending in

However, there are ways for asylum seekers to engage with the local community if they are able to avoid the asylum seeker label. Carla, one young woman from Angola, explained that she took pride in using the Norfolk greeting of 'You alright?' (Carla, 17 February 2003). She said that when she goes to London to get her hair styled, she likes to think of herself as a Great Yarmouth girl from Norfolk. At the pub with her local girlfriends she enjoys calling out 'Alright?' to the boys and they will call back 'Alright, darl'n?' (Carla, 17 February 2003). Carla is aware of the significance of this greeting as a colloquial expression with working class origins which identifies the speaker's sense of local belonging. Thinking of herself as a 'Yarmouth girl' does two things. First, it is a spoken expression of the embodiment of an identity that transcends an asylum seeking identity. Participation in this banter also emphasizes her sexuality and allows her to claim acceptance by the local community. Second, it establishes her belonging to a regional area and acknowledges a set of relations and meanings that are localized and unique and that reinforce her identity when she is outside her local district. Carla draws on local British identity rather than Angolan, African or asylum seeker identities, as this is much more conducive to achieving a sense of belonging.

Similar to the young Canadian Oromos in Kumsa's (2006) study, asylum seekers in East Anglia adopted strategies to avoid the labels of asylum seeker and refugee. As Hawar and Eduardo explained, these labels stood in the way of interactions with locals:

> HAWAR: ...if you say that you are a refugee or an asylum seeker, they will treat you differently.
> EDUARDO: Differently.
> HAWAR: Yeah, we either say we are, you know, like, immigrating to here, or we are students. That's all. [...]
> EDUARDO: But people can be good. But, they'll be treating you like you were poor and they'll always want to help you and stuff. I want to...
> HAWAR: ...which is quite annoying.
> EDUARDO: It is annoying! Because I want to live normal, you know.
> HAWAR: Yeah.
>
> (Eduardo and Hawar, 13 August 2003)

Even when the asylum seeker label evokes sympathy rather than hostility, it still presents a barrier to integration and 'living normal'. Attending a local college enables Eduardo and Hawar to call themselves students, which is an acceptable identity and a way of blending in. Along with adopting locally accepted roles and local dialects, another way for asylum seekers in East Anglia to remain inconspicuous is to discard the clothes traditionally worn in their homeland and wear similar clothing to the locals, even if this compromises their religiosity.

Distancing and avoidance

Racialization and the stigma attached to their insecure status make many asylum seekers sensitive to social interactions. As Fuglerud (1999: 105) points out, it is in a situation where one has to communicate with others that the possibility of conflict arises. For example, when Tanja, an asylum seeker from Kosovo, was asked if she thought that people in Great Yarmouth were friendly, she seemed to think that this was a silly question. She said it was the same anywhere. But when she elaborated it was evident that she was able to remain on good terms with locals by keeping a low profile:

> I think that some friendly and some are not. But mostly friendly. Always I am quiet and smile and say 'Thank you', then there is no problem. Some refugees only want to make trouble. I no make trouble if I am quiet and

smile and say only 'Please' and 'Thank you'. I do not want trouble so I say, 'No, sorry my English is not good', or, 'I no speak English' because I only want to say, 'Hello, you alright', and 'Goodbye'.

(Tanja, 19 June 2003)

Keeping quiet in contexts where people know about her asylum seeker status is a way of countering the image of the refugee as a trouble maker or a problem. This image is frequently invoked in justifications of the asylum seeker dispersal policy as a burden-sharing mechanism. Meanwhile the British media represents asylum seekers as excessively demanding and as 'undeserving recipients of better treatment than the average British citizen' (Buchanan *et al.* 2003: 25; see also Leudar *et al.* 2008). In the context of the impending war in Iraq and the widespread fear of terrorists, it was especially important to adjust one's identity from one situation to another in order to minimize the risk of causing trouble. On one occasion at the drop-in centre, Tanja used the tactic of avoidance when she was approached by a local resident who spoke to her in slow and deliberate English, perhaps unwittingly reinforcing the boundary between his local and her asylum seeker status. A short time later, Tanja was observed communicating easily with a Zimbabwean student who even commented on her excellent use of English. Tanja evidently felt secure enough to engage with the student who spoke to her in a relaxed and casual manner but chose not to understand the local resident who treated her like an asylum seeker.

The asylum seeker comments presented here reflect an awareness of the suspicion and fear held by local residents that are propelled by broader government and media discourses around difference, terrorism, burden and excess. Asylum seekers employ responses that range from avoiding public spaces that might harbour threats to their safety and avoiding contact by keeping a low profile, to hiding their refugee status by highlighting more acceptable aspects of their identity and adopting local cultural practices to blend in. These tactics represent various ways of attempting to negotiate integration in a policy environment that does not encourage bonding among asylum seekers or actively support bridge building between newcomers and established residents. The work of integration is one-sided and its success is uncertain. In a region with an overwhelmingly white British population, asylum seekers and refugees are easily identified as strangers. Since the various refugee labels are indistinguishable to most in the community, it will be challenging for the refugee integration policy to achieve its goals.

South Australia

Until recently, South Australia's capital city Adelaide has had a multicultural population that consisted mostly of European migrants who settled here from the late nineteenth century, with a significant proportion of southern and eastern European migrants settled since the 1950s. A number of Indo-Chinese refugees arrived in the 1980s, but it was in the early 2000s that South Australia's refugee intake became global with increasing numbers of African and Middle Eastern arrivals. While most African refugees were resettled according to plan through the established Australian humanitarian program, a large proportion of Adelaide's refugee population from Middle Eastern countries arrived as asylum seekers by boat or as sponsored humanitarian migrants. They experienced a much cooler welcome than the resettled refugees, first in mandatory immigration detention, then on temporary protection visas which gave them few rights to welfare and services and no certainty of continued abode in Australia. Although five years had passed since the 9/11 attacks which dominated public discourses, refugees still struggled with widespread assumptions that they posed a threat to Australian society. African refugees also faced stigmatization following statements by senior politicians about the alleged difficulties with integrating Africans (Martin 2007). Such concerns about the country's ability to accommodate cultural difference trigger stronger pressures to assimilate or integrate.

Insecurity and assimilation

Several interview participants contested allegations that refugees pose a threat to social and national cohesion. One critic, Jessica, arrived in Adelaide in the early 1990s when being African was still positively associated with the multicultural student body of South Australia's three universities. In the late 1990s, when refugees from Africa started to arrive in greater numbers, Africanness became increasingly attached to the refugee label and refugees of African descent were viewed through the prevalent asylum and integration debates. In Jessica's view, the growing Sudanese refugee population was getting on well with the local population and giving no cause for the government to question their ability to integrate. Drawing comparisons with other ethnic groups – 'one suburb is fully Italian, one suburb is fully Asian, one suburb is fully Lebanese' – Jessica pointed out that her own community was behaving exactly how the government expected them to:

> The Sudanese should be instead an example for all other ethnic groups in Australia because they have integrated and mixed in. They didn't just choose one suburb for themselves alone. They are in every suburb and they mix very well because they want to learn the culture. The Sudanese are the people that love to learn and they are friendly people so they want to be part of Australia.
>
> (Jessica, 4 November 2007)

The image of African refugees as an integration problem was based, she thought, on false or insufficient information disseminated through television and newspapers. This misinformation had a direct impact on her sense of security in public spaces:

> One time this week I was attacked by somebody in the bus stop and they told me to go back to Sudan. This is because of the comment they heard on

the television because otherwise how do they know I'm from Sudan? I didn't tell them myself I was from Sudan. I'm just an African person.

(Jessica, 4 November 2007)

In Jessica's view, anxieties about potential threats to the nation from culturally different people combined with latent racism to make her and other refugees' lives in Australia harder and more unsafe. There is also the sense that it is unfair and unrealistic to expect 'someone to come from a totally different country and come here with their life experiences and everything and be able to change just like that overnight' (Stephanie, 4 November 2007). Stephanie argued that the new arrivals needed time to settle down and develop a sense of security to successfully 'assimilate'.

Nevertheless, a strong theme emerging from the South Australian interviews is that being accepted as a refugee significantly boosts a displaced person's sense of security. Many commented on their relief about being in a safe and peaceful country far from war and armed conflict and being able to enjoy the basic freedoms guaranteed by a functioning state and legal system. This was also emphasized by the majority of those refugee respondents who had spent time in the Australian immigration detention system facing an uncertain future, and/or on temporary protection visas which provided only temporary security of residence. However, once existential safety is assured, other factors impinging on a person's sense of security come to the fore. These factors include a perceived lack of acceptance by the host country and administrative and financial barriers to family reunion and skills recognition, which stand in the way of creating a new life in Australia. Particularly those who arrived as asylum seekers saw their lives affected by these problems, as Peter made clear in his interview. He said he came to Australia because his life was under threat and 'it's a safer country' but was suffering because his family was still unsafe in another country. It proved difficult to bring them to Australia: 'everything is very restricted here and everything is really tough', leaving Peter to reflect that 'We are living in Australia now, we are in a free country, freedom, but you are not free' (Peter, 6 April 2007).

Blending in and integrating

In an Australian context, marked by practical multiculturalism and ideological integrationism, refugees are sometimes struggling to balance the security of co-ethnic bonds within the refugee community with the challenge to adapt to a new cultural value system. Dan was a refugee for more 15 years before being resettled in Australia in 2003 and claiming citizenship a couple of years later. From this relatively secure position, he saw the host society's acceptance of his cultural traditions and values as an important aspect of integration. Rather than migrants having to drop their identity and culture in order to embrace Australian values, he advocated a more selective approach which involves taking the best from each culture. Like everywhere, including in his home country, in Australia 'there are really good positive values, whereby I believe, but there are some values that you cannot really believe' because they either conflict with his own values or they are merely rhetoric (Dan, 25 October 2007). Respect for cultural difference was claimed to be part of the Australian value system, he said, but was not necessarily implemented by the government and the broader community.

For refugees from Muslim countries, their assumed religion presents a major obstacle to integration. Nodir was living in Australia for over six years and had recently become an Australian citizen. However, his ability to integrate is constrained by his name which identified him as a Muslim and potential terrorist to Australians, who are often unaware of the persecution he suffered at the hands of Islamic fundamentalists.

> Will society accept me? This is the question. Again the society will judge me as [name] or Nodir or whatever or Mohammad and then [...] I have to change my name and hide my background; is this okay, lying to the people?
> (Nodir, 12 June 2007)

Having to hide his identity and his background in order to be acceptable does not chime with the notion of integration as a two-way process where both sides accept and adapt to each other. Nodir viewed the broader community as 'not willing to accept us' and the government's position on integration as 'just words – no-one works practically, no-one says, "Okay, let's really join with them"' (Nodir, 12 June 2007).

Visible markers of Islamic faith such as the head scarf draw insults and abuse from the broader community and schoolchildren are advised not to say that they are Muslim or come from a Muslim country: 'Whenever we say that we are from Afghanistan, the first reaction that we see from the other side, they say, "Oh, do you know Osama Bin Laden?"' (Adil, 3 May 2006). Another refugee reported that he often did not reveal his provenance from a Muslim country 'because I have to hide to have a peaceful life here' (Cameron, 9 July 2007). For him, hiding is 'not very hard, you know, because when I am walking on the street they don't know who I am – because my face is different, like Chinese or Japanese or Korean, like Asian'. The multicultural cityscape offers some degree of cultural anonymity but his job as a taxi driver requires his name to be on display, prompting a few of his clients to request to be let out for fear of sharing the car with a potential terrorist. Cameron's approach is 'to live like them, to act like them, as Australian, because if I don't combine myself with the Australian society, [it] is very hard to live here. So I have to respect every culture, every ideology' (Cameron, 9 July 2007). This is a draining process of one-sided integration where respect for cultural difference is frequently not reciprocated.

Bridging distance and questioning integration

In contrast to asylum seekers in East Anglia, Australian refugees, or citizens of refugee background, are able to participate in practical steps that bring refugees together with members of the broader community as a way of overcoming distance and fostering mutual understanding. After arriving as an asylum seeker by boat in 1999, spending time in immigration detention and on a temporary protection visa, Adil was able to find work as a community liaison worker with a settlement services provider. He viewed integration as requiring effort on both sides whereby 'the broader community has more responsibility than the small minority group for the integration process' and the government and non-governmental organizations (NGOs) have a key responsibility in providing accurate information about the backgrounds of refugees to help deconstruct the stereotypes surrounding the Muslim 'other' (Adil, 3 May 2006). Refugees should be encouraged to engage with the broader community through practical measures that facilitate direct encounters, he argued, rather than only attending citizenship lessons and information sessions. Adil gave the example of a project where local councils or church organizations in regional towns invited recent refugee arrivals to spend a couple of days of holiday, sharing food, talking and sightseeing: 'And this was a kind of integration process. An understanding of each other that we are not different from each other' (Adil, 3 May 2006). In this view of integration as a two-way process, links between the newcomer and the established community are facilitated by the latter, sometimes through projects funded by the Australian government's Settlement Grants Program. According to Jupp (2007), such multicultural programmes receive only a fraction of the funding that security agencies receive for hunting terrorists. But according to Adil, they are highly effective in building bridges and, once the initial bridging capital is invested, newcomers can cross the bridge.

Social connection only flourishes when refugees get a 'fair go', as Australians colloquially term equal opportunity. This principle is, however, often compromised in the current arrangements for asylum seekers, refugees and other marginalized groups in Australian society. There are deep-seated inequalities and historical injustices in Australia's make-up that refugees become increasingly aware of as they become part of the nation's citizenry. Based on his experience of living in Australia for over a decade, Maradona put refugee integration in the broader context of Australian society and history. He noted a lack of national cohesion in Australia, which was exemplified for him in the debates over Australia Day between those who see it as a celebration of the first fleet of settlers and others who see it as a celebration of colonial invasion. This marks Australia as an emerging nation, rather than fully formed, one that is still in the process of defining its identity and values and hence lacking a clear idea of what newcomers should integrate into. At the same time, it opens a space for newcomers to make the nation. As Maradona sees it, the challenge is not just for the government but also for all Australians: 'we have to come up with something else that is more inclusive, that includes everybody' (Maradona, 30 August 2007).

Social connection and the integration process

In the new millennium, asylum seekers and refugees face a challenging environment when they reach the relative safety of the countries of the Global North.

We focused on two aspects of that environment. One is the tightening asylum policies and a proliferation of refugee labels with attendant differences in entitlements, status and security. The other is a shift away from multiculturalism, with its focus on cultural rights and equal opportunity, to an integrationist model centred on shared core values and civic rights and responsibilities. Both are linked by a concern about social cohesion and national unity in the face of rapid global change, transnational threats and social fragmentation, though it is beyond the scope of this chapter to question the legitimacy of those concerns. The asylum and integration policies encountered in both case study countries appear to counteract each other in many respects. For example, asylum seekers in Britain may live in the country for several years, excluded from the UK integration policy and neither entitled nor encouraged to do the kinds of things that are known to promote integration, such as participate in the labour market and the education system. Meanwhile, public and media discourses portray asylum seekers as a social and economic burden, potential terrorists and likely to self-segregate rather than integrate. The Australian government, too, has created different classes of refugees through its mandatory detention policy and temporary visas for those who arrive undocumented and by boat, with far-reaching impacts on their ability to feel secure and achieve a sense of belonging. With their illusions of Australia as a beacon of security and humanitarianism shattered by detention and unequal treatment, some refugees are unsure what kind of country they are asked to integrate into and at what cost.

Nevertheless, there are important differences in the way refugees in Australia and asylum seekers in England engage with the wider communities. For the South Australian refugees, the possibility of integration is more tangible as their inclusion is actively supported through government initiatives and programmes. The interview material reveals a great willingness to interact with the wider community through work and cultural exchange and to fulfil perceived social obligations of contributing and 'giving back' to society. This is also likely to be the case for refugees in the UK, although the refugee integration policy defines integration rather narrowly and one-sidedly as empowering refugees to 'contribute to the community and access the services to which they are entitled' as members of 'British Society'. While newcomers are urged to 'self-integrate' to avoid 'self-segregation', for the receiving society it appears to be sufficient to 'provide protection' (UK Border Agency 2009: 8). While asylum seekers in East Anglia are excluded from this official integration process, they still undertake practical steps that enable them to integrate into the local community. This includes adopting identities as students or migrants that are more acceptable to the community or blending in by using local expressions and dress. Those unable to assimilate in these ways try to minimize the potential for conflict by avoiding some public places or contact with particular kinds of local people. Unlike refugees, asylum seekers are more preoccupied with their uncertain status, the suspicions it raises, and the extent to which it can be concealed. As a result, accessing social connections and bridges into communities is much harder for them.

However, in many circumstances is impossible for a member of the local community to distinguish between an asylum seeker and a refugee, or whether this refugee has 'jumped queues' or lined up patiently in a refugee camp. Nodir, Adil and Cameron continue to be defined by their ethnic and religious difference which is interpreted as a possible security threat by members of the broader population. Narrow integration strategies that target only refugees are unlikely to succeed as suspicion and racialization do not discriminate between asylum seekers and refugees, or indeed other types of non-white migrants.

The continual preoccupation among policy makers in the Global North with multiculturalism and whether it encourages social integration or ethnic segregation undermines the effectiveness of many local and even state sponsored efforts to recognize cultural difference. Despite the multiculturalism backlash in political and public discourse in Europe and elsewhere, 'this set of policy reorientations has not emerged with the eradication, not even much to the detriment, of actual measures, institutions and frameworks for minority cultural recognition' (Vertovec and Wessendorf 2009). These encouragements to claim public space on the basis of cultural distinctiveness are difficult for refugees to reconcile with their experiences of rejection and government rhetoric about integration. The Australian government appears to have recognized this and is taking steps to rehabilitate multiculturalism, but there are no such indications in Britain, where 'state multiculturalism' continues to be blamed for encouraging 'different cultures' to 'live separate lives' (BBC News Online 2011). Clear, coherent and sustained policies, based on sound research-based evidence, are needed to promote the social, economic and cultural inclusion of refugees in the Global North. This in turn may help to shift the tide of ever tighter, more hostile asylum laws towards greater hospitality and respect for the human rights of displaced people.

Notes

1 *Negotiating existence* is an ethnographic study of the experience of seeking refuge in the predominantly white and rural region of East Anglia, UK. This study considers how asylum seekers' interactions with the local British community, the immigration system and support organizations, as well as with other asylum seekers, shaped tactics to further the likelihood of a successful status outcome. These interactions are contextualized by the broader factors of the second war in Iraq, the fear of terrorism that impacted on new arrivals and communities in Britain, and the commencement of government initiated dispersals of asylum seekers into East Anglia, drawing the issue of immigration to the fore of public and media attention.
2 *From Stranger to Citizen* was funded by an Australian Research Council (ARC) Discovery Grant in 2006 and 2007 and jointly conducted with Jane Haggis, whose intellectual contribution to the project we acknowledge. It explores how individuals who come to Australia from a developing country in the Middle East or Africa interpret, embrace, critique and resist what they perceive 'being Australian' to constitute and how local institutions and organizations interpret and practise government policies in shaping newcomers' understanding of what Australian cultural practices and values are.
3 'White British' is the term used by National Statistics to refer to people of Anglo-Saxon origin. The 2001 census uses two other categories of 'white' – 'white Irish' and

'white other' – to describe people who may be considered to be 'white' but whose origins are not encompassed in the previous two categories. See National Statistics (2003).

Bibliography

Ager, A. and Strang, A. (2008) 'Understanding integration: a conceptual framework', *Journal of Refugee Studies*, 21(2): 166–91.

Banting, K. and Kymlicka, W. (2010) 'Canadian multiculturalism: global anxieties and local debates', *British Journal of Canadian Studies*, 23(1): 43–72.

Barker, M. (1981) *The New Racism: Conservatives and the Ideology of the Tribe*, London: Junction Books.s

BBC News Online (2011) '"State multiculturalism has failed", says David Cameron', 5 February. Available at: www.bbc.co.uk/news/uk-politics-12371994 (accessed 11 February 2011).

Bloch, A. and Schuster, L. (2005) 'At the extremes of exclusion: deportation, detention and dispersal', *Ethnic and Racial Studies*, 28(3): 491–512.

Boswell, C. (2001) *Spreading the Costs of Asylum-Seekers: A Critical Assessment of Dispersal Policies in Germany and the UK*, London: Anglo-German Foundation.

Bowen, C. (2011) 'The genius of Australian multiculturalism', address to the Sydney Institute, 16 February. Available at: www.chrisbowen.net/media-centre/speeches.do?newsId=4154 (accessed 16 September 2011).

Brighton, S. (2007) 'British Muslims, multiculturalism and UK foreign policy: "Integration" and "cohesion" in and beyond the state', *International Affairs*, 83(1): 1–17.

Briskman, L., Latham, S. and Goddard, C. (2008) *Human Rights Over Board: Seeking Asylum in Australia*, Melbourne: Scribe Publications.

Buchanan, S., Bethan, G. and Threadgold, T. (2003) *What's the Story? Results from Research into Media Coverage of Refugees and Asylum Seekers in the UK*, London: Article 19.

Castles, S., Korac, M., Vasta, E. and Vertovec, S. (2001) *Integration: Mapping the Field*, Oxford: Centre for Migration and Policy Research and Refugee Studies Centre, University of Oxford.

Crock, M., Saul, B. and Dastyari, A. (2006) *Future Seekers II: Refugees and Irregular Migration in Australia*, Annandale: Federation Press.

Department of Immigration and Citizenship (2007) *Life in Australia*, Canberra: Australian Government.

Due, C. and Riggs, D.W. (2008) '"We grew here you flew here": claims to "home" in the Cronulla riots', *Colloqui Text Theory Critique*. Available at: www.colloqui.monash.edu.au/issue16/due-riggs.pdf (last accessed 1 February 2011).

Finney, N. and Simpson, L. (2009) *"Sleepwalking to Segregation?" Challenging Myths About Race and Migration*, Bristol: Policy Press.

Forrest, J. and Dunn, K. (2007) 'Constructing racism in Sydney, Australia's largest ethnicity', *Urban Studies*, 44(4): 699–721.

Fuglerud, O. (1999) *Life on the Outside: The Tamil Diaspora and Long Distance Nationalism*, London; Sterling: Pluto Press.

Fuglerud, O. and Engebrigtsen, A. (2006) 'Culture, networks and social capital: Tamil and Somali immigrants in Norway', *Ethnic and Racial Studies*, 29(6): 1118–34.

Gilroy, P. (1992) 'The end of antiracism', in J. Donald and A. Rattansi (eds) *Race,*

Culture, and Difference. London; Newbury Park, California: Sage Publications in association with the Open University.

Griffiths, D., Sigona, N. and Zetter, R. (2006) 'Integrative paradigms, marginal reality: refugee community organisations and dispersal in Britain', *Journal of Ethnic and Migration Studies*, 32(5): 881–98.

Haddad, E. (2008) *The Refugee in International Society: Between Sovereigns*, Cambridge: Cambridge University Press.

Hage, G. (2003) *Against Paranoid Nationalism: Searching for Hope in a Shrinking Society*, Annandale: Pluto Press.

Hardwick, S.W. and Meacham, J.E. (2005) 'Heterolocalism, networks of ethnicity, and refugee communities in the Pacific Northwest: the Portland story', *The Professional Geographer*, 57(4): 539–57.

Harte, W., Childs, I.R.W. and Hastings, P.A. (2009) 'Settlement patterns of African refugee communities in Southeast Queensland', *Australian Geographer*, 40(1): 51–67.

Hewitt, R. (2005) *White backlash and the politics of multiculturalism*, Cambridge: Cambridge University Press.

Home Office (2005) *Integration Matters: A National Strategy for Refugee Integration*, London: UK Home Office.

Hugo, G. (2003) *Migrants and Their Integration: Contemporary Issues and Implications*, UNESCO.

Hugo, G. (2008) 'Immigrant settlement outside of Australia's capital cities', *Population, Space and Place*, 14(6): 553–71.

Jupp, J. (2007) 'The quest for harmony', in J. Jupp, J. Nieuwenhuysen and E.W. Dawson (eds) *Social Cohesion in Australia*, New York: Cambridge University Press.

Kalra, V.S. and Kapoor, N. (2009) 'Interrogating segregation, integration and the community cohesion agenda', *Journal of Ethnic and Migration Studies*, 35(9): 1397–415.

Khawaja, N.G., White, K.M., Schweitzer, R. and Greenslade, J. (2008) 'Difficulties and coping strategies of Sudanese refugees: a qualitative approach', *Transcultural Psychiatry*, 45(3): 489–512.

Kumsa, M.K. (2006) '"No! I'm not a refugee!" The poetics of be-longing among young Oromos in Toronto', *Journal of Refugee Studies*, 19(2): 230–55.

Leach, M. and Mansouri, F. (2004). *Lives in Limbo. Voices of Refugees Under Temporary Protection*, Sydney: UNSW Press.

Leudar, I., Hayes, J., Nekvapil, J. and Baker, J.T. (2008) 'Hostility themes in media, community and refugee narratives', *Discourse and Society*, 19: 187–221.

Marfleet, P. (2006) *Refugees in a Global Era*, Houndmills: Palgrave Macmillan.

Marston, G. (2003) *The Consequences of Temporary Citizenship for Refugees on TPVs*, Melbourne: Centre for Applied Social Research, RMIT University.

Martin, L. (2007) 'Why, my beloved country?' Melbourne: The Age Education Resource Centre. Available at: http://education.theage.com.au/cmspage.php?intid=135&intversion=220 (accessed 24 April 2012).

Moran, A. (2005) *Australia: Nation, Belonging and Globalization*, New York: Routledge.

National Statistics (2003) *Region in Figures: East of England*, London: The Office for National Statistics.

Phillimore, J. and Goodson, L. (2008) 'Making a place in the global city: the relevance of indicators of integration', *Journal of Refugee Studies*, 21(3): 305–25.

Phillips, D. (2006) 'Parallel lives? Challenging discourses of British Muslim self-segregation', *Environment and Planning D: Society and Space*, 24: 25–40.

Pickering, S. (2001) 'Common sense and original deviancy; news discourses and asylum seekers in Australia', *Journal of Refugee Studies*, 14(2): 169–86.

Putnam, R. (1993) 'The prosperous community: social capital and public life', *American Prospect*, 13: 35–42.

Robinson, D. (2005) 'The search for community cohesion: key themes and dominant concepts of the public policy arena', *Urban Studies*, 42(8): 1411–27.

Robinson, V. (1998) 'Defining and measuring successful refugee integration', paper presented at ECRE International Conference on Integration of Refugees in Europe, Brussels.

Robinson, V. (2003) 'Dispersal policies in the UK', in V. Robinson, R. Andersson and S. Musterd (eds) *Spreading the 'Burden'? A Review of Policies to Disperse Asylum Seekers and Refugees*, Bristol: Policy Press.

Schneider, J. and Crul, M. (2010) 'New insights into assimilation and integration theory: introduction to the special issue', *Ethnic and Racial Studies*, 33(7): 1143–8.

Simich, L., Beiser, M. and Mawani, F. (2002) 'Paved with good intentions: Canada's refugee destining policy and paths of secondary migration', *Canadian Public Policy*, 28(4): 597–607.

Stratton, J. (1998) *Race Daze. Australia in Identity Crisis*, Annandale: Pluto Press.

Taguieff, P. (1999) 'The new cultural racism in France', in M. Bulmer and J. Solomos (eds), *Racism*, Oxford: Oxford University Press.

Tate, J.W. (2009) 'John Howard's "nation": multiculturalism, citizenship, and identity', *Australian Journal of Politics and History*, 55(1): 97–120.

Threadgold, T. and Court, G. (2005) *Refugee Inclusion: A Literature Review. Produced for the Welsh Refugee Council and the Welsh Assembly Government*, Cardiff: Cardiff University.

UK Border Agency (2009) *Moving on Together: Government's Commitment to Supporting Refugees*, London: UK Government Home Office.

Valentine, G., Sporton, D. and Nielsen, K.B. (2009) 'Identities and belonging: a study of Somali refugees and asylum seekers living in the UK and Denmark', *Society and Space*, 27(2): 234–50.

Vertovec, S. and Wessendorf, S. (2009) 'Introduction: assessing the backlash', *The Multiculturalism Backlash. European Discourses, Policies and Practices*, Routledge.

Viviani, N. (1996) *The Indochinese in Australia, 1975–1995: From Burnt Boats to Barbecues*, Melbourne: Oxford University Press.

Williams, L. (2006) 'Social networks of refugees in the United Kingdom: tradition, tactics and new community spaces', *Journal of Ethnic and Migration Studies*, 32: 865–79.

Woolcock, M. (1998) 'Social capital and economic development: towards a theoretical synthesis and policy framework', *Theory and Society*, 27(2): 151–208.

Zetter, R. (2007) 'More labels, fewer refugees: remaking the refugee label in an era of globalization', *Journal of Refugee Studies*, 20(7): 172–92.

Zetter, R., Griffiths, A., Sigona, N., Flynn, D., Pasha, T. and Beynon, R. (2006) *Immigration, Social Cohesion and Social Capital: What Are the Links?* York: Joseph Rowntree Foundation.

Zetter, R., Griffiths, D. and Sigona, N. (2005) 'Social capital or social exclusion? The impact of asylum-seeker dispersal on UK refugee community organizations', *Community Development Journal*, 40(2): 169–81.

8 Transnational practices, social inclusion, and Muslim migrant integration in the West[1]

Fethi Mansouri

Introduction

The debate about the perceived permeability of national borders is indicative of the complex set of problems posed by migration at national and global levels. From a simple statistical point of view, the increase in human mobility may be gauged by a review of basic statistics about international migration flows. In 1910 'some thirty-three million of 1.7 billion in the world's population lived in countries as migrants. Figures collated in the year 2000 show that there were about 175 million of six billion people at some distance from their countries of origin' (Benhabib and Resnik 2009: 1). Notably, these figures do not account for internally displaced people and domestic migrants within the same country. Despite this marked increase in the volume of international migration, such figures represent less than 4 per cent of the world's population. This relatively small figure is due to the fact that there are few significant émigré societies around the world that pursue an active immigration programme as the USA, Canada or Australia have done over the past few decades.

The size and pace of human mobility aside, transnational migration poses serious challenges to the Westphalian nation-state model and its classical emphasis on political membership as a process regulated by national citizenship. In recent years, a new debate has arisen about the ethical limitations of citizenship rights in light of the emergence of a more rigorous call for adherence to universal human rights frameworks, in particular, the Human Rights Declaration of 1948 and the Refugee Convention of 1951. Universal human rights paradigms are not without their critics, however. In relation to transnational forced migration involving asylum seekers, for example, human rights norms face an inherent paradox: they recognize an individual's right to emigrate (leave one's country) but not to immigrate (enter a new country). More critically, they remain incapable of invoking signatory states' obligations towards forced migrants.

These conceptual debates are played out against the backdrop of increased transnational migratory movements, both voluntary and forced. Indeed, the perceived rise in transnational migration, especially towards Western countries, is the result of a number of interconnected global forces. Such forces include increased international interconnectedness especially at the levels of transportation and communication; the proliferation of transnational networks; increased economic integration; and rising political instability around the world. An example of this fluid global context is the so-called Arab Spring that started in early 2011 and led to hundreds of thousands of refugees fleeing from Tunisia and Libya and crossing Italy's border through the tiny island of Lampedusa. The bulk of this forced migration occurred in the space of only two weeks. Such a sudden flux of human movement on a relatively large scale, even if on a temporary basis, can pose challenges to the Western state and may be seen to create tensions at the national and transnational levels.

These tensions and pressures engendered by migration do not relate exclusively to international relations. They can also have a profound effect on societies from within. In this context, debates are intensifying about the extent to which multicultural societies could and should accommodate different dimensions of migrants' cultural and religious identities. Such debates have thrown down a significant challenge to the ideas of liberalism and cultural pluralism. The challenge posed by cultural and religious diversity relates to the perception that minority groups may attach stronger loyalties to external communities, networks, and value systems than to those within their local societies. For example, while many Muslim migrants identify themselves via their nationality – as British, American, French, or Australian – some identify themselves first and foremost as Muslim and and thus give their allegiance to the global Muslim community before the nation in which they live.

These and other similar debates about the place of Islam and Muslims in the West and the suitability of contemporary models of integration in liberal states, which tend to either support the (culture-blind) liberal citizenship approach at one end of the spectrum or the multiculturalist perspective at the other end, can be traced back historically to the radical tradition of Enlightenment. It was during the eighteenth century Enlightenment period in Europe that public intellectuals began to develop the idea of liberalism and to advocate the importance of the principle of secularism – the separation of religion and state – as a way of achieving equal citizenship and overall social progress. The argument advanced in this context was that religion was an impediment to progress and modernity as it curtailed the potential for applying reason and logic and as such it was essential for society and state to restrict the practice and influence of religion to the private sphere.

Against this historical background, this chapter discusses the social experiences of Muslim migrants in a number of Western (secular) cities. It focuses on the challenges of national belonging and social inclusion as they relate to local and transnational ties, as well as on subjective (personal) indicators of local inclusion and belonging.

The overall argument underpinning this chapter, and the wider research project from which it is extracted, is that a new approach to diversity and migrant integration is needed in culturally pluralist societies. It is argued here that such an approach can best be sustained if it reflects the realities of transnational mobility and is grounded and articulated in a discourse of cosmopolitan ethics that builds on Benhabib's (2004) 'discourse theory of ethics', with its emphasis on universalist morality. This approach emphasizes the critical recognition of the cultural and religious rights of human beings, not just fellow citizens. In other words, this chapter will illustrate that normative notions of citizenship, premised on primordial attachments and contributory rights with their associated privileges, are insufficient to meet the complex social realities of culturally diverse societies. More specifically, members of cultural and religious minority groups, such as Muslim migrants in non-Muslim majority societies, present a new conceptual and policy challenge: namely how to reconcile demands for a more flexible mode of inclusion and belonging that can reflect the possibilities of multiple attachments.

Thus, it is important to discuss the interrelated themes that underpin this chapter about transnationalism and multiculturalism in the context of Muslim migrants in the West.

Transnational human mobility and the challenge of national belonging

Globalization has produced new trends and patterns of migration where human mobility exhibits more fluidity, circularity and ongoing transnational practices. In contrast, and in resistance to conservative views of immigration – where migrant populations only exert 'a limited influence culturally and politically on the host nation' because of the limiting influence of assimilation – the trend has shifted in favour of an environment in which migrants no longer feel the need to completely forsake their heritage or cultural identities for a mainstream identity based on their new place of residence (O'Sullivan 2003: 26–29).

This shift in the nature of human migration is facilitated by the emergence of mass communications and transportation systems (Castles 2002). Such technological advancements have created a situation in which the settler model of migration (where new immigrants move permanently to another country and are incorporated into the mainstream society by way of assimilationist policies) has been transcended by the temporary migration model (where temporary migrant workers re-locate into a particular country for a period but maintain ties with their country of origin). The consequence of this shift is that 'new modes of migrant belonging' have emerged whereby people are no longer attached to one country, but become a combination of two or more national orientations (Castles 2002: 1143–1153; Vertovec 2004; Lubeck 2002; Sinclair and Cunningham 2000: 2).

Transnational practices which are in many ways linked to globalization and modernity have challenged the primacy of 'clearly demarcated parameters of geography, national identity, and belonging' (Evans Braziel and Mannur 2003: 1). They question traditional assumptions about 'the national boundedness of the ethnic experience' (Sreberny 2000; see also Sinclair and Cunningham 2000: 15). Transnational migration, nowadays, is engendering an environment in which migrants are able simultaneously to maintain ties with their old and new homelands (Sinclair and Cunningham 2000: 10; Mummery 2005; Jupp 2001: 261). Migrants' identities, therefore, are increasingly embodying a form of transcendence of national borders. Migrants themselves are no longer automatically torn between one national identity over the other (Dunn and Geeraert 2003), but can retain and even pass on a 'sense of pride in their origins' to their children (Jupp 2001: 261). However, while these developments are often perceived as potentially positive for individual migrants and their ethnic communities, mainstream society sometimes views in them as problematic.

On a practical level, the transnational practices of migrants refer to activities that 'cross state boundaries but do not necessarily originate with state agencies or actors' (Sklair and Robbins 2002: 82). While the state still has a role in engaging transnational practices in a more general manner, the existence of such practices which occur outside the sphere of the global system is an indication of the limited influence of state actions on informal transnational practices. This is particularly relevant in examining the processes of both voluntary and forced migration, as well as the overall settlement process, The 'sustained ties of persons, networks and organisations' (Faist 1999: 2) that exist across national borders can have a significant impact on patterns of cultural maintenance, identity formation, and general settlement practices among refugees and migrants.

For all these reasons, transnationalism has often challenged simple theories of assimilation and multiculturalism that portray culture as a zero sum phenomenon. It has confounded the notion that, upon resettlement in another country, the culture of a migrant group is either wholly retained or largely discarded in favour of the culture of the receiving society (as was advocated by the Chicago School (of Anthropology) in the USA in the first half of the twentieth century). With the rise and prominence of transnational practices, nation-states are no longer the predominant containers of cultural, social, economic, and political processes. Rather, migrants and refugees with easier access to 'transnational capabilities' (Al-Ali *et al.* 2001: 581) are able to 'develop subjectivities and identities' embedded in networks and connections that stretch within and beyond the borders of the settlement society (Sherrell and Hyndman, 2004: 3). In this context, transnationalism can lead to a greater mobility of ideas, information, and various forms of cultural capital which engender an increased capacity for people to sustain cultural and national loyalties to interest groups and movements across national borders. For individual migrants these ties can have a significant local influence on the process of acculturation (Kennedy and Roudometof 2002; Faist 1999).

But transnational practices may also be seen to have the potential to alter the culture of both countries of origin and host societies in a number of ways. These include through economic and political activities such as transnational electoral participation and political lobbying, through social and cultural engagements such as cross-border 'marriage alliances, religious activity, media and commodity consumption' (Vertovec 2001: 575), and through networks for maintaining contact with family, friends, and ethnic, political, or religious groups (Al-Ali *et al.* 2001). The following section will explore these issues in the context of Muslim migrants and their various transnational practices and ties.

Transnational ties and Muslim migrant settlement in the West

Reflecting the wider discussion above, the relationship between transnational ties and the integration of Muslim migrants in Australia and other Western émigré societies would appear to be even more complex. Not least because of the problematized perception of Islam and its association with political violence and radicalism (Akbarzadeh and Mansouri 2007). In the Australian context, for example, Muslim migrants find themselves in a society that is not only multicultural in terms of its political policies and social values, but that is also experiencing heightened public anxiety towards Islam and Islamic practices, in line with other Western societies. Some scholars link this phenomenon to a broader anti-religion framework within the context of secularism.

The secular Enlightenment theory that conceives of political community as an abstract collection of equal citizens emerged in response to the inequalities that characterized the absolutist states of medieval Europe, many of which legitimized their authority on religious grounds. Radical Enlightenment public intellectuals such as Baruch Spinoza and Giambattista Vico were influential in challenging the hierarchy imposed by religious authorities, which represented one of the first steps towards a more institutionalized secularization in European history. For Muslims living in the West, their visibility in public spaces and their claims for cultural recognition have been compounded by new approaches to multiculturalism that are more instrumentalist than cosmopolitan.

Against this broader historical background, it is useful to reflect on the social experiences of Muslims in Western (secular) cities and examine their sense (or otherwise) of local integration and transnational connections. Within an increasingly securitized social milieu, Muslim migrants find at their disposal a growing array of communication technologies that enhance continuing links to their homelands, and as such, further the possibilities of a global Muslim *ummah* – a transnational community of fellow Muslims (Hassan 2002). Bowen (2004) outlines three dimensions that transnational Islam may entail:

a   Islamic concepts and ideas of personal conduct being articulated globally through Muslims moving across national borders for cultural, political, or economic reasons;
b   Muslims being increasingly associated with religious movements that promote cross-national exchanges and cross-national communication; and
c   Muslims debating issues pertaining to the nature and role of Islam in Western countries.

In terms of systematic examination and critical appraisal, it is this third dimension of transnational Islam that has been most neglected (Bowen 2004). Yet, debates and discussions among Muslims about the nature and role of Islam in Western countries (Ramadan 2004) are crucial in informing Muslim migrants' abilities to negotiate a satisfactory balance between their religious identity and their sense of social integration into a predominantly secular society.

However, it is insufficient to posit that a coalescence of faith-based Muslim values on the one hand and Western-secular ideals on the other could engender a sense of integration or otherwise. Muslims' non-integration into Western societies and their resistance to certain aspects of its value systems may be attributable less to antagonisms between Islamic and Western culture and more to the economic, cultural, and political inequalities frequently experienced by Muslim migrants within their 'new' societies. This is despite host societies' stated ideals of multiculturalism and equal citizenship. In light of this, the following section discusses the concepts of multiculturalism and citizenship and the extent to which they are contestable in the context of collective cultural claims by minority groups.

Critical reflections on 'multiculturalism'

From its genesis as a policy framework aimed at providing settlement services to newly arrived immigrants, in the second half of the twentieth century, multiculturalism has developed into a concept that articulates and characterizes society's growing ethno-cultural diversity. Since its early days in Australia and Canada, multiculturalism has become a contested and controversial policy that has been subject to much scrutiny, especially during the past decade with its political upheavals, perceived global insecurity and widespread socio-economic challenges (Koleth 2010). Thus it is important to distinguish between multiculturalism as a policy, as a moral position, and as the description of a demographic reality. The argument against multiculturalism as a demographic fact is problematic because the majority of nation-states across the globe are multicultural in their composition. To extrapolate criticism of multiculturalism can only lead to one extreme policy outcome, namely a repatriation of migrants and their descendants (Turner 2006).

Australian multiculturalism, while not under immediate threat, over the past decade or so has been challenged and subjected to closer scrutiny. The critiques of multiculturalism are varied but generally relate to three broad themes: its ability to support cultural diversity, the value and relevance of its ideals and its practical implementation if it is to foster genuine intercultural dialogue and understanding.

Australia has one of the most culturally diverse populations among the developed countries, with 20.3 per cent of its population born overseas as opposed to 18.9 per cent for Canada, under 13 per cent for the USA and just over 12 per cent for the UK (UNESCO 2009; Global Commission on International Migration 2006). The existence of such a diverse population in Australia presents novel challenges to policy makers at all levels of government.

Australian multiculturalism was adopted in the 1970s as a cornerstone of the government's strategy to settle newly arrived migrants and in the process manage the country's growing levels of cultural diversity. The advantage of multicultural policies, it was argued, was that they provided guidelines for reconciling cultural differences and thus facilitate greater social cohesion. The policy was originally meant to supplant the more aggressive paradigms of migrant settlement which expected individuals to assimilate into the overarching Anglo-Saxon population and thereby lose their cultural identity. Multicultural policies, it was argued, would allow minority groups to participate in Australian society while retaining their cultural distinctions. In theory the cultural diversity that this multicultural approach sanctioned was seen as beneficial to society because it fostered a positive form of social belonging for migrants and enriched the mainstream community by opening it up to new ideas.

In recent years, however, the concept of multiculturalism has been questioned as a meaningful concept for informing and shaping debates about managing diversity and framing national identity. It is increasingly being challenged, and in some countries replaced, by a new emphasis on liberal principles of social inclusion and civic citizenship, which encourage a commitment to the core values of each country's mainstream national identity.

Recent studies of multiculturalism in countries such as Canada, Britain, and Australia recognize that the future of multiculturalism as an ideology is deeply intertwined with global geopolitics and the impact of such politics on attitudes towards Islam and the experiences of Muslims everywhere (Abbas 2005; Dunn 2005; Dunn *et al.* 2007; Forrest and Dunn 2006; Jakubowicz 2007; Meer and Modood 2008; Nesbitt-Larking 2008; Poynting 2004; Ramadan 2004; Turner 2006). In Australia, Muslims are confronted with the dual pressure of conforming to dominant essentially Anglo-Saxon 'core values', or risk marginalization and social exclusion (Jakubowicz 2007; Mansouri 2005). At this juncture 'it is important to distinguish between multiculturalism as a social policy, as a moral argument about diversity and as the empirical description of a state of affairs in which a population is heterogeneous' (Turner 2007: 75).

Turner suggests that 'multiculturalism means the existence within the same society of a diversity of different cultures and communities, but the principal debate about multiculturalism is in reality about the cultural diversity that is produced by migrant communities' (Turner 2007: 76). In the recent history of Australia, this increased diversity triggered the emergence of paranoid versions of Australian nationalism, which were inflamed during the mid-1990s when Pauline Hanson's right wing One Nation party came onto the federal political scene. Hanson's form of paranoid nationalism, which raised concerns about the high level of Asian immigration and the incompatibility of Islam with Australian culture, highlights the potential for an essentialized discourse of identity to degenerate into a blatant racism that calls for the exclusion of certain cultures from the country. It is within this context that multiculturalism in Australia has come under a renewed scrutiny that questions its relevance and utility as a social policy tool.

The status of multiculturalism in other Western émigré societies is even more problematic than is the case in Australia. In 2011, a number of European leaders, including the German Chancellor Angela Merkel and the British Prime Minister

David Cameron, declared that multiculturalism has failed in their respective countries. Such comments must be regarded within the post-9/11 context, which is characterized by a rise in security fears compounded by contemporary economic woes; thus these remarks may be seen to reflect mainly populist reactions from a nervous electorate looking for scapegoats. In truth, neither the UK, nor Germany in particular, had anything like a fully-fledged multicultural policy. Germany is a multiethnic country that never really adopted a proactive multiculturalism policy as was the case in Australia. The UK has had a policy of accommodating cultural diversity, yet historically has stopped short of adopting social and settlement policies to support the cultural aspirations of its migrant communities.

Against this background of a retreating multiculturalism, Muslim migrants in the West are engaging with and challenging restrictive notions of social inclusion and national belonging. The empirical findings reported below relate specifically to transnational ties and local inclusion as perceived by Muslim migrants in three culturally pluralist cities, namely Melbourne, Paris and Sheffield. This data enables a useful analysis of the three different policy approaches to cultural diversity that these countries have adopted. The empirical findings will also allow a further examination of the way these approaches impact on notions of belonging and inclusion among Muslim migrants.

Current study

The data used in this chapter has been extracted from a broader study that examined the role of local governments in managing intercultural relations in Australia, France, and the UK between 2008 and 2010. The study investigated whether the local level of governance was effective in managing intercultural relations and whether it represented an optimal conduit for ensuring full and active citizenship for local citizenry. The specific objectives of the larger study were: (a) to assess the level of local support for multiculturalism and cultural diversity in the community; and (b) to examine attitudes towards Muslim migrants as an increasingly visible religious group in multicultural spaces. The chapter draws on data provided by Muslim residents, which has been extracted from a more general data set elicited from a larger pool of participants surveyed randomly in the three case studies. That is, Muslim residents were not the targeted sample per se within the larger study from which the following data emanates.

Data collection

The community sample for this study was collected using a random selection approach whereby every fifth household in a specified local area was approached and asked to complete the survey. No specific communities or individuals were targeted, as the diverse cultural make-up of the target local areas ensured a sufficiently representative sample. The final figures for the community surveys indicate a close reflection of the total demographic profile for the areas in question.

Transnational practices, social inclusion 135

In terms of analysis, the quantitative data was coded, entered, and analysed using frequency counts and general tallying techniques. Raw figures as well as ratios were generated to compare data within the same sample and across the two surveys. The qualitative data was analysed through a systematic thematic content analysis and using NVivo as a data-management program. The chosen themes for analysis reflected the study's key focal areas, namely attitudes towards multiculturalism and cultural diversity, perceptions of Muslim migrants, and views on the role of local governments and grass-root organizations in managing intercultural relations.

This chapter incorporates quantitative data from the broader project's fieldwork conducted in Australia, France and the United Kingdom. The total number of surveys administered in Australia was 497 for community residents and 194 for council staff; while both for France and the UK the number of surveys was equal reaching 100 for each. The community surveys in the three localities included surveys completed by residents who self-assigned Islam as their religion. These surveys by Muslim migrants which form the basis for the analysis in this chapter amounted to 29 surveys in France, 21 in Australia and 24 in the UK.

Focus on data from Muslim migrants:

- City of St Denis, France – 29 respondents
- City of Whittlesea, Australia – 21 respondents
- City of Sheffield, United Kingdom – 24 respondents

The Muslim participants, like the wider sample for this study, were randomly selected as part of the larger community survey. The figures have been extracted and isolated to facilitate a customized analysis focusing on transnational ties and perceptions of belonging and inclusion among this demographic group.

Data analysis

The overall data set from which this cohort of responses has been taken was collected by way of household surveys in three local council areas in the cities of

Table 8.1 Summary of data

	Australia	France	United Kingdom
	City of Whittlesea (W) and City of Shepparton (S)	City of St Denis	City of Sheffield
Diversity survey (Council staff)	95 (W)+99 (S)=194	–	–
Diversity survey (Residents)	299 (W)+198 (S)=497	100	100
Interviews with community leaders	13	11	18

Paris, Melbourne, and Sheffield. The data sample analysed for this chapter focuses exclusively on respondents who self-identified as being adherents to the Islamic faith. Given that Muslim respondents were not targeted participants but rather came from within the broader sample, the data set focusing on Muslim respondents is smaller than the overall data pool.

The empirical findings reported below relate to the local and transnational ties maintained by Muslim migrants in the three local cities. Figure 8.6 also provides data on perceptions among Muslim respondents of the meanings of local inclusion. The three local council areas were St Denis in Paris, the City of Whittlesea in Melbourne, and the City of Sheffield in Yorkshire. These three areas all have Muslim and Arabic-speaking populations that exceed the respective national averages. Because of this demographic characteristic, these three cities represent optimal sites within which to explore local and transnational solidarities and ties among Muslim migrants. Figures 8.1, 8.2 and 8.3 report data for each site and display the quantitative findings that relate to the contacts that Muslim respondents have developed with other Muslim groups both locally and transnationally.

Figures 8.1, 8.2 and 8.3 show the participants' answers to a question about sustained contacts with other Muslim groups both locally and internationally. For the purposes of this study 'Sustained contacts' are defined as contacts that happen more than once and which give a sense of solidarity and support between Muslim respondents and other Muslim groups (be they local or transnational).

The data in Figure 8.1 show that Muslim residents in Whittlesea tend to develop stronger ties with other Muslim individuals and groups at a local level more than on a transnational level, even if the difference is only marginal. This may be seen as indicative of a capacity among these respondents to draw on

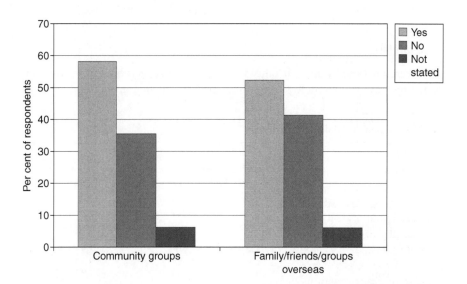

Figure 8.1 Contact with other Muslims: City of Whittlesea, Australia ($N=21$).

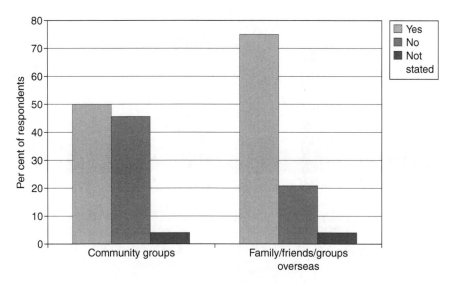

Figure 8.2 Contact with other Muslims: United Kingdom (*N*=24).

local social networks. Such networks provide the respondents with opportunities for social interaction, solidarity, and cultural expression still available to Muslim migrants in Australia.

The data from the UK (Figure 8.2) shows that Muslim migrants in Sheffield tend to develop stronger ties with other Muslims overseas (transnationally) than they do at a local level. This may suggest that the opportunities and spaces for local social networking and cultural expression are more restricted and limited in comparison with Australia.

Transnational links are even more common in the data collected from Muslim migrants in St Denis in Paris (Figure 8.3), showing a similar trend among the respondents to developing stronger transnational links as opposed to local ties to other Muslims. This trend is even more pronounced in St Denis than in Sheffield reflecting a stark reverse 'correlation' between local ties and transnational connections. In other words, the data would seem to suggest that weaker notions of local engagements seem to correlate with stronger transnational ties and vice versa.

A simple comparative analysis of the data from the three groups shows that in St Denis and Sheffield transnational ties with relatives, friends, and community groups are very high (75.9 per cent in St Denis and 75 per cent in Sheffield), compared with the City of Whittlesea (52.5 per cent). This may be indicative of the fact that Muslim migrants in the St Denis and Sheffield are more active in providing financial and social support to their countries of origin, such as Algeria, Morocco, Tunisia, Pakistan, Somalia, and other Muslim countries. In the case of France, with its close proximity to the North African countries from which the migrants originate, it is perhaps not surprising that such ties are

138 F. Mansouri

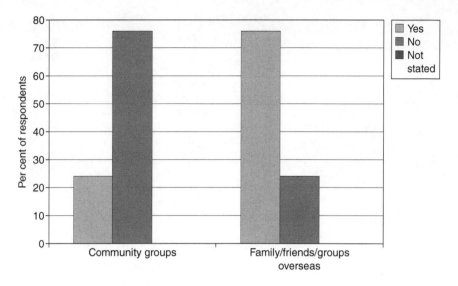

Figure 8.3 Contact with other Muslims: France (*N*=29).

exchanges are possible and sustainable. Many of those surveyed in the France as well as the UK indicated that they kept in touch with members of their extended families and other Muslim friends living in their 'host' countries.

Of course there may be other possible explanations for these divergent transnational practices among Muslim respondents. A closer look at the data collected from Sheffield indicates that there was a higher percentage of young adults in the sample (20.8 per cent under 20 years, 79.1 per cent 35 years and under) which may account for the more frequent transnational connections via social networking sites such as Facebook.

Figure 8.4 shows that contact with local Muslim community groups is relatively high in the City of Whittlesea (58.3 per cent) and the City of Sheffield (50 per cent) but very much lower in the City of St Denis (24.1 per cent). One possible explanation for this is that participation in local ethno-specific groups in Whittlesea and Sheffield allows the respondents to engage with a form of bonding social capital that is not permitted publicly in France's aggressive approach to colour-blind 'integration'. The comparatively more tolerant Australian social policy context may be seen to help Muslim migrants negotiate and resist the complex forms of prejudice and racism they may encounter as members of a minority ethno-religious group.

As the discussion on multiculturalism earlier in this chapter showed, progressive government multicultural policies in Australia and, to a lesser degree, the UK have supported the formation and survival of community groups and their settlement support services. By contrast, in St Denis ties with local Muslim community groups are much lower, as the government emphasizes a more civic

Transnational practices, social inclusion 139

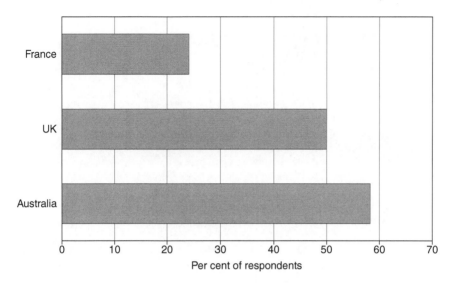

Figure 8.4 Ties with local Muslim community groups.

approach to migrant integration and therefore participation in ethno-specific groups is discouraged by the state.

Comparative insights into the empirical findings

This section discusses briefly some comparative findings for Muslim migrants' contacts with local Muslim groups (Figure 8.4), Muslim contacts with overseas groups (Figure 8.5), and a final set of data on the subjective perceptions of Muslim migrants of local belonging (Figure 8.6).

Local and transnational ties between Muslim migrants are often sustained over a long period of time and can engender solidarity and support, which have the potential to build broader social capital.

The comparative analysis of the data in Figure 8.5 shows that in France and the UK transnational ties between the Muslim respondents and Muslims overseas are higher (75.9 per cent in St Denis and 75 per cent in Sheffield) than in Australia (52.5 per cent in Whittlesea). Whereas, Figure 8.4 shows that ties with local Muslim community groups are relatively high in Australia (58.3 per cent, City of Whittlesea) and the UK (50 per cent, City of Sheffield), but much lower in the City of St Denis in France (24.1 per cent).

This inverse relationship between local and transnational ties points to the existence of a clear link between local policy dynamics and transnational practices. That is, the stronger one's local ties – in terms of bridging the gap between the individual and the wider society as well as bonding within one's own community – the less need one has for systematic and intense transnational connections.

140 F. Mansouri

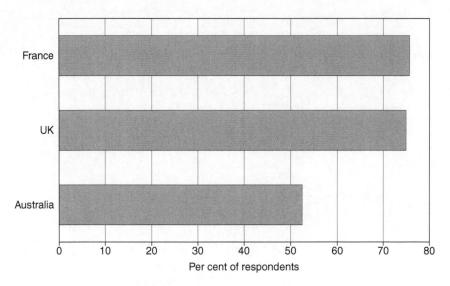

Figure 8.5 Ties with Muslim relatives/friends/groups overseas.

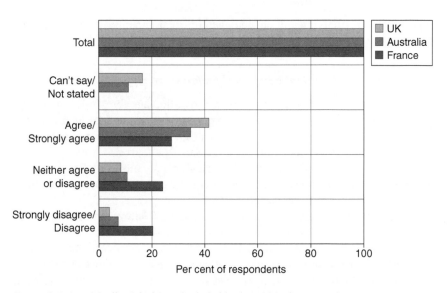

Figure 8.6 As a Muslim I feel I am included in the national community.

These findings may be explained in terms of many factors, for example, age, socio-economic status, gender, and settlement period. However, the data on perceptions of inclusion in the national community contained in Figure 8.6 may provide insights that explicate these findings. The responses in Figure 8.6 reflect

Muslim respondents' perceptions of a much less inclusive environment in France than perceptions of inclusion in Australia and the UK.

Despite the small size of the data pool reported in this chapter, there appear to be links as well as an inverse relationship between local and national inclusion outcomes and migrants' tendencies to develop and maintain transnational ties. Such an analysis of the quantitative data has been corroborated by insights elicited in the in-depth qualitative interviews. The three sites in which the study took place have varying degrees of local tensions, where racial targeting has prompted differential outcomes at the level of social exclusion. In the following excerpts, members of the Muslim migrant communities across the various sites reflect on these tensions and dilemmas as they engage on a daily basis with local authorities and the citizenry at large. For one member of the Muslim community in Sheffield, it was a question of not only achieving belonging but, more critically, being able to survive:

> The community don't understand what we're trying to do and what we're fighting. They don't understand how hard it is [for us]. We're fighting the [local] council and the community are fighting us.

In the following excerpt, a Muslim migrant in France challenges the racialization of Islam and its incompatibility with the secular values of the French Republic:

> When one is born here, you are a Muslim from this country, and not a Muslim from Morocco, North Africa, etcetera, and actually it only takes some travelling to shed any illusions about this. Now once that is settled, it is all about how to read the values we hold, and this can be applied to all religions, and social justice can be read in the Koran as well as the Bible, or in secular literature. [But in France it is] as if Islam were an alien thing, and we say, but Islam comes from here, and we are the living proof of it, Islam is part of this society.

Such perceptions and a more pronounced sense of being targeted (through Islamophobia) are also underlined by a French Muslim who works closely with interfaith networks, migrant groups, and women's groups:

> Islamophobia has been linked to immigration, to a physical appearance. If you have dark hair and are of North African type, you are a Muslim, a fundamentalist, a terrorist, and insecurity is your fault. So we have felt this very strongly, even among NGOs with whom we work and who also want to promote diversity, people are starting to be afraid of this context.

This testimony suggests that the assertion of a French identity by Muslims may be seen as threatening to the wider secular tradition which privileges the *Francais de souche* or 'Real French'. It is these types of racialized exclusions that may result in Muslim migrants relying on transnational connections as a sustainable means of achieving a sense of solidarity and support. This is something that can be seen in real terms at the level of spiritual leadership, economic support, and overall welfare of individuals and their communities.

Conclusion

Transnational ties and their consequent configurations for social inclusion are shaping the way new political relationships are being constructed within the nation-state. This chapter has examined the interrelationship between transnational practices on the one hand and subjective perceptions of local integration of Muslim migrants on the other. Transnational ties among Muslim migrants in the West exhibit complex manifestations in relation to local policies. Perceived transnational ties have often been problematized, especially when these take place within a context of heightened international tensions, ethnic segregation, and societal anxieties regarding religious activism and religiosity. This chapter explored in a limited empirical capacity whether an upholding of transnational ties can, in some cases, confound migrants' development of a sense of connection to their local milieu. The empirical data reflect on the complex relationship between transnational practices and issues pertaining to national belonging and social inclusion.

Today, with the 'retreat' of progressive social policies in many Western states (Benhabib 2004), there is an increased scrutiny of multiculturalism driven, in particular, by state policies that act in the name of the nation. The findings reported in this chapter suggest that multiculturalism – and the associated cultural recognition of religious minorities – in most cases does not pose a threat to Western values, nor will it lead to the possibility of separatist disintegration (Taylor 1994; Kymlicka 1997). As the discussion outlined in this chapter shows, it is important that religious and cultural minorities are recognized and supported through local government as a way of achieving social inclusion, equal citizenship and full participation in society.

In a national and global context, where demographic boundaries are continually redrawn and where racialized inequalities are increasingly challenged, grassroots action at the local level may be the optimal conduit through which to generate appropriate policies and initiatives aimed at supporting migrant integration. Migration has historically served Australia and other Western nations well. It is to be expected that migrants be empowered to gain access to full and active citizenship rather than be pushed towards social dislocation and economic marginalization.

Émigré societies in the twenty-first century are still struggling to come to grips with the notion that national identity and active citizenship can no longer be the exclusive domain of primordial attachment (Benhabib 2004; Benhabib, Shapiro and Petranović 2007). What is needed now is a more grassroots approach to moral universalism and cosmopolitanism. Within such an approach, classical understandings and applications of normative citizenship can be augmented by a new emphasis on a discourse of human rights that transcends the particularities of nation-state polity with its increasingly out-dated emphasis on political membership and tributary rights (Turner 2007). this chapter and the larger study from which is extracted show that government policies, citizenship approaches, and national discourses on identity and belonging do often shape in a significant manner migrants' subjective sense of belonging and their social connectedness practices.

Note

1 This chapter is based on a large research project, *Local Governance, Multiculturalism and Active Citizenship: The Case of Arab-Muslim Diaspora in the West*, funded by an Australian Research Council discovery grant (2007–10). The research team was led by Professor Fethi Mansouri and included Professors Sue Kenny and David Walker. The author would like to acknowledge the significant contribution of Dr Michele Lobo as the research fellow on the project, Professor Gary Craig and Dr Hannah Lewis who collaborated on the case study in Sheffield and Dr Rim Latrache who assisted with the French part. The author would like to acknowledge the crucial input of the local councils and all the participants in Australia, France and the UK.

Bibliography

Abbas, T. (2005) 'Recent developments to British multicultural theory, policy and practice: the case of British Muslims', *Citizenship Studies*, 9(2): 153–166.

Akbarzadeh, S and Mansouri, F. (2007) *Islam and Political Violence: Muslim Diaspora and Radicalism in the West*, London/New York: I.B.Tauris/Palgrave Macmillan.

Al-Ali, N., Black, R. and Koser, K. (2001) 'Europe as Emerging Transnational Communities', *Ethnic and Racial Studies*, 24(4): 578–600.

Benhabib, S. (2004) *Another Cosmopolitanism*, Oxford: Oxford University Press.

Benhabib, S. and Resnik, J. (2009) *Migrations and Mobilities: Citizenship, Borders and Gender*, New York: New York University Press.

Benhabib, S., Shapiro, I. and Petranović, D. (eds.) (2007). *Identities, Affiliations, and Allegiances*, Cambridge: Cambridge University Press.

Bowen, J.R. (2004) 'Beyond migration: Islam as a transnational public space', *Journal of Ethnic and Migration Studies*, 30(5): 879–894.

Castles, S. (2004) 'The factors that make and unmake migration policies 1', *The International Migration Review*, 38(3): 852–884.

Castles, S. (2002) 'Migration and community formation under conditions of globalisation', *International Migration Review*, 36(4), 1143–1168.

Castles, S. (1996) 'The racisms of globalisation', in E. Vasta and S. Castles (eds) *The Teeth are Smiling: The Persistence of Racism in Multicultural Australia*, St Leonards: Allen and Unwin.

Dunn, K. (2005) 'Repetitive and troubling discourses of nationalism in the local politics of mosque development in Sydney, Australia', *Environment and Planning: Society and Space*, 23: 29–50.

Dunn, K.M. and Geeraert, P. (2003) 'The geography of 'race' and racisms', *GeoDate*, 16(3): 1–6.

Dunn, K., Klocker, N. and Salabay, T. (2007) 'Contemporary racism and Islamophobia in Australia: racializing religion', *Ethnicities*, 7(4): 564–589.

Evans Braziel, J. and Mannur, A. (2003), 'Nation, migration, globalisation: points of contention in diaspora studies', in J. Evans Braziel and A. Mannur (eds) *Theorizing Diaspora*, London: Blackwell Publishing.

Faist, T. (1999) *Transnationalization in International Migration: Implications for the Study of Citizenship and Culture*. Transnational Communities Working Paper. Institute for Intercultural and International Studies, Bremen. Available at: www.transcomm.ox.ac.uk/working%20papers/faist.pdf (accessed 11 October 2011).

Forrest, J. and Dunn, K.M. (2006) '"Core" culture hegemony and multiculturalism: perceptions of privileged positions of Australians with British background', *Ethnicities*, 6(2): 203–230.

Global Commission on International Migration (2006) *Estimates of the Remittances of Working Migrants*. Available at: www.gcim.org (accessed 16 March 2011).

Hassan, R. (2002) *Faithlines: Muslim Conceptions of Islam and Society*, Karachi, Pakistan: Oxford University Press.

Jakubowicz, A. (2007) 'Political Islam and the future of Australian multiculturalism', *National Identities*, 9(3): 265–280.

Jupp, J. (2001) 'The institutions of culture: multiculturalism', in T. Bennett and D. Carter (eds), *Culture in Australia: Policies, Publics and Programs*, Cambridge: Cambridge University Press.

Kennedy, P. and Roudometof, V. (2002) 'Transnationalism in a global age', in P. Kennedy and V. Roudometof (eds), *Communities across Borders: New Immigrants and Transnational Cultures*, London: Routledge.

Koleth, E. (2010) *Multiculturalism: A Review of Australian Policy Statements and Recent Debates in Australia and Overseas*, Research Paper no. 6, Canberra: Australian Parliament Library.

Kymlicka, W. (1997) *States, Nations and Cultures*, Amsterdam: Van Gorcum.

Lubeck, P. (2002) 'The challenge of Islamic networks and citizenship claims: Europe's painful adjustment to globalisation', in N. Al Sayyad and M. Castells (eds) *Muslim Europe or Euro-Islam: Politics, Culture, and Citizenship in the Age of Globalisation*, Lanham: Lexington Books.

Mansouri, F. (2005) 'Citizenship, identity and belonging in contemporary Australia', in S. Akbarzadeh and S. Yasmeen (eds) *Islam and the West: Reflections from Australia*, Sydney: UNSW Press.

Meer, N. and Modood, T. (2008) 'The multicultural state we're in: Muslims, "multiculture" and the "civic re-balancing" of British multiculturalism', *Political Studies*, 1: 25.

Mummery, J. (2005) 'Being not-at-home: a conceptual discussion', in C. van den Driesen and R. Crane (eds), *Diaspora: The Australasian Experience*, New Delhi: Prestige Books.

Nesbitt-Larking, P. (2008) 'Dissolving the diaspora: dialogical practice in the development of deep multiculturalism', *Journal of Community and Applied Social Psychology*, 18: 351–362.

O'Sullivan, J. (2003) 'How not to think of immigration', in L. Kramer (ed.), *The Multicultural Experiment: Immigrants, Refugees and National Identity*, Sydney: Macleay Press.

Poynting, S. (2004) *Living with Racism: The Experience and Reporting by Arab and Muslim Australians of Discrimination, Abuse and Violence since 11 September 2001*, Report to The Human Rights and Equal Opportunity Commission, Australia.

Ramadan, T. (2004) *Western Muslims and the Future of Islam*, New York: Oxford University Press.

Sherrell, K. and Hyndman, J. (2004) *Sharing the Wealth, Spreading the 'Burden'? The*

Settlement of Kosovar Refugees in Smaller BC Cities, Working Paper No. 04–06. Vancouver: RIIM.

Sinclair J. and Cunningham S. (2000) 'Diaspora and the media', in J. Sinclair and S. Cunningham (eds), *Floating Lives: The Media and Asian Diaspora*, St Lucia: University of Queensland Press.

Sklair, L. and Robbins, P. (2002) 'Global capitalism and major corporations from the Third World', *Third World Quarterly*, 23(1): 81–100.

Sreberny, A. (2000) 'Media and diasporic consciousness: an exploration among Iranians in London', in S. Cottle (ed.), *Ethnic Minorities and the Media: Changing Cultural Boundaries*, Buckingham, UK/Philadelphia, USA: Open University Press.

Taylor, C. (ed.) (1994) *Multiculturalism. Examining the Politics of Recognition*, Princeton NJ: Princeton University Press.

Turner, B. (2006) 'Citizenship and the crisis of multiculturalism', *Citizenship Studies*, 10(5): 607–618.

Turner, B.S. (2007) 'New and old xenophobia: the crisis of liberal multiculturalism', in A. Akbarzadeh and F. Mansouri (eds), *Islam and Political Violence: Muslim Diaspora and Radicalism in the West*, London/New York: Tauris Academic Studies.

United Nations Educational, Scientific and Cultural Organization (UNESCO) (2009) *UNESCO Framework for Cultural Statistics*, Canada: UNESCO Institute for Statistics.

Vertovec, S. (2001) *Transnational Challenges to the New Multiculturalism*. ESRC Transnational Communities Program Working Paper, Oxford. Available at: www.transcomm.ox.ac.uk/working%20papers/WPTC-2K-06%20Vertovec.pdf.

Vertovec, S. (2004) 'Migrant transnationalism and modes of transformation 1', *The International Migration Review*, 38(3): 970–1001.

Securing long-term belonging

9 Equal valued status
Belonging, identity and place

Hurriyet Babacan and Alperhan Babacan

Introduction

In the past decade we have witnessed the questioning of policies relating to cultural diversity, multiculturalism and citizenship. This has been exacerbated by the advent of 'globalized terrorism' in the wake of September 11 and has resulted in the adoption of protective measures both nationally and internationally. The discourses on fighting the war on terror have been conjoined with other issues such as border protection, ethnic crime and threats to 'Australian culture' from immigration and have added to negative public opinion relating to cultural diversity. A climate of concern over safety and security has been created. The adoption of a 'protective framework' has been accompanied by an erosion of civil liberties, freedoms and human rights which were traditionally associated with Western democracies. This has had impacts on minorities' sense of belonging in countries, such as Australia, with significant immigrant populations.

The erosion of civil liberties and pre-emptive war are directed at preserving the global economic and political order and in a more interconnected world. As Beck (2000) points out, all that happens on the planet is no longer a limited local event and all inventions, victories and catastrophes affect the whole world. In Australia, the public discourses relating to terrorism have been strongly linked with the process of creating 'the other' as 'the threat'. The manner in which the debates have been handled has resulted in suspicion of those who are deemed to be different. The discussion and debates have been interwoven with issues relating to Australian values and national identity and have ultimately reinforced particular types of patriotism. There has been an attempt to create a unique and homogenous national identity by the Federal Government that tries to unite some parts of the community while excluding others. New forms of patriotism have emerged which are racialized and draw boundaries of inclusion and exclusion. Who is an Australian, what are Australian values, who makes up the 'Aussie battler' have been redefined and have had significant consequences for those who are included and excluded. Kershan (2005) argues that these developments would not be novel in host–migrant relations. The recurrence of key elements such as socioeconomic disadvantage, media hostility and the real or imagined anxiety that immigration is 'out of control' is a feature of the politics of immigration over the last century. However, Kershan notes that what is different is the combination of enduring and new variables, together with the changing global context of migration processes, which brings a sharp edge to the contemporary political saliency of immigration.

In this chapter, we visit the key issues in immigrant integration and migrant security in the context of Australia. We critically examine the so-called threats posed by migrants to Australian society, excavating the links between identity, nation building and immigration, social inclusion–exclusion and racism and fear. In the past decade, the public discourses on immigration have been negative where groups such as refugees, asylum seekers, Asians and Muslims are demonized and vilified in the media, although the government has maintained existing immigration levels. Questions have been raised about the value that immigrants bring, whether multicultural policies are divisive of the nation, whether Muslim Australians integrate into the Australian 'way of life' and how to stop asylum seekers. Such important debates have been conjoined with issues of safety and security and presented as a danger to the Australian way of life.

We argue that a key challenge to social inclusion is a lack of recognition with 'equal valued status' (both in material and subjective terms) and that there are groups and classes of people, in this case immigrants and refugees, who are at value-risk or already devalued in society. Borrowing from the concept of 'social role valorisation' (Thomas and Wolfensberger 1999), 'equal valued status' refers to the enablement, establishment, enhancement, maintenance and/or defence of valued social roles for people who are deemed fundamentally different from and of less value than everyone else. We argue that to achieve a socially inclusive society there is a need for minorities to be valued, while a more comprehensive approach to human security and citizenship is needed to meet the challenges of a globally mobile world.

Immigration, nation building and identity in a globalized world

The twenty-first century is characterized as a globally mobile world, with more frequent movements of people across the globe which lead to greater levels of diversity and cultural interaction within the borders of the nation-state. Ferguson (1994) argues shared objective traits such as languages become meaningful within the framework of subjective consciousness, which in turn becomes a powerful force in shaping common objectives of state-determined policies of 'nation building'. Nation building efforts are confronted with the dilemmas of unity of the people of a country and the diversity that minorities and immigrants bring. The nation-state is increasingly challenged in relation to the role it plays and the impact it has. This section explores the connections between immigration, identity and the Australian nation-state.

'Globalization' is a broad term that is used to refer to the interconnectedness of the world. It refers to processes that are primarily economic but increasingly social, cultural and political (Beck 2000). An important feature of globalization is the permeability of political and geographic borders and the greatly increased speed with which interactions take place, whether through trade, tourism or electronically (Waters 1995). Appadurai (1990) points out key global flows: ethnoscapes, technoscapes, financescapes, mediascapes and ideoscapes. These flows represent the shifting and fluid movements of people, technology, finance, media and ideas. The contemporary processes of globalization include an ideology that endorses the primacy of the free market and theorizes that it can solve social problems and provide for human good and social justice (Heron 2008).

The globalized world is one in which there are large numbers of people on the move. In the year 2010, the International Organization for Migration (IOM) identified 214 million people as international migrants (IOM 2011). The United Nations High Commission for Refugees (UNHCR) states that by the end of 2009, the total 'population of concern' was estimated at 36.5 million people, broken down as refugees, asylum seekers and internally displaced peoples (UNHCR 2010: 7). The reasons for the movement, processes of settlement and adjustment and their reception in the host countries show great variability. Migration experiences alter the understanding of society and shift interactions between people, political bodies and other institutions, with far reaching consequences for social relations, public policies and international relations (Freeman and Jupp 1992).

International migration is never a simple individual action in which a person decides to move, but is organized and coordinated through a network of government and international agencies. Migration requires infrastructures and institutions of transport, communication and regulation. Contemporary travel involves strict regulation and control. Nation-states seek to maximize the opportunities from transnational corporations and selectively open their doors to the different forms of movement of people. Migration processes must be viewed through the lens of networks of political, military and cultural relations which lie with either nation-states, transnational corporations or international bodies (Held *et al.* 1999; Castles and Miller 1998).

Movements of people have resulted in diversity of 'ethnic mixes' in many countries of the world, including Australia. Notions of belonging are changing and the traditional allegiances to homelands are altered (Westwood and Phizacklea 2000). Global changes are experienced as crises of the national economy and social relations, often minority relations. The recent development of racist movements in many Western developed nations has been linked to the crisis countries face as global economic decisions cause societal changes. The modern nation-state is increasingly under pressure from the processes of neo-liberal globalization. The power exerted by media giants and large multinational corporations is very significant in terms of their being able to influence legislation and regulation and reduce the ability of governments to respond to the needs and demands of the polity (McChesney 2001). In a shrinking world, the impact of states is lessening with economic globalization undermining the ability of governments to deliver on significant elements of the social contract (Jayasuriya 2003). When the state is unable to respond effectively to the demands of its citizens, it faces a crisis of legitimacy and has to look for new ways to engender loyalty and affiliation (Gopalkrishnan 2007). In an attempt to be relevant to its citizens and to maintain loyalty, the state, it is argued, will shift to appease populist views. Often these are connected with taking policy positions against minorities.

In contemporary Australia, the construction of national identity has been accompanied by a grand narrative, which has been interwoven with issues relating to Australian values, national identity and fear of the 'other', and has ultimately reinforced particular types of patriotism. There has been a deliberate attempt to create a unique and homogenous national identity that attempts to unite some parts of the community while excluding others (Babacan and Babacan 2006a). This is a unilateral debate, driven mainly by the nation-state and aided by the media (Brett 2004). This involves the construction of Australian identity to reflect particular cultural groups and exclude others in the national interest. National identity is constructed as a particular way of life and a particular set of values represented by those who are white and of Anglo-Saxon/Celtic backgrounds (Markus 2001). The discourse of nationalism has set out to determine who is Australian and who is un-Australian. 'Un-Australian' draws lines of acceptability – delineating what is regarded as reasonable, proper and decent forms of public speech and behaviour. Who is an Australian, what are Australian values, who makes up the 'Aussie battler' and what is 'un-Australian' have been redefined in particular ways, which privilege Anglo-Saxon norms and have had significant consequences for those who are included and excluded.

The new forms of nationalism are reinforced by the manner in which the nation-state engages with key functions of immigration regulation, security and border control and citizenship rights. Nation-states have become more involved in the control and regulation of wanted and unwanted citizens through regulation of rules of entry and exit. In Australia, a key focus of discussion has become to what extent can and does the state control its borders and take measures against certain unwanted immigrants, for example, through the detention of asylum seekers and tightening of regulations and rules of entry (Brochmann and Hammar 1999). Another key element is the relationship between sovereignty and security of the nation-state. There are clear links between international relations and domestic foreign policy and immigration policies of nation-states (Ghosh 2000). The final issue for the state is the incorporation of immigrants in host countries, including what citizenship rights are to be given, the provision of welfare support and legal entitlements and the determination of a national identity which is representative of multicultural demographics and policies of inclusion more broadly (Brubaker 1992).

'Citizenship', in both the legal and more normative sense, has become more restrictive in Australia and is about limiting who can access social, civil and political rights. Citizenship and belonging are portrayed as a privilege rather than a right. These are evidenced by the introduction of testing to become an Australian citizen, which did not previously exist. Under a neo-liberal philosophy, problems such as crime or unemployment have been portrayed as problems that are engaged in by individual choice and that coercive legislation and punishment, rather than state assistance, are the solutions to these problems. Groups or individuals (for example, youth, asylum seekers, refugees, immigrants) who were once considered as being 'at risk' and requiring the support of the state are now portrayed as groups and individuals who are a 'risk' to society (McCulloch 2004). The consequence is that a sense of anxiety and insecurity is created among the community (McCulloch 2004) which Hage (2003a) calls 'the worrying nation'. The Australian Government has now been able to sell the idea of a trade-off between security and civil liberties, enabling harsher legal and security measures and fewer social services and leading to the erosion of the social contract (Jayasuriya 2003; Babacan and Babacan 2006b).

Regular pronouncements by public figures and the media 'license' notions of who belongs, while feeding feelings of dominance. Dominance is internalized in the dominant group and leads to rejection of others (Dudgeon and Oxenham 1989). Powerful discourses invoke images of meritorious Aussie 'battlers' or ordinary Australians who deserve more respect and support. As Carole Johnson observed, 'ordinary Australians are not Aboriginal, Asian, homosexual, lesbian, feminist or migrant' (2000: 64–5).

Solutions to anxiety about risks from the 'other' are presented in the form of a powerful political campaign which 'emphasises a return through cultural renewal to a more secure – often mythical – idea of community' (Jayasuriya 2003: 3) and an increasing concern about social solidarity, social order and cohesiveness. The concept of 'social cohesion' has entered the lexicon of Western governments and is used broadly to encompass a large number of ideas, including social capital, civic and political participation, trust, ethnic harmony, personal and national security and peace (Colenso 2005: 412). There is little agreement about what social cohesion is, what a socially cohesive society would look like and how public policy actions could help sustain or improve it. The nation-state achieves social cohesion through a unity of its people through a set of values, identity and emotions. National identities are essential to promote the legitimacy of nation-states as they enable the populace to identify with commonalities, whether real or imagined (Anderson 2006). An analysis of nationalism in Australia demonstrates that the Australian state shapes national identity according to the prevailing economic and social needs of the nation and prevailing philosophy of the times, so that ethnicity becomes a legitimacy device through which the state either pursues political agendas or meets the nation's needs (Wong 1994). Reflecting on the contemporary state of affairs in Australia, Krongold (2006: 8) states that a 'discursive framing of asylum seekers and by association their Australian Muslim brethren as the demonized "Other" was juxtaposed against the white teleology of nationhood to produce the most explicit attack on multiculturalism since its inception'. The government's public discourses on Australian values and its portrayal of itself as the protector of Australia's boundaries, sovereignty and culture resulted in conservative elements of Australian society being able to attack 'cultural diversity'. This in turn is linked with social exclusion, racism and fear.

Social exclusion, racism and fear

The fear politics pursued by the government has had a massive impact on race relations in Australia (Poynting and Noble 2004). Turner and Hogg (1987) present 'depersonalisation' as a process that permits social stereotyping, group cohesiveness, ethnocentrism, altruism, emotional contagion and empathy, collective action and other processes. As Wazana states:

> creating such categories becomes the only way of justifying in the face of international condemnation, the acceptance of some and the refusal of others. This discourse of fairness and unfairness resonates intensely with the average citizen, which no doubt explains the government's reliance on it. It also helps to situate the illegal refugee in a context of lawlessness and degeneracy, juxtaposed with the nation itself, seen as lawful and civilised.
>
> (Wazana 2004: 89)

Immigrants, however, in any context of migration, want to be included and belong to their host country, without giving up their history, backgrounds and identity. Western governments, paradoxically, have engaged with social inclusion and exclusion as a way of overcoming disadvantage in fields such as education, housing and employment. Being socially included means:

- To participate as valued, appreciated equals in the social, economic, political and cultural life of the community
- To be involved in mutually trusting, appreciative and respectful interpersonal relationships at the family, peer and community levels

(Crawford 2003: 5)

There is ample research across the globe to demonstrate that exclusion takes place (Dekker and Bolt 2005; Social Inclusion Board 2010). Factors that contribute to exclusion are multiple and mutually exacerbating. The discussion and definition of social exclusion are highly contentious, with multiple factors being emphasized by different writers. In general, social exclusion is defined as:

> A multi-dimensional disadvantage which severs individuals and groups from the major social processes and opportunities in society such as housing, citizenship, employment, adequate living standards and may be manifested in various forms, at various times and within various sections of the population.
>
> (Barry and Hallet 1998: 1)

Writings on social exclusion have focused on this concept as exclusion from the labour market, economic exclusion (including poverty), exclusion based on social isolation, geographic or spatial exclusion and exclusion based on institutional processes and systems (Young 1999). The majority of the literature on social exclusion focuses on factors such as class, ability and gender but makes no mention of exclusion based on 'culture', 'ethnicity' and 'racism'.

'Culture' is a constructed, dynamic and interactive process by which society determines its rules, structures, symbols, traditions, customs and institutions which mould all aspects of life (Woodward 1997). The political and institutional approach by the state towards culture, ethnicity, language, identity and history are crucial elements in the discourse and reproduction of national identities (Gutmann 2003). In multicultural societies such as Australia, discourses on race and culture have formed the basis of nation building (Stokes 1997; Vasta and Castles 1996). Castles *et al.* (1988) point out that Australian national identity has been forged on a process of exclusion of and racism towards Indigenous and ethnic minorities. Policies of multiculturalism in the 1970s and 1980s were an attempt to use cultural difference as a way to gain leverage for state recognition for minorities, resource allocation and equality. The new liberal forms of multiculturalism that has emerged in the 1990s and the 2000s question the validity of such claims and separate out issues of social justice and equality from that of cultural difference. Boyd (1996) points out that this may one of the major sites of repression and that the problem gets hidden behind safe platitudes talked about in obfuscatory terms such as one nation, community relations and harmony.

It is important to acknowledge that social exclusion can take place on the basis of 'culture' and 'race'. New forms of racism no longer rely on biological definitions of inferiority or superiority. They bring into play exclusions based on cultural considerations. Defining 'racism' is a difficult task as it changes its forms and meanings in different historical contexts. These forms are multiple, historically specific, situationally variable and often contradictory. They also are gendered and interconnect with nationalist and religious identities in complex ways (Hollinsworth 2006). Zelinka defines racism as:

> a belief in the superiority of one particular racial or ethnic group and, flowing from this, the exclusion of other groups from some or many aspects of society. This exclusion (and often exploitation) is seen as legitimate simply because of the difference or supposed inferiority of the other group's race, ethnicity or nationality.
>
> (Zelinka 1996: 1)

Racism operates through relational, systemic and institutional practices that serve to devalue, exclude, oppress or exploit people. It is an act of power and a means of maintaining privilege and racialized hierarchies of power characterize social structures (Back and Solomos 2000; Babacan *et al.* 2009). There is considerable evidence that racism leads to social exclusion on the basis of culture, language, ethnicity and perceived perceptions of 'race'. Studies indicate that the life chances of racialized minorities are adversely affected (Hollinsworth 2006; Bonnet 2000). Dunn *et al.* (in a research project on racism for which one of the authors is also principal researcher) in a large national study demonstrated that

78 per cent of Australians believe humankind is made up of separate races, 41 per cent believe that there are cultural groups that do not fit into Australian society and 85 per cent believe there is racial prejudice in Australia; paradoxically, 87 per cent believe that it is a good thing for society to be made up of different cultures. The same study found anti-Asian sentiment (24 per cent), anti-Indigenous sentiment (28 per cent), anti-Muslim sentiment (49 per cent) and anti-Semitic sentiment (23.3 per cent). Experiences of racism were also identified in this national study, with 18 per cent in the workplace, 17 per cent in educational settings, 18 per cent in a shop or restaurant and 16 per cent at public or sporting events. Significantly, 23 per cent identified as being treated less respectfully, 27 per cent identified as being called names or insulted and 16 per cent identified as not being trusted due to 'ethnicity, culture or race' (Dunn et al. 2004). Social signification based on 'race and culture' facilitates social exclusion and hinders inclusion, although much of this literature is presented only in terms of barriers in accessing services.

The impacts of exclusion based on racism are both 'distributional' and 'relational' (Silver and Miller 2002). The distributional relates to material elements of life such as access to goods and services, employment, housing and so on. The relational includes the sense of belonging, trust, connections and networks, social inclusion, neighbourhood and community participation and recognition and respect for identity. The interplay of dimensions of racism in both these areas leads to social stratification and disadvantage. Both distributional and relational elements impact on the ability of individuals and communities to exercise their citizenship rights (Babacan et al. 2009). These go to the heart of social inclusion, belonging and migrant security. Johnson et al. (2005) caution that the social capital of one community may be created at the expense of another's, or the strength of one community may be to the detriment of others. Osburn (2006: 5) identifies the process of devaluation as people being perceived and interpreted as 'deviant' due to their negatively-valued differentness; being rejected by community or society or being cast into negative social roles, some of which can be severely negative, such as 'subhuman', 'menace' and 'burden on society'; being put and kept at a social or physical distance; having negative images (including language) attached to them and being the object of abuse and violence. Resorting to fear politics has facilitated and promoted new racisms in Australia (Gopalkrishnan and Babacan 2007). This impacts on people's ability to forge relationships and friendships in the community, with their neighbours, within school communities and at work. The 'old racism' in which ethnic communities were viewed as inferior has been largely replaced by 'new racism' (also termed 'cultural racism').

There is a growing literature, however, that seeks to articulate how 'new racism' operates in subtle forms that are difficult to identify (Henry et al. 2000; Dunn et al. 2007; Babacan 2008). This literature explores how racism can still be articulated without denouncing democratic principles, through a transformation into more 'legitimate' and contemporary concerns. Social messages are perpetuated through coded public discourses on immigration, multiculturalism, refugees and citizenship. Such 'codes' reflect unequal power to represent others, to negatively evaluate others and to make these representations and evaluations prevail in public domains and, as such, are key features of new racism (van Dijk 2000; Babacan and Babacan 2006b).

Management of diversity continues to be a central issue for Australia as it grapples with the public opinion that negatively targets immigrants, refugees and asylum seekers. Racism is powerful in its capacity to generate fear of 'others', a phenomenon that is widely understood as being a powerful tool for governments and corporations by which to shape public discourse and behaviours (Gopalkrishnan 2007). The last few decades have also seen the rise of fear and hate-based politics, with Pauline Hanson in Australia, Georg Haider in Austria and the Bharatiya Janata Party in India just some of the examples of where fear of the 'other' has been effectively transformed into political capital (Gopalkrishnan 2003, 2007; Waymer 2009).

The use of fear is not new. Gopalkrishnan (2007) points to the process of globalization and its impacts on the nation-state. He notes the adoption of neo-liberal philosophies, resulting in 'de-stating', where the state divests itself of its roles to the market, in social services and even in some cases in the provision of the bottom-line safety net. The process involves liberalization, privatization and deregulation and the state restricts much of its functions to focusing on maintenance of internal and external security and a minimum of other roles. The increasingly changed role of governance gives rise to questions around the relationship between the polity and the elected government. In a world based on neo-liberalism, the use of fear has achieved a new level of sophistication and reach. Technology has enabled a world where reality and fiction are easily blurred, while the enormous power of the media is very effective in presenting narratives in convincing forms. The role of the media in creating an atmosphere of fear is crucial and is well facilitated by the highly concentrated ownership of the media and the global nature of media networks (Glassner 2004). The messages of fear become even more ominous when they are targeted on racial lines (Stratton 1998; Gopalkrishnan 2003, 2007). Fear has the capability of building cohesion within the chosen members of the in-group, normally the majority, around the core value of safety (Furedi 2005). Fear of an external or internal foe can easily supplant day-to-day issues around job insecurity, changing power relationships in the workplace, increasing indebtedness, loss of social support frameworks, alienation and a sense of helplessness in the face of powerful forces. Used in this context, fear becomes an instrument of rule used in various ways by political leaders, either because it helps them to pursue a specific political agenda and/or lends support to their beliefs (Robin 2004).

The use of fear has become increasingly important in the Australian landscape. The definition of who is to be targeted as 'other' has shifted over time in Australia. While the perceived threats were once Indigenous or Asian communities, more recently Arab and Muslim communities have been added to the list (Dunn et al. 2004). Collectively, the 'other' have been labelled as 'criminals', 'queue jumpers' or 'terrorists' who are not worthy of Australia's compassion or assistance (Koo 2005). Today the stereotypical notion of the stranger as asylum seeker, migrant or refugee exists before the arrival of migrants, perpetuated through the media and other networks. However, as Lawrence (2006: 2) argues, fear continues to fuel cycles of worry in Australia at a time when the country has never been safer, with increased life expectancy, reduced child mortality, lessened civil strife and moderate murder levels. The climate of fear has made it seem reasonable and rational to engage in assaults on human rights and civil liberties. Gopalkrishnan (2007) identifies the processes in which fear is used and coins this 'infeartainment'.

> Infeartainment represents the use of fear by the powerful to contain the population while also providing them with entertainment as a form of distraction. It involves a set of processes set within a narrative framework and ensures compliance while also identifying visible targets to focus fear on. Infeartainment relies on misdirection as a tool to be used on behalf of the powerful in society and provides the moral framework within which the use of political and social controls as well as violence can be justified.
> (Gopalkrishnan 2007: 25)

The grand narrative of infeartainment is built on stereotypes and labels that can be easily used to marginalize groups of people in society. It provides a moral basis for hate and fear of the 'other' and also creates an environment where these emotions can be acted on and justified. An example of this is in the aftermath of September 11, when a narrative was easily generated that enabled individual assaults on innocent people, based on whether they looked different from the mainstream. In Australia, Muslims, as well as members of other communities such as the Sikhs, bore the brunt of the hate unleashed post-September 11. The broader ramifications of this narrative are that ethnic communities are differentiated as being a 'threat to the cultural integrity' of the Anglo-Celtic host society (Dunn et al. 2004). Questions as to who does or does not belong to Australian society, who is included and who is excluded, and what and who are or are not Australian are integral aspects of the intolerance of some groups and the new racism in Australia (Dunn et al. 2004).

Space, place and belonging

The discourses of fear are played out in public places and spaces. The nature of global migration allows people to occupy transnational spaces. The result is that identity formation becomes a spatially situated process, physical, virtual and symbolic. Place and space are important to identity construction, sense of security, belonging and integration. The idea of 'home' is built on notions of the 'inside '(and hence inclusion and belonging) and implies 'normal life' that is relevant, unlike the outside world that is alien (Steinbock 1995). The construction of social spaces involves the materiality of places as they are constructed and the recursive shaping of people's identities, actions and interactions with their physical environment. The settlement process for migrants arriving in a new country is closely connected to the spatial experience in the new environment. The process of adjustment requires establishment of roots, a sense of belonging and validation of the self. The sense of place is established through physical and cultural factors (Fortier 2000; Mason 2000). Sarup (1994) reminds us that places are socially constructed and that this construction is about power. Spaces and places can silence, obscure and disenfranchize some while providing security for those who hold power. An important consideration is the way space and place are implicated in the experience of fear. Tuan (1979) calls this the 'landscapes of fear', a metaphor which covers real threats and imagined fears. Diken (2002) points out that in contemporary societies, the logic of discipline, control and terror is the paradigm that dominates spaces and places.

Representations of public spaces are important, especially when minorities feel they do not 'fit' in and have very few means to impact on the dominant images. The public spaces (of work, recreation and consumption) offer both opportunities and threats; however, taking up the opportunities requires social capital. The threats are more immediate and punitive, resulting in social exclusion. In a national study conducted between 2001 and 2004, Babacan and Babacan (2006b) identified issues of migrant security in relation to spatial considerations. The study found that ethnic communities continually negotiate their belonging, engaging in creating spaces in confused ways and transforming the urban landscape of contemporary cities. Thus their spatial practice is 'a negotiated reality' that involves both symbolic and material expressions of local and translocal connections, as well as their engagement with the receiving society. The key areas of engagement included consumption, culture and faith, business, recreation and social elements (for example, health and education). While there is no scope in this chapter to visit the full findings of the study in relation to place and space, the findings in relation to belonging and migrant security are important.

Work, finance, resources and cultural capital determined the capacity to engage. For newly arrived immigrants and particularly refugees, this capacity was not there and many felt torn between lived practice and ways to influence public spaces. The participants in the study demonstrated concern over the pervasive climate of fear and conflict in their new spaces. This included crime, insecurity, counter-terrorism and surveillance measures, police attitudes and racism. For many members of ethnic communities, elements of fear prevented proactivity in engagement with places, for putting forward ideas for shaping places and spaces and to feeling a sense of belonging. Interestingly, powerful institutions of society, such as the government, corporations and the police, were also seen as forming a part of the threat in the landscape, with their pre-eminent capacity to impose and render those who do not belong as the 'other'.

The study illustrated that the dimensions of space and place are closely connected with migrant security, identity formation processes and use of fear. These factors were critical in inclusion, social participation and integration which in turn determine outcomes for life chances for many ethnic minorities. Spatial factors link with other differences and create inequality in access to space and place. Relations of power, structures of inequality and practices of domination and subordination are embedded in spatial design and relations (Babacan and Babacan 2006b).

Towards equal valued status and social inclusion

'Social inclusion' involves entry points for vulnerable communities and establishment of human relationships. Interest in inclusion arises from five values: social justice, diversity, choice and opportunity, entitlement to rights and services and working together (Cushing 2003: 15). In the context of migration, social inclusion enables the recognition of the social and life history of ethnic communities and their contribution to society as equals. The key elements of social inclusion include: access to social goods and services with appropriate resource allocation across the social contract; empowerment of communities who are skilled and have genuine participation in the decision making structures of society; institutional trust and building democratic governance bodies; and building understanding and bridges between people (Phillipson *et al.* 2003). Crawford (2003) summarizes social inclusion as people wanting to:

> participate as valued, appreciated equals in the social, economic, political and cultural life of the community (i.e., in valued societal situations) and to be involved in mutually trusting, appreciative and respectful interpersonal relationships at the family, peer and community levels.
>
> (Crawford 2003: 7)

At a more systemic level, social inclusion is about overcoming structural barriers and extending rights to the most vulnerable, thereby strengthening processes and outcomes which lead to equality. It is a process that may manifest itself as a struggle for space in the public arena and for policy making, appropriate resource allocation and interventions (Pierson 2001).

Social inclusion of immigrants involves a consideration of the status given to this broad category of people. All people strive for intangible elements of security beyond the material aspects, such as belonging, status and acceptance. It is useful to draw upon status theories here to answer the question, 'Why do beliefs that attach different amounts of status to different categories of people become consensually held by the members of a society?' The status of individuals and groups within society has different outcomes for inclusion, equality and social rewards. Status structures are defined as:

> rank-ordered relationships among actors describing the interactional inequalities formed from actors' implicit valuations of themselves and one another according to some shared standard of value. Status refers to one's standing in a social hierarchy as determined by respect, deference and social influence.
>
> (Ridgeway and Walker 1995: 28)

Mark et al. (2009) point out that status hierarchies are formed in any cooperative interaction. Following on from our earlier discussion, status-belief generation can occur in people who previously did not hold any status beliefs. Beliefs about status affect the positions people occupy in those hierarchies. Thus, a pattern of interactional inequality emerges that rank orders members of the group. Berger and Fisek (2006) note that regularly observed inequalities (and associated expectations) govern opportunities, participation, evaluation and influence. Huberman et al. (2004) argues that status signals competence and provides access to power and resources. Status beliefs result in loss or support for social capital, and have distributional and relational consequences. Status is an important factor in achieving resources. Lin (1999) differentiates between personal and social resources. She argues that resources exert an important and significant effect on attained statuses, beyond that accounted for by personal resources (Lin 1999: 468). Lin also posits that social capital, in terms of both access to and mobilization of resources, enhances the chances of attaining better statuses. However, social capital is contingent on initial positions in the social hierarchies as well as on extensity of social ties.

An ethnic community's social capital encompasses resources available to an individual through their membership in that community or group. It involves the shared feelings of social belonging that enable groups to set up institutions and other networks that members can access. Social capital in these communities exists in the social relations among community members and with institutions of society (Giorgas 2000). Many writers point out that culture and ethnicity can be considered a distinct form of social capital which is constructed from one's cultural endowments and includes obligations and expectations, information channels and social norms (Coleman 1988; Zhou and Bankston 1994). Construction of identity (at personal and community levels) is an important consideration in building social capital. Giorgas (2000) studied six immigrant groups: Germans, Dutch, Hungarians, Poles, Italians and Greeks. She found that levels of social capital among the last two were relatively high. Greek and Italian immigrants had a collective sense of identity. This was because they saw themselves not only as individuals and family members, but part of the Italian/Greek-Australian community. Giorgas argued that this made them better able to organize and unite for a common purpose and gave them greater collective command over resources. Similarly, from a UK study of refugees, Loizos found that refugees turn to one another to reconstruct their networks in exile as a means of support and to establish a meaningful sense of social life and identity. Loizos states that 'the package of customs, beliefs and practices from before their dislocation ... continued to serve them in diasporic adjustment' (Loizos 2000: 132). Identity, however, is two-pronged, involving self-perception and perception by others. It is not simply imposed but can be chosen by the individual or the group and actively used within particular social contexts and constraints. The other side of identity is the perception of others. Stereotyping by dominant groups and repression can occur in society. Against dominant representations of 'others', identity offers a tool for resistance. In the context of contemporary post-September 11

Australia, accessing and mobilizing ethnic and mainstream social capital are difficult for immigrant communities. These pose serious challenges for building an inclusive society.

As pointed out by Huberman *et al.* (2004), status has intrinsic value beyond the material and people make tradeoffs to gain status. The implication of this is very important for an inclusive society. It implies that people who are marginalized or excluded in some way want to be given 'equal valued status' and successful integration of immigrants will be determined by this. However, this is difficult to achieve for immigrants in a climate of fear and demonization of some groups. Furedi (2005) argues that the use of fear and the focus on tough measures of security, surveillance and curtailment of civil liberties are accompanied by a disengagement by citizens from the political process. This disengagement takes the form of fear to engage, apathy or being forced to disengage through exclusionary practices of the state. The result is a move towards politics of blame, distrust and a move away from compassion for each other, particularly those who are deemed to be different (Hage 2003b). Trust, reciprocity, belonging, networks and mutual support are the key elements of social capital (Coleman 1988) and social inclusion. These are constantly eroded through the politics of fear. Fear impacts on people's ability to forge relationships and friendships in the community, with their neighbours, within school communities and at work. Stokes (1997) states that:

> A person or group of people can suffer real damage, real distortion if the people or society around them mirrors back to them a confining or demeaning or contemptible picture of themselves. Nonrecognition or misrecognition can inflict harm, can be a form of oppression, imprisoning someone in a false, distorted and reduced mode of being.
>
> (Stokes 1997: 19)

To achieve social inclusion and migrant security more broadly requires a move away from notions of security as law and order responses to ones of human rights and citizenship, where the notion of 'valued equal status' is aimed at, to provide the platform for the recognition of minorities as equal, enabling opportunities and creating the conditions to utilize citizenship rights (Cushing 2003). This means supporting initiatives that build social capital, improve status beliefs about ethnic communities and refute stereotyping as this diminishes status. Zetter *et al.* (2006: 14) point out that social capital building among immigrants is important for a range of reasons, including: combating and adjusting to social exclusion; celebrating and reinforcing different cultural identities; mediating a response to social needs; organizing to participate in wider social activities and establishing an identity and presence in order to define a negotiating position vis-à-vis other groups or institutions and agencies who may control public resources.

The conditions for social inclusion can only occur if the fear politics and anxieties created by being the 'worrying nation' (Hage 2003a) are stopped, as this makes the nation inward looking, focusing on self and lacking in compassion for others. Freiler (2002: ix) provides us with the cornerstones for social inclusion: valued recognition – respect of others' difference extended through systems; human development – nurture people's skills and growth to make own choices; involvement and engagement – right and support to be involved/control decisions affecting you; proximity – share public space; integrated schools; exposure to diversity and material well-being – housing, food and social activity. Cultural and spatial dimensions of inclusion – exclusion need greater consideration in our evidence base to inform policy making.

The nation-state has devoted resources to keeping an exclusive nation with large border protection measures and a strict control of who has eligibility for social, civil and political rights (McMaster 2001). Despite views on citizenship that emphasize citizen participation, membership and democratic community, most of the discussion has been centred on citizenship as a singular concept in the legal sense (Rubenstein 2002). Social inclusion needs a strong argument for the virtues of citizenship in the broader sense, which can include concepts such as group rights (Kymlicka 2001), multicultural citizenship (Jayasuriya 2003), post-national citizenship (Soysal 1994) and global cosmopolitanism (Appadurai 1990). Although we do not have scope to examine these concepts here, they offer the potential to think beyond the narrow forms of belonging and inclusion.

Conclusion

This chapter has visited some of the key challenges facing migrant security in Australia. The process of globalization will continue to mean that people will be mobile across the globe. Australia is committed to a migration process because of demographic, economic and social imperatives. Ethnic and cultural identities are now diverse and demand recognition in public spaces and places. Greater cultural, ethnic and religious plurality confronts perceptions of a cohesive national identity and citizenship and generates questions about shared identities within the nation-state. In a post-September 11 era, there is an increasing focus on security and safety, much of this based on narrow definitions of security and focusing on law and order, war on terror and border security. This is conjoined with discourses on asylum seekers, integration of immigrants, citizenship and welfare rights for immigrants and ethnic crime.

The notion of migrant security has to be broader and has to encompass social and developmental variables. Overall, human security can only be enhanced through the strengthening of human rights and civil liberties and through the development of more inclusive multicultural policies based on social justice, human rights and citizenship. Kalantzis (2000) points to four key principles associated with multicultural citizenship: (i) there needs to be equality of citizenship at the outset; (ii) a recognition that formal equality of rights does not necessarily translate into equal access to opportunities and resources; (iii) opportunities need to be provided for group representation and participation; and (iv) there needs to be differential treatment for people with different needs. The challenge for governments is to effectively balance the need to protect, while simultaneously safeguarding civil liberties, human rights and social inclusion. Cushing (2003: 3) points to the dual approaches which must be taken: 'process conditions' changing, such as structures, policies and opportunities that help people to participate; and an alteration of 'attitudinal conditions' relating to current public understanding of, or feelings towards, immigrant or disadvantaged groups.

To be successful, social inclusion requires changes in attitude, and power and resource sharing on the part of the dominant group. History has shown that such sacrifices of interest are not easily ceded (Cushing 2003: 3). Taylor reminds us that the 'neutral public sphere' is not, in fact, neutral but biased towards the ethos and values of the dominant group (Taylor 1992: 44). Multiples of factors, identified through this chapter, need honest appraisal and diverse strategies for successful social inclusion of immigrants to achieve a broader sense of migrant security. The consequences are not only for immigrants but for society as a whole, since the 'other' is not outside of us but within.

Bibliography

Anderson, B. (2006) *Imagined Communities: Reflections on the Origin and Spread of Nationalism*, (rev. ed.). London: Verso.

Appadurai, A. (1990) 'Disjuncture and difference in the global cultural economy', in M. Featherstone (ed.) *Global Culture: Nationalism, Globalization and Modernity*, London: Sage Publications.

Babacan, A. and Babacan, H. (2006b) 'Fear politics, new racism and the Cronulla riots', *Migration Action*, 28(1): 15–20.

Babacan, H. (2008) 'Addressing denial: the first step in responding to racism', 4Rs Conference, University of Technology, Sydney, 1–3 October 2008.

Babacan, H. and Babacan, A. (2006a) 'Locating identity: sense of space, place and belonging', *International Journal of Diversity in Organisations, Communities and Nations*, 5(5): 113–24.

Babacan, H., Gopalkrishnan N. and Babacan, A. (2009) *Situating Racism: the Local, National, and the Global*, Cambridge: Cambridge Scholar's Press.

Back, L. and Solomos, J. (2000) *Theories of Race and Racism: A Reader*. London: Routledge.

Barry, M. and Hallet, C. (1998) *Social Exclusion and Social Work: Issues of Theory, Policy and Practice*, Dorset: Russel House Publishing Ltd.

Beck, U. (2000) *What is Globalization?* Cambridge: Polity Press.

Berger, J. and Fisek, M.H. (2006) 'Diffuse status characteristics and the spread of status value: a formal theory', *The American Journal of Sociology*, 3(4): 1038–79.

Bonnet, A. (2000) *Anti-Racism*, London: Routledge.

Boyd, D. (1996) 'Dominance concealed through diversity: implications for inadequate perspectives on cultural pluralism', *Harvard Educational Review*, 6(3): 609–31.

Brett, J. (2004) 'The new liberalism', in R. Manne (ed.) *The Howard Years*, Melbourne: Black Inc. Agenda.

Brochmann, G. and Hammar, T. (1999) *Mechanisms of Immigration Control: A Comparative Analysis of European Regulation Policies*, Oxford: Berg.

Brubaker, R. (1992) *Citizenship and Nationhood in France and Germany*, Massachusetts: Harvard University Press.
Castles, S. and Miller, M.J. (1998) *The Age of Migration: International Population Movements in the Modern World*, Houndmills: Macmillan Press.
Castles, S., Kalantzis, M., Cope, B. and Morrisey, M. (1988) *Mistaken Identity: Multiculturalism and the Demise of Nationalism in Australia*, Sydney: Pluto Press.
Coleman, J.S. (1988) 'Social capital in the creation of human capital', *American Journal of Sociology*, 94 (Supplement): S95–120.
Colenso, P. (2005) 'Education and social cohesion: developing a framework for education sector reform in Sri Lanka', *Compare*, 35(4), December: 411–28.
Crawford, C. (2003) 'Towards a common approach to thinking about and measuring social inclusion', Social Inclusion Research Conference, Ottawa: The Canadian Council on Social Development and Human Resources Development.
Cushing, P. (2003) *Report on Social Inclusion and Exclusion Policies*, Toronto: The Roeher Institute.
Dekker, K. and Bolt, G. (2005) 'Social cohesion in post-war estates in the Netherlands: differences between socioeconomic and ethnic groups', *Urban Studies*, 42(13): 2447–70.
Diken, B. (2002) 'Zones of indistinction: security, terror and bare life', *Space and Culture*, 5(3), August: 290–307.
Dudgeon, P. and Oxenham, D. (1989) 'The complexity of Aboriginal diversity: identity and kindredness', *Black Voices*, 5(1): 22–39, Townsville: James Cook University.
Dunn, K., Forrest, J., Burnley, I. and McDonald, A. (2004) 'Constructing racism in Australia', *Australian Journal of Social Issues*, 39(4), November: 409–30.
Dunn, K.M., Klocker, N. and Salabay, T. (2007) 'Contemporary racism and Islamaphobia in Australia: racialising religion', *Ethnicities*, 7(4): 564–89.
Ferguson, Y. (1994) 'Ethnicity, nationalism and polities great and small', *Mershon International Studies Review*, 38: 241–6.
Fortier, A. (2000) *Migrant Belongings: Memory, Space, Identity*, Oxford: Berg.
Freeman, G.P. and Jupp, J. (1992) *Nations of Immigrants: Australia, the United States, and International Migration*, Oxford: Oxford University Press.
Freiler, C. (2002). 'Forward: the Laidlaw Foundation's perspective on social inclusion', in C. Frazee (ed.) *Thumbs Up*, Toronto: Laidlaw Foundation Working Paper Series Perspectives on Social Inclusion.
Furedi, F. (2005) *Politics of Fear: Beyond Left and Right*, London: Continuum International Publishing.
Ghosh, B. (2000) *Managing Migration: The Need for a New International Regime*, Oxford: Oxford University Press.
Giorgas, D. (2000) 'Social capital within ethnic communities', TASA 2000 Conference, Flinders University, Adelaide, 6–8 December.
Glassner, B. (2004) 'Narrative techniques of fear mongering', *Social Research*, 71(4): 819–26.
Gopalkrishnan, N. (2007) 'Neo-liberalism and infeartainment: what does a state do?' in N. Gopalkrishnan and H. Babacan (eds) *Racisms in the New World Order: Realities of Cultures, Colours and Identity*, Cambridge: Cambridge Scholar's Press.
Gopalkrishnan, N. (2003) 'Fear, diversity and the globalisation paradigm', *International Journal of Diversity in Organizations, Communities and Nations*, 3: 601–9.
Gopalkrishnan, N. and Babacan, H. (eds) (2007) *Racisms in the New World Order: Realities of Cultures, Colours and Identity*, Cambridge: Cambridge Scholar's Press.
Gutmann, A. (2003) *Identity in Democracy*, Princeton: Princeton University Press.

Hage, G. (2003a) 'Against paranoid nationalism', *Searching for Hope in a Shrinking Society*, Annandale: Polity Press.
Hage, G. (2003b) *White Nation: Fantasies of White Supremacy in a Multicultural Society*, Annandale: Pluto Press.
Held, D., McGrew, A., Goldblatt, D. and Perraton, J. (1999) *Global Transformations: Politics, Economics and Culture*, Cambridge: Polity Press.
Henry, F., Tator, C., Mattis, W. and Rees, T. (2000) *The Colour of Democracy: Racism in Canadian Society*, Toronto: Harcourt Brace and Company.
Heron, T. (2008) 'Globalization, neoliberalism and the exercise of human agency', *International Journal of Politics, Culture, and Society*, 20: 85–101.
Hollinsworth, D. (2006) *Race and Racism in Australia*, 3rd edn, Melbourne: Thomson and Social Science Press.
Huberman, B.A., Loch, C.H. and Önçüler, A. (2004) 'Status as a valued resource', *Social Psychology Quarterly*, 67(1), March: 103–14.
International Organization for Migration (IOM) (2011) *Facts and Figures*, International Organization for Migration. Available at: www.iom.int/jahia/Jahia/about-migration/facts-and-figures/lang/en (accessed 9 May 2011).
Jayasuriya, L. (2003) 'Australian multiculturalism: past, present and future,' paper presented at Managing Diversity Conference, Melbourne, 1–3 October.
Johnson, C. (2000) *Governing Change: From Keating to Howard*, St Lucia: University of Queensland Press.
Johnson, D., Headey, B. and Jensen, B. (2005) *Communities, Social Capital and Public Policy: Literature Review*, Policy Research Paper Number 26, Canberra: Department of Family and Community Services.
Kalantzis, M. (2000) 'Multicultural citizenship', in W. Hudson and J. Kane (eds) *Rethinking Australian Citizenship*, Cambridge: Cambridge University Press.
Kearns, A. and Forrest, R. (2000) 'Social cohesion and multilevel urban governance', *Urban Studies*, 37(5/6): 995–1017.
Kershan, A.J. (2005) 'The 1905 Aliens Act', *History Today*, 55(3): 13–19.
Koo, K.L. (2005) 'Terror Australis: security, Australia and the "war on terror" discourse', *Borderlands e Journal*, 4(1). Available at: www.borderlandsejournal.adelaide.edu.au/vol4no1_2005/leekoo_terror.htm (accessed 1 March 2011).
Krongold, J. (2006) 'A breach of trust: the vitiated discourse of multiculturalism at the turn of the twenty first century', *Australian Critical Race and Whiteness Studies Association E Journal*, 2(1): 1–13.
Kymlicka, W. (2001) *Politics in the Vernacular: Nationalism, Multiculturalism and Citizenship*, Oxford: Oxford University Press.
Lawrence, C. (2006) *Fear and Politics*, Victoria: Scribe Short Books.
Lin, N. (1999) 'Social networks and status attainment', *Annual Review of Sociology*, 25: 467–87.
Loizos, P. (2000) 'Are refugees social capitalists?', in S. Baron, J. Field and T. Schuller (eds) *Social Capital: Critical Perspectives*, Oxford: Oxford University Press.
Mark, N.P., Smith-Lovin, L. and Ridgeway, C.L. (2009) 'Why do nominal characteristics acquire status value? A minimal explanation for status construction', *The American Journal of Sociology*, 115(3), November: 832–62.
Markus, A. (2001) *Race: John Howard and the Remaking of Australia*, Crows Nest: Allen and Unwin.
Mason, A. (2000) *Community, Solidarity and Belonging*, Cambridge: Cambridge University Press.

McChesney, R.W. (2001) 'Global media, neoliberalism, and imperialism', *Monthly Review*, 52: 1–19.
McCulloch, J. (2004) *National Insecurity Politics in Australia: Fear and the Federal Election*. Available at: www.statewatch.org/news/2004/jun/jude-mccullogh.pdf (accessed 27 April 2012).
McMaster, D. (2001) *Asylum Seekers: Australia's Response to Refugees*, Melbourne University Press.
Osburn, J. (2006) 'An overview of social role valorization theory', *The SRV Journal*, 1(1): 4–13. Available at: www.srvip.org/overview_SRV_Osburn.pdf (accessed 9 March 2011).
Phillipson, C., Allen, G. and Morgan, D. (2003) *Social Networks and Social Exclusion: Sociological and Policy Perspectives*, Aldershot: Ashgate.
Pierson, J. (2001) *Tackling Social Exclusion*, New York: Routledge.
Poynting, S. and Noble, G. (2004) *Living with Racism: The Experience and Reporting by Arab and Muslim Australians of Discrimination, Abuse and Violence Since September 2001*, Report to the Human Rights and Equal Opportunity Commission. Available at: www.hreoc.gov.au/racial_discrimination/isma/research/index.html (accessed 17 February 2009).
Ridgeway, C.L. and Walker, H.A. (1995) 'Status structures', in K. Cook, G. Fine and J. House (eds) *Sociological Perspectives on Social Psychology*, Upper Saddle River, NJ: Pearson Education.
Robin, C. (2004) 'The politics and antipolitics of fear', *Raritan*, New Brunswick, 23(4).
Rubenstein, K. (2002) 'Citizenship, sovereignty and migration: Australia's exclusive approach to membership of the community', *Public Law Review*, 13, June: 102–9.
Sarup, M. (1994) 'Home and identity,' in G. Robertson (ed.) *Travellers Tales: Narratives of Home and Displacement*, London: Routledge.
Silver, H. and Miller, S. (2002) 'Social exclusion: the European approach to social disadvantage', *Poverty and Race*, 11(5), October.
Social Inclusion Board (2010) *Social Inclusion in Australia: How Australia is Faring*, Canberra: Commonwealth of Australia. Available at: www.socialinclusion.gov.au/sites/www.socialinclusion.gov.au/files/publications/pdf/SI_HowAusIsFaring.pdf (accessed 27 April 2012).
Soysal, Y. (1994) *Limits of Citizenship: Migrants and Postnational Membership in Europe*, Chicago: University of Chicago Press.
Steinbock, A.J. (1995) *Home and Beyond: Generative Phenomenology after Husserl*, Evanston, Illinois: Northwestern University Press.
Stokes, G. (ed.) (1997) *The Politics of Identity in Australia*, Cambridge: Cambridge University Press.
Stratton, J. (1998) *Race Daze: Australia in Identity Crises*, Annandale: Pluto Press.
Taylor, C. (1992) *Multiculturalism and the Politics of Recognition*, Princeton: Princeton University Press.
Thomas, S. and Wolfensberger, W. (1999) 'An overview of social role valorization', in R.J. Flynn and R.A. Lemay *A Quarter Century of Normalization and Social Role Valorization: Evolution and Impact*, University of Ottawa Press.
Tuan, Y.F. (1979) *Landscapes of Fear*, Oxford: Blackwell.
Turner, J.C. and Hogg, M.A. (1987) *Rediscovering the Social Group: A Self Categorization Theory*, Oxford: Basil Blackwell.
United Nations High Commissioner for Refugees (UNHCR) (2010) *Statistical Yearbook 2009: Trends in Displacement, Protection and Solution*, United Nations High

Commission for Refugees. Available at: www.unhcr.org/4ce530889.html (accessed 20 May 2011).
Van Dijk, T. (2000) 'New(s) racism: a discourse analytical approach', in S. Cottle, *Ethnic Minorities and the Media*, Buckingham, UK: Open University Press.
Vasta, E. and Castles, S. (1996) *The Teeth are Smiling: The Persistence of Racism in Multicultural Australia*, St Leonards: Allen and Unwin.
Waters, M. (1995) *Globalization*, London: Routledge.
Waymer, D. (2009) 'Walking in fear: an autoethnographic account of media framing of inner-city crime', *Journal of Communication Inquiry*, 33(2): 169–84.
Wazana, R. (2004) 'Fear and loathing down under: Australian refugee policy and the national imagination', *Refuge*, 22(1): 83–95.
Westwood, S. and Phizacklea, A. (2000) *Trans-Nationalism and the Politics of Belonging*, London: Routledge.
Wong, L. (1994) 'Ethnicity, the state and the public agenda', in M. Muetzelfeldt (ed.) *Society, State and Politics in Australia*, Sydney: Pluto Press.
Woodward, K. (ed.) (1997) *Culture, Media and Identities: Identity and Difference*, London: Sage.
Young, J. (1999) *The Exclusive Society: Social Exclusion, Crime and Difference in Late Modernity*, London: Sage.
Zelinka, S. (1996) *Understanding Racism in Australia*, Human Rights and Equal Opportunity Commission, Canberra: Australian Government Publishing Service.
Zetter, R., Griffiths, D., Sigona, N., Flynn, D., Pasha, T. and Beynon, R. (2006) *Immigration, Social Cohesion and Social Capital: What are the Links?* York: Joseph Rowntree Foundation.
Zhou, M. and Bankston III, C.L. (1994) 'Social capital and the adaptation of the second generation: the case of Vietnamese youth in New Orleans', *International Migration Review*, 18(4): 821–45.

10 Citizens of nowhere

Refugees, integration criteria, and social inclusion

Eileen Pittaway

> Sometime I wish that I had not come to Australia. I feel, as an African, we are not treated as people. We are treated with no dignity … and yet only the colour of our skin is different.
>
> (Refugee man from Sudan)

A sense of belonging, social inclusion, and access to citizenship has a very special meaning for one group of people who are part of current transnational movements. They are refugees and asylum seekers. They are people who do not choose to leave their countries of origin, but are forced to flee because of persecution and conflict. They do not choose the countries in which they first seek refuge. The small percentage who are resettled by governments to developed countries each year have little choice about where they will be sent. Nor do they have the choice to return to their country of origin if they are not happy in their new home.

In this chapter, we will focus on the experience of resettled refugees and asylum seekers living in Australia. Resettlement is one of the three 'durable solutions' for refugees designated by the United Nations High Commissioner for Refugees (UNHCR). Countries of resettlement accept a nominated number of refugees each year from refugee camps. An average of 73,000 resettlement places is offered internationally each year (UNHCR 2010b). Australia has always had a generous resettlement program, settling on average 13,500 refugee and humanitarian entrants annually. Refugees invited to resettle in Australia are granted permanent residency on arrival and provided with a range of services to assist their settlement. They have to wait four years before they can apply for citizenship and the rights it implies, such as the right to vote, to hold a passport, or to take public office.

Most refugees want to return to their homeland, but years living in insecurity and being on the margins of society leave them with few options. Resettlement to a third, often unknown, country is their only chance for safety. They believe it is a final opportunity to achieve a secure life for themselves and their children. Having lived for years as 'citizens of nowhere' (refugee woman from Bangladesh 2007), resettlement offers them a chance to regain this status.

Other refugees seek asylum directly in developed countries, often joining the many migrants, both legal and illegal, who are seeking work and an income for their families which cannot be obtained in their country of origin. In the name of 'domestic security' and as a strategy for addressing uncontrolled international migration, increasingly developed nations are tightening their national borders to control the arrival of asylum seekers and illegal migrants. Australia has been at the forefront of developing stringent border protection measures despite the fact that we are little touched by the mixed-flows migration which many European nations are experiencing. As we have increased border security in an attempt to stop unauthorized asylum seekers arriving by boat, we have expanded our resettlement programme.

While refugee advocates applaud the increase in resettlement places, this trend toward more stringent border protection fundamentally changes the notion that every global citizen has the right to seek asylum in another country if persecuted in their own country. It goes further than the right of governments to assess the legal rights of refugees to claim asylum and passes into the realm of political and moral judgement about who we want to accept into host societies. It calls into question the rights of refugees to claim asylum (van der Klaauw 2009). Importantly, it influences public perception about refugees and asylum seekers, often with negative impact on resettlement outcomes. 'I am an Australian citizen, yet people still yell at me, "Heh, black man, go back to where you came from". I wish I could' (refugee man from Sudan).

The policy initiatives currently guiding the resettlement of refugees into Australia and in other countries of resettlement are those based on the concepts of social inclusion, citizenship, and integration. There is an assumption that, if these are achieved, refugees will be successfully settled and contributing members of society. In this chapter, we will explore some of the currently accepted meanings of these concepts and their strong interlinkage. We will then look at some of the challenges to achieving these posed by the pre- and post-arrival experience of refugees and asylum seekers as they strive to settle into Australia.

Method

Unless stated otherwise, the quotes used throughout this paper have come from interviews and consultations conducted by the University of New South Wales Centre for Refugee Research (CRR) between 2007 and 2010 in three research projects with over 500 refugees in Sydney, Wagga, Brisbane, and Townsville (Pittaway *et al.* 2009; Doney *et al.*, 2009a; Doney *et al.* 2009b). Seventy-two per cent of the participants were women, 28 per cent men. The methodology in each case was based on community consultation and participatory action research approaches, which were developed by Eileen Pittaway and Linda Bartolomei of CRR. It uses an introduction to human rights as the context in which to guide refugees and asylum seekers through an examination of issues of critical concern to their communities. Many of the refugees were relatively new arrivals and not yet eligible for citizenship. It is not known how many of the other respondents had acquired Australian citizenship, as this was not the focus of the consultations. What was notable was that the meaning of belonging and citizenship was a recurrent theme, raised by the refugees themselves in more than 200 unsolicited responses and in group discussions. It was an unintended output of the research.

Some of the longer-term refugees did identify as having acquired Australian citizenship and saw this as a positive contribution to their feeling of belonging in Australia. '... before I was nothing, I was lower than nothing, but there – here they give me citizenship, they give me rights, they give me back a life' (refugee man from Rwanda). Others questioned the value of citizenship in terms of its ability to provide the sense of security and belonging that they craved. Most discussed citizenship in the context of a feeling of exclusion from their new society. There was no suggestion that this suddenly changed when citizenship was obtained. 'So I have my passport now and my kids are "Australian". What does that mean? Do I belong here? No! There is no life for me here. I don't know where I will go to die' (refugee woman from the Democratic Republic of the Congo, DRC).

Who is a refugee?

The Convention on Refugees defines a refugee as someone who:

> owing to well-founded fear of being persecuted for reasons of race, religion, nationality, membership of a particular social group or political opinion, is outside the country of his nationality and is unable or, owing to such fear, is unwilling to avail himself of the protection of that country.
>
> (1951 Convention Article 1A(2))

There are currently over 15.4 million mandated refugees and 27.5 million people of concern to the United Nations High Commoner for Refugees (UNHCR 2011a). In their flight to hoped-for security, most seek refuge in neighbouring countries, mainly in the developing world.

Many people in Australia have little understanding of why people become refugees and the Australian resettlement programme. Refugees and asylum seekers often find themselves treated with suspicion and are marginalized in the communities in which they hoped to find security. The majority of people who seek asylum in Australia are found to have a genuine claim by the Australian refugee determination system and are allowed to stay. However, many have to endure extreme hardship in Australian detention centres before this is granted and are often incorrectly labelled as illegal immigrants and economic refugees.

> I could hardly speak to my father – he had promised safety in Australia, a land that believes in human rights. We were in terrible danger on this horrible boat – my mum lost a baby because it was so horrible. Then we got to

Australia and they threw us into a detention centre in the middle of the desert.

(Refugee youth from Iraq)

Any discussion of resettlement outcomes has to include an acknowledgement of the pre-arrival experience of the majority of refugees. They come from a space in which they have lost their homes, family members, friends, and often the citizenship of their country of origin. UNHCR estimates that eight million refugees have been living in protracted refugee situations for at least five years, some for over 30 years (UNHCR 2011a).

[In the camp] we have no money, we have no good food, no nourishing food. We have to go very far away and bring the water ... dirty water but we have to drink it. Women get raped fetching the water. Because we don't have enough bamboo and enough leaves, the whole rainy season the roof is leaking and the children have got so many kinds of diseases.

(Refugee woman from Zambia 2011)

Camps are dangerous and violent. Food, education, and medical services are minimal. Men are not permitted to undertake their roles as providers, while women's traditional roles as mothers and wives are eaten away by conflict and the institutionalism of camp life. Death of family and friends from hardship or violence is common. Many children and young people were born in refugee camps and have known no other life. The rape and systematic sexual abuse of women and girls, which happens to the majority of them, erode their sense of self and hope for the future (UNHCR 2011b). 'They rape the little children, they rape grandmothers, no-one is safe' (refugee woman from Burma).

In these difficult situations, refugees suffer from serious challenges to their cultural heritage and their ability to maintain family and community life. They struggle to maintain their capacity to create a sustainable lifestyle for themselves and their families. It is a testimony to their strength and determination that so many succeed and prosper in Australia. 'Mum held the family together despite all she went through ... losing her husband, children, and not even being able to bury them' (refugee woman from Burma).

Integration, social inclusion, and citizenship: three planks of belonging and successful settlement?

One of the challenges to achieving social inclusion and security in a new country is the stringent integration criteria, which, in the name of national security and social harmony, many countries are using to select refugees for resettlement. Integration is a contested notion, which has changed over time. In some cases, it is used as an indicator of a humanitarian response to address the challenges mentioned above and to understand and improve the settlement outcomes of refugees. In other situations, it is being used as an indicator of assimilation potential and as a basis for refugee selection or rejection, regardless of need.

While in Australia we do not formally endorse 'integration criteria' for our refugee intake, a former Minister for Immigration stated that:

> The Government will put more emphasis on new 'integration criteria' when assessing applications from people seeking to settle in Australia on a long-term basis ... considering the capacity of 'would be' migrants [including humanitarian entrants] to integrate and would include an assessment of the applicants adaptability and resourcefulness.
>
> (*Sydney Morning Herald* 2007)

The use of integration theory has become the focus of academic endeavour around the world, as researchers seek to understand its potential for achieving successful settlement (Smyth *et al.* 2010).

Ager and Strang have proposed a useful conceptual framework using ten domains for achieving integration based on common understandings of what constitutes successful integration (Ager and Strang 2008). The most obvious include access to employment, housing, education, and health services. Other prerequisites are those of social bonding with members of one's own community, social support from within refugee communities and social bridges with other communities, including the host community. The acquisition of language, cultural knowledge, and safety and security are identified as 'facilitators' of local integration. Underpinning all of these is the experience of citizenship and rights.

Social support from within refugee communities is seen as critical to providing a direct social relationship to the pre-arrival experience and, indirectly, to facilitating access to and attainment of essential services by providing culturally appropriate assistance and knowledge (Simich *et al.* 2005: 259). Contrary to the sometimes-expressed opinion that this form of social connection consolidates people of similar ethnicity for the sake of maintaining cultural exclusivity, it is argued that social bonding promotes distinct identities, which grow out of 'shared needs and aspirations of specific groups' (Zetter *et al.* 2006).

> It's good especially when you came to a new world and you find someone who speaks the same language as you and takes you shopping. Because my community guide [Adult Migrant Education Service Resettlement Services staff] was a refugee, he will understand my suffering before we start talking about it. We cry together ... we laugh together. I do not have to explain everything.
>
> (Refugee man from Afghanistan)

It builds on the theory of social capital, which highlights the value of social relations within and between social networks, both formal and informal. It also explores the value of reciprocity between these networks as a demonstration of the cooperation and confidence building necessary to achieve collective results (Putnam 2000).

Under the Humanitarian Settlement Strategy, the Australian Government provides or funds services to newly arrived refugees in each of the domains in the Ager and Strang model. These include education about the host population, information provision for new arrivals, poverty alleviation through activities designed to bring diverse communities together with a common purpose, and torture and trauma treatment services. Yet despite these services, many refugees are still experiencing social exclusion and living with feelings of insecurity.

> Until I can learn English, I can do nothing here. No work, no study, no future. But I have tried and I cannot learn, I cry at night. They do not understand what I need, I am not stupid but I feel stupid.
> (Refugee woman from Eritrea)

It is useful to consider these ten domains when considering the challenges to achieving social inclusion faced by newly arrived refugees.

The challenges of resettlement

In 2008, an Auditor General's report in Western Australia found that recent humanitarian arrivals had complex and specific needs not seen in previous groups and that '[t]hese needs reflect the conditions in which they have lived before coming here. They have often suffered torture and trauma and spent long periods in refugee camps without basic services' (Auditor General for Western Australia 2008: 5).

Refugees come from cultural backgrounds which can be very different from the host community.

> I am confused with the meaning of community in Australia. I do not know how I can divide myself into being a member of my Eritrean community and at the same time being part and parcel of my new found home Australia.
> (Refugee man from Eritrea)

Many new arrivals find learning English or entering the education system extremely difficult due to interrupted or non-existent schooling. Some have never had the opportunity to become literate in their first language. 'I have been here for years and I still can't speak English – it is like being in a basket. I cannot help my children with their schoolwork yet I am not a stupid person' (refugee woman from Burma).

Refugees put a high premium on education and have great expectations of their children. While many do succeed, for others it is a struggle. Children bear the weight of failure in the school system and not living up to the expectations of their parents.

Yet when they come here they are put into school according to their age. How can they cope? They can't. They feel discouraged and then they won't go to school and they go to the streets. We are so worried.

(Refugee man from Sudan)

Years spent in protracted refugee situations have denied many the opportunity to undertake tertiary education, practise their professions, or to update their qualifications. Previous professional or occupational experience is sometimes redundant or is not easily transferable to a 'technological and urbanised environment' such as Australia's (Desmond Cahill cited in Lower 2008).

Work is the number one problem. Some of us have overseas qualifications; most of them are not recognized by Australia. Where can we get Australian experience from? We just arrived. Some doctors are working as taxi drivers and they have to cope with that ... English, English – without it you are nothing here. I speak six languages but I am nothing. We cannot communicate, not work, not even become a citizen.

(Refugee woman from Sudan)

Housing is expensive and difficult to obtain and landlords are often racist and cling to ethnicity-based stereotypes. Refugee families are often large, with six or more children common in some groups. Refugees in all states have stated that finding affordable, safe, and secure housing large enough to house their families is critical to their wellbeing, yet finding good housing is one of their greatest challenges.

When I was here for one year and a half then came the problem that I had to leave the house in two months. I had three children. When I applied for ten houses and I was not getting any, then at that time all the trauma came up. The doctor said I had heart problems, but I told him it was trauma.

(Refugee woman from Ethiopia)

The experience of unresolved trauma can prevent refuges from participating in Australian society and chronic health problems may be diagnosed after years of no health care. 'The nightmares are so bad I dread going to bed at night. Then I cannot cope the next day. My little son cries when he remembers the bodies in the street. What can I say to him?' (refugee woman from Afghanistan). Lack of security and distrust of authority figures in conflict, flight, and in refugee situations can also translate to fear of authority figures in Australia. 'The police were torturers in our country, how can we trust them here' (refugee woman from Sierra Leone).

Women and girls who have been raped, abused, or sexually tortured, single women, and single-headed households face particular problems upon resettlement. They may have children born of rape and thus not be accepted into their own community. Shame compounds trauma and they do not seek psychological support. The earlier experience of violence makes them vulnerable to further abuse upon resettlement. 'I am afraid to live in my community because they know what happened to me over there. But I want my community – it is strange here and I am lonely' (refugee woman from Somalia).

Separation from families is a major problem for all refugee communities and one which impacts very strongly on their ability to settle into a new country.

> I have thrown my phone away – I cannot talk to them again. They need money for food, for medicine, they are sick, they are starving. What can I do? I cannot pay rent here. I cry all day and I cry all night.
>
> (Refugee man from Uganda)

Males often feel that their traditional roles have been stripped away from them, women assume new roles with more freedom and autonomy than they previously held, and adolescents have freedoms which they never dreamed of in their previous lives.

> Child protection took my kid. They said we were not good parents because we did not want her going out at night. They put her in a place for kids who don't live with their parents.... She was doing well in school, every teacher said she was intelligent, and she is pregnant now and living with her boyfriend and she is only 16.
>
> (Refugee woman from Sudan)

Refugees have complained that they have little knowledge or understanding of such things as women's and children's rights, nor of the Australian legal system. This is causing significant problems within refugee communities. 'Women here think they can go out when they like, they think they have their own money. They think their husbands cannot beat them even if they are bad wives. This is not right and the men are angry' (refugee man from the DRC).

These issues are also causing problems between generations as refugee children and youth learn English more quickly and start to challenge the culture of their parents. '...our kids know their rights as soon as they can walk, they call the police, they call child protection. There's no relationship between us and the police, they pay more attention to our kids and they ignore us' (refugee woman from Sudan).

These changes in social structures are causing challenges to refugee communities as they seek to re-establish their lives. To add to these problems, some sections of the Australian public are extremely racist and this impacts on refugees' sense of belonging (Pittaway and Muli 2009; Kaplan and Webster 2003; Pittaway 1991). 'My little daughter tried to scrub the brown colour from her skin in the bath. She said the children at school were laughing at her' (refugee woman from Sudan). Importantly, 'Racism silences communities' (refugee man from Somalia). It stops refugees from expressing their fears and insecurities and leads to resentment and anger. Instead of the hoped-for security, refugees can find themselves still on the margins of society. Their years of hardship continue.

Given these challenges, we question whether the access to and achievement of the domains proposed by Ager and Strang are by themselves sufficient for achieving successful settlement and what else is needed to make this possible.

Social inclusion

> I work as a community worker, I have been here for ten years, and yet I have never been invited into a [white] Australian's home.
>
> (Refugee man from Sudan)

'Social inclusion' is widely used in government policy and academic debate as a prerequisite to social cohesion and security. However there are many critiques of the concept, the main being that social inclusion lacks a clear definition and a coherent theoretical core. Different concepts of social exclusion and inclusion are used in Europe, the UK, the USA, and Australia and these shift over time in response to political and economic imperatives (Buckmaster and Thomas 2009).

Social inclusion first came into the political discourse in Australia in 2002 and was adopted by the Rudd Government in 2007. It targeted employment, participation, mental health, homelessness, child poverty, community development, and Indigenous communities as key areas for action. The current Australian Government's vision of a socially inclusive society is one in which all Australians share similar values and have the opportunity to participate fully in the life of our society. In practical terms, this means that people will have the resources, opportunities, and capabilities to access education, training, and work. They will also actively participate in civil, cultural, and recreational activities (Department of Immigration and Citizenship 2008). 'We are part of this great country, we are proud to be Australians. My family is doing well here, we will do anything to succeed ... I never want to go back [to Sudan] where I was no-one' (refugee man from Sudan).

As a corollary to social inclusion, many academics and politicians are using the term 'social exclusion' to describe those people who are detached from the normative prescribed activities of the society in which they live. They are people who live in poverty and without access to the means to enable them to enjoy their full rights as citizens. In the United Kingdom, social exclusion was conceptualized as both 'wide' forms of exclusion, experienced by large sectors of society, and 'deep' social exclusion, felt by the most excluded and at risk groups (Buckmaster and Thomas 2009: 5). We could argue that, compared with their lives pre-arrival, on arrival many refugees encounter 'deep' exclusion.

> Although I came here literate, I had completed high school, I struggled a lot and I was really depressed.... They hire us for the size of our bodies, not the size of our brains. I think people who commit suicide [in Australia] are right ... you are just like in a prison.
>
> (refugee man from Sudan)

In discussing the issue of social inclusion, Buckmaster and Thomas pose the question, 'Inclusion into what?' (Buckmaster and Thomas 2009: 4). What is the nature of the society into which one is included? A common principle across many integration-based resettlement programs is that 'basic knowledge of the host society's language, history and institutions is indispensable for integration' (Civil Liberties, Justice and Home Affairs 2009: 48). This reflects the general belief that cultural homogeneity is essential for social harmony. Does this imply that when we invite refugees to resettle, we are suggesting that the price of social inclusion is a significant adaptation to the Australian (or any other) society, which will inevitably involve the loss of much of their cultural and ethnic heritage? Can this be done in a way that both respects diversity and yet promotes social harmony? 'I feel as if I don't belong in Australia. Is this where I want to grow old and where my children should grow old? No. We are not at home here' (refugee from Sudan). This is particularly relevant for refugees who have come to Australia from very different social, linguistic, cultural, and religious backgrounds and whose recent experience has been vastly different from that of the average Australian, whether from an Anglo-Protestant background or from one of the many countries of migration. 'We love learning about our new culture, barbecues, the beach, about our rights. But we bring you our culture, too, our wonderful drums, our food and our friendliness. Please let us in to your lives' (refugee woman from Sierra Leone).

Since the mid-1970s in Australia, multiculturalism has been regarded as part of our nation building, a pragmatic and modest policy approach to achieving social cohesion (Jupp *et al.* 2007: 17). It was designed to provide services for migrant inclusion and respect for cultural difference but also had the aim of building a stronger social structure for all Australians. However, it is argued that, currently, multiculturalism has taken on a different meaning. We value diversity, which provides a rich ethnic and cultural mix, food, and quaint customs, but not difference, which implies a rejection of our values and religious and political beliefs and is usually seen as negative or even threatening to our way of life (Pardy 2009). The boundary between acceptable diversity and unacceptable difference means different things to different people. Often refugee communities have differences which are unacceptable to many Australians and this has also led to social exclusion.

> The neighbours complained to the local paper that we sang so loud in our church that they needed headphones to block the noise and they made a big joke about us. Don't they understand how important our Christianity is to us, and how much that hurt us? It's not as if we were singing at night or doing anything bad.
>
> (Refugee woman from DRC)

A critical factor is the way in which refugees are perceived and presented in the media and by the public. Politicians in many developed countries increasingly use defamatory terms such as 'queue jumpers', 'illegal immigrants' and 'economic refugees' to describe refugees (Every and Augoustinos 2008; Mares 2002). At the height of the controversy about so-called 'boat people' and the push for border security, John Howard, a previous Australian prime minister, famously stated, 'We will decide who comes to this country and the circumstances in which they come' (Howard 2001), implying that no-one had the right to seek asylum in Australia. This negative discourse shapes public opinion and works against notions of social inclusion. It is fuelled by the commercial media, in particular radio 'shock jocks', who influence the views of listeners on refugee issues. This discourse has a very negative impact on refugees, as they struggle to make a new and secure home in Australia.

Citizenship and security

> [Citizenship] constitutes membership of a polity, and as such citizenship inevitably involves a dialectical process of inclusion and exclusion.
> (Kivisto and Faist 2007: 1)

Acquisition of citizenship is linked to social inclusion by a number of academics and is commonly defined as '"full membership in a community," which encompasses civil, political and social rights and responsibilities' (Yuval-Davis 1991: 59). Membership has a set of reciprocal duties and rights which are inherent features of democracy (OHCHR 1996–2012: para. 3). However, traditional concepts of citizenship are being threatened by globalization, capitalism, individualistic tendencies, neo-liberalism, and the erosion of the nation-state on which notions of citizenship are predicated. The human rights regime rhetorically leans towards notions of world citizenship, which further challenges the notion of sovereign power (Kabeer 2005). Conversely, and at the same time, many governments are pressing for the integration of refugees and migrants and making strong links between citizenship and inclusive societies.

For most refugees, 'citizenship' has a very clear meaning. It symbolizes justice, freedom, security, rights, self-determination, and inclusion. They do not see themselves as having the luxury of dual citizenship or the right to return home. They have a strong desire to belong, to be accepted into the new society, while maintaining their cultural and ethnic difference. This is one of the few things they are able to bring with them, along with their social capital, their capacity to survive, and their determination to make a new life for themselves and their families. 'I will only really be a citizen of this place when my children are truly equal to all other children – and that has not happened yet' (refugee woman from Somalia).

Isin and Wood (1999) note that involvement in public life (a common theme in the integration and social inclusion discourses) is also an important part of a contemporary multifaceted citizenship and critical to identity. Citizenship is one of the many identity markers which we all bear, such as 'ethnicity', 'teacher', and 'mother'. Some of these markers are self-assigned, some are attributed by others. Some are positive and some are negative. Most importantly, identity is a fluid concept (Pittaway and Pittaway 2004).

> I am a refugee ... a dirty, helpless woman, hopeless, a hungry person and ignorant person, a troublesome person, yet another burden for the world to feed, another burden for the world to care, that is who they say we are ... BUT ... being a refugee is not by choice. If it is a choice, I wouldn't be a refugee anywhere. Looking at myself, I believe I am not a victim, but I am a survivor, a very strong person, a refugee woman.
>
> (Refugee woman from Sudan)

In order to understand the process of social inclusion, we must examine what happens when one group has so many negative identity markers that they are completely marginalized by the population in which they wish to be involved. These identity markers may include 'refugee', 'hopeless person', 'Muslim', 'black', 'poor', 'illiterate', 'unemployed', and many others. As new arrivals, refugees are often passive recipients of welfare without involvement in public life and thus 'bludgers' is a common identity marker assigned to them. Identity is also a political concept. Majority groups assign negative labels as a tool of domination or to legitimate the status quo. The social context and, most importantly, the ways in which the people with whom we interact assign labels to us dictates which identity is predominant at a particular point in time.

> [W]hen we look for the sources of identity, we cannot look to one set of conditions or one definition to serve all our needs: cultural, ethical, national, and gender identity all have their own dynamics, which shift according to who does the asking and who does the telling.
>
> (Janack 1999: 326)

To this, we would add the impact of the refugee experience and the power of assigned identities. 'You ask about my culture – try "refugee culture". I have lived nearly 40 years as a refugee. I don't even know how my parents really lived' (refugee woman from Angola).

The identity marker 'refugee' has different meanings according to who is using it. For some, it is an identity that calls forth sympathy or empathy and the willingness to help. It can also be a negative label, evoking pathetic and helpless people, without agency. It is used to refer to people perceived as trying to enter Australia illegally and take advantage of our social and economic security. 'I don't pay my taxes to support illegal immigrants' (author's notes, community meeting 2009).

Refugees adopt different identities as they seek to make space for themselves in host communities. 'We never say we are refugees. People hate refugees, they think we are lazy and dishonest' (refugee from Sudan). This has important consequences for refugees struggling to survive in a new environment and to establish a positive identity for themselves. In recent times in Australia, the refugee identity has been used as a primary tool of oppression. When the weight of this oppression becomes too great, it is possible that self-associated identities of some can become subsumed under the imposed labels of the oppressing group (Pittaway and Pittaway 2004). 'My people never admit to being a refugee. They are ashamed because of what is said in the media. They would rather not have services than say they are a refugee' (Afghan community worker).

If the predominant identity markers used by the society in which they are living are negative, then whatever their preferred labels, refugees will find it difficult to achieve social inclusion. The negative identity markers are an active agent of social exclusion and makes domestic security difficult to achieve. They also fuel discontent and a sense of injustice. Therefore, a major challenge in the successful inclusion of refugees into Australian society is the fostering of positive refugee identities which respect the right of individuals to either retain or discard the identity of 'refugee' when they see fit (Zetter 2007).

> Even if I get to be a citizen, I will always be a refugee as long as I am not at home. They cannot take away the pain ... and I do not want my children to forget what happened to our country, why we are here.
> (Refugee man from Iraq)

In their analysis of social inclusion, Buckmaster and Thomas consider the work of Marshall (1950) who developed the concept of citizenship to include civil, political, and social citizenship. Marshall argued that modern citizenship is predicated on notions of equality of status supported by a social infrastructure which makes this possible. Buckmaster and Thomas suggest 'Locating social inclusion within a revised and more contemporary citizenship framework would most likely strengthen it as a concept' (Buckmaster and Thomas 2009: 1). This would seat the policy of social inclusion within a rights-based framework, which will 'transform beggars into claimants. Claimants have their dignity and strength derived from these entitlements' (Frankovits 1996: 85).

In Australia, human rights, social justice, and gender equality are now part of our social and legal policy discourse. However, many refugee families come from patriarchal family structures and may not have been exposed to these changes. Years in conflict and in protracted refugee situations have sometimes eroded their cultures or, in some cases, caused a modification of cultural practice or a regression to traditional practice that had been dying out, in order to meet new circumstances.

> We always had dowry, but in my tribe it was become more like a gift to help the newly married couple. Now it is something else. Young girls are being sold because the families are desperate and they have no other way of getting money. They call it our culture, but it isn't.
> (Refugee woman from Sudan)

Their exposure to concepts such as human rights has been ad hoc and often rejected, particularly by men from patriarchal societies who see such concepts as a further erosion of their roles in the family and society. 'In the camps, they are always teaching women about their rights. What about our rights? They just take them away' (refugee man from Burma). This reality merits serious consideration when developing policy aimed at integration and social inclusion. 'You tell me I am a bad parent and take away my children but you do not teach me about the law' (refugee woman from the DRC). However, many appreciate the rights framework even as they struggle with it. 'We have a better life than we ever dreamed of. If this means we have to learn some new ways of looking [at family dynamics], then we shall learn' (refugee man from Ethiopia).

A key message from a recent consultation with young women was that, even though there are many difficulties in settlement, they are now 'proud to be young women who are respected, valued, and encouraged to participate' (refugee woman from Burma). Prior to coming to Australia, these young women did not have passports and felt they were not able to participate as active members of society. In Australia, however, they feel they have come to learn about their rights and have developed a strong sense of self-worth and identity (Doney *et al.* 2009b). 'The best thing about being in Australia is that we live in freedom with no fear and we are safe' (refugee woman from Iraq).

Conclusion

The comments from refugees used in this chapter pose more questions than they answer and point to the need for much more research in this area. The fact that so many refugees settle successfully, their children succeed in school, and they achieve the hoped-for sense of belonging, security, and citizenship is as much a testament to their social capital and individual capacity as to the services which are provided to assist in their resettlement.

'Australia is one place you can do something normal, live a normal life in a multicultural place that is secure' (refugee from Sudan).

While many succeed, others are struggling. In order to bridge the nexus between theory and reality, assisting refugees and asylum seekers achieve security involves an active acknowledgement that the principles of social inclusion must be proactive and must be incorporated into our legal and social infrastructure. However, to ensure that this happens for the majority of refugees resettling in Australia, more concerted and focused action will need to be taken. This will involve a deeper acknowledgement that refugees have special needs on arrival which must be addressed before they achieve successful settlement. These include recognizing that, for many refugees, authority figures and government offices are people and places of fear. Services offered to resettled refugees must also recognize the gender dimension of the refugee experience, so that women and girls are given assistance to recover from trauma and sexual abuse and to participate as equals in society. 'Australia gave me my rights. I never had rights before I came to Australia. As a black Muslim woman I am proud to be who I am' (refugee woman from Somalia).

These services must incorporate an understanding of the impacts of torture and trauma: protracted periods spent as a refugee affect a person's ability to participate actively in a new and alien society. They must also be culturally appropriate for the target population. For example, services for refugees who have survived torture and trauma are sometimes rejected by refugees who identify them with negatives perceptions and the stigma of mental health problems. 'We are sad, not mad' (refugee woman from Chile).

The horror of family separation must be acknowledged as a barrier to feelings of security and belonging. We must also consider the impact on a refugee's sense of security if they do not feel welcomed in their new country, the country in which they believed they would finally find safety and peace. What impact does the negative connotation of the term 'refugee' have on this process? Even if the structures for social inclusion are in place, how do xenophobia and racism in the media impact on refugees?

> I think the perception is that this person is from Africa, oh, he is not good for the kids, he does not love his wife. Well, one of the options is educating them, inviting them to let us know them.
>
> (Refugee man from Sudan)

Responsibility is a critical part of the rights discourse. However, much of the responsibility for achieving social inclusion is placed on the shoulders of the refugees themselves. The government plays a role by providing the means for them to do this. Active participation in the host society is mentioned in all areas as being critical to social inclusion, integration, and citizenship. However, research has increasingly regarded integration as a process which is influenced by the institutional environment of the receiving society as well as the personal capacities of the settling population (Valtonen 2004). If the host population is not welcoming, it is very difficult for refugees to feel secure.

> I struggle to cope with the isolation and loneliness. You have no-one to talk to, no-one to share with. Where we came from, we had neighbours and families, here we have no-one.
>
> (Refugee woman from Somalia)

Governments of host countries also have the responsibility to ensure that the services offered are accessible, adequate, and effective. The host community has to take responsibility for welcoming refugees (and migrants) and accepting the social changes that they will inevitably bring. People cannot achieve a sense of inclusion or belonging in a hostile environment.

Citizenship and social inclusion have been linked to a rights-based framework of service provision, which challenges service providers to examine the philosophical basis of the work they undertake. Such a framework ensures the centrality of human wellbeing and self-determination. It focuses on entitlement rather than charity and articulates the specific duties of governments and service providers. It introduces notions of accountability to service provision and has an equal focus on social and cultural as well as civil and political rights. This framework is predicated on the agency of the service recipients as equal participants in achieving effective outcomes, in this case, successful settlement. It leads to empowerment, a strong respect for existing community systems and strengths, community debate, and engagement (Doney et al. 2009a). It reflects the human rights framework in which policies of social inclusion are said to be grounded and could provide a blueprint to guide services aimed at achieving integration, social inclusion, and domestic security. This shift to meaningful social inclusion was exemplified by one refugee who stated, 'We need to stop calling ourselves refugees – we must become citizens of this new home of ours' (refugee woman from the DRC).

Refugees have the potential and willingness to contribute significantly to Australian society. They bring skills, capacity, and the strength that has enabled them to survive the horrendous refugee experience. There are some excellent examples of settlement services recognizing this potential and providing pathways for this to occur, but these are few and far between. Refugees also bring a strong desire to settle well and for their children to succeed in Australian society. 'We don't want our children working in factories. For us it is too late, that is all there is, but for them – they can go to university' (refugee from Sudan). They are survivors and have tremendous resilience. They have a strong interest in and commitment to succeeding in their new life. In a relatively short time, many learn English, find work, pursue higher education, and begin to rebuild their lives for a secure and successful future. 'We are here and I am doing well. I am contributing now and I will contribute in the future. I am a citizen of Australia' (refugee woman from Sudan).

It is critical that countries of resettlement provide the structures and climate for these things to occur. These involve an acknowledgement that, in the act of inviting strangers to our home, we are actually inviting them to be active agents of change in a fluid society. Without this, it is extremely difficult for refugees to achieve the sense of belonging and social inclusion that contribute to domestic security. Unless this happens, their commitment and loyalty to Australia or any other country of asylum will always be problematic.

Resettlement has been likened to a massive social experiment which is poorly monitored and with few established criteria for success. Unless it can be demonstrated that the majority of refugees and asylum seekers can find a measure of domestic security and a sense of inclusion in their new home, then the experiment can be deemed to have failed.

Bibliography

Ager, A. and Strang, A. (2008) 'Understanding integration: a conceptual framework', *Journal of Refugee Studies*, 21(2): 166–91.

Auditor General of Western Australia (2008) *Lost in Transition: State Services for Humanitarian Entrants. Performance Examination*, West Perth, Western Australia: Office of the Auditor General.

B's Independent Pro-Peace Initiative (2008) *Wars, Conflicts, International and Intranational crises*. Available at: www.bippi.org/bippi/menu_left/conflicts.htm (accessed 28 April 2011).

Bartolomei, L., Pittaway, E. and Pittaway, E. (2008) 'Who am I? An examination of the role of identity and citizenship in the experiences of women in Kakuma Refugee Camp in Northern Kenya', *Development*, 46(3): 87–93.

Buckmaster, L. and Thomas, M. (2009) 'Social inclusion and social citizenship – towards a truly inclusive society', *Social Policy*, 8.

Civil Liberties, Justice and Home Affairs (2009) *Problems and Perspectives of the European Citizenship: The Fifth Report on Citizenship of the Union*, Brussels: European Parliament.

Colc-Peisker, V. and Tilbury, F. (2007) 'Integration into the Australian labour market: the experience of three "visibly different" groups of recently arrived refugees', *International Migration*, 45(1): 59–83.

Dahinden, J. (2010) 'Transnational belonging, non-ethnic forms of identification, and diverse motilities: rethinking migrant integration?', Migrations: Interdisciplinary Perspectives Symposium, University of Vienna.

Department of Immigration and Citizenship (2008) *Fact Sheet 66: Integrated Humanitarian Settlement Strategy*, Canberra: Department of Immigration and Citizenship. Available at: www.immi.gov.au/media/fact-sheets/66hss.htm (accessed 28 April 2011).

Doney, G., Eckert, R. and Pittaway, E. (2009a) *African Women Talking: "We want the best thing for our family"*, Logan, Queensland: Access Services.

Doney, G., Eckert, R. and Pittaway, E. (2009b) *Unsung Heroes: An Evaluation of the AMES Community Guides Program*, Sydney: Adult Migrant Education Service and the Centre for Refugee Research.

Every, D. and Augoustinos, M. (2008) 'Constructions of Australia in pro- and anti-asylum seeker discourse', *Nations and Nationalism*, 14(3): 562–80.

Feller, E., Türk, V. and Nicholson, F. (2003) *Refugee Protection in International Law, UNHCR's Global Consultations on International Protection*, Cambridge: Cambridge University Press.

Frankovits, A (1996) 'Rejoinder: the right way to development', *Food Policy* 21(1): 123–28.

Galbally, F. (1978) *Migrant Services and Programs: Report of the Review of Post-Arrival programs and Services for Migrants*, Canberra: AGPS.

Howard, J. (2001) 'John Howard's policy speech', *Australian Politics*, Available at: http://australianpolitics.com/news/2001/01-10-28.shtml (accessed 27 April 2012).

Iredale, R., Mitchell, C., Pe-Pua, R. and Pittaway, E. (1996) *Ambivalent Welcome: The Settlement Experiences of Humanitarian Entrant Families in Australia*, Canberra: Department of Immigration and Multicultural Affairs.

Isin, E.F. and Wood, P.K. (1999) *Citizenship and Identity*, London: Sage Publications.

Janack, M. (1999) 'Struggling for common ground: identity politics and the challenge to feminist politics', *Social Theory and Practice*, 25(2).

Jupp, J., Nieuwenhuysen, J.P. and Dawson, E. (2007) *Social Cohesion in Australia*, Cambridge: Cambridge University Press.

Kabeer, N. (2005) 'The search for inclusive citizenship, meanings and expressions in an interconnected world', in N. Kabeer (ed.) *Inclusive Citizenship, Meaning and Expression*, London: Zed Books.

Kaplan, I. and Webster, K. (2003) 'Refugee women and settlement: gender and mental health', in P. Allotey (ed.), *The Health of Refugees*, Victoria: Oxford University Press.

Kastoryano, R. (2010) 'Codes of otherness', *Social Research: An International Quarterly*, 77(1), Spring. Available at: http://socialresearch.metapress.com/app/home/journal.asp?referrer=parent&backto=homemainpublications,1,1.

Kivisto, P. and Faist, T. (2007) *Citizenship: Theory, Discourse and Transnational Prospects*. Oxford: Blackwell.

Lower, G. (2008) 'Fatal brawl that doused so much hope and potential', *The Australian*, 24 November. Available at: www.theaustralian.com.au/news/nation/fatal-brawl-that-doused-so-much-hope-and-potential/story-e6frg6nf-1111118119921 (accessed 28 October 2010).

Malik, K. (2010) 'Multiculturalism undermines diversity', *Guardian*, 17 March. Available at: www.guardian.co.uk/commentisfree/2010/mar/17/multiculturalism-diversity-political-policy (accessed 10 December 2010).

Mares, P. (2002) *Borderline: Australia's Response to Refugees and Asylum Seekers in the Wake of the Tampa*, Sydney: UNSW Press.

Marshall, T.H. (1950) 'Citizenship and social class', in T.H. Marshall (ed.) *Citizenship and Social Class and Other Essays*, Cambridge: Cambridge University Press.

Office of the High Commissioner for Human Rights (OHCHR) (1996–2012) *Universal Periodic Review, Office of the High Commissioner for Human Rights*. Available at: www.ohchr.org.

Pardy, M. (2009) 'Multicultural incarnations: race, class and urban renewal', paper presented at The Future of Sociology: Annual Conference of The Australian Sociological Association, Canberra.

Pittaway, E. (1991) *Refugee Women – Still at Risk in Australia*, Bureau of Immigration Research, Canberra: Australian Government Publishing Service.

Pittaway, E. (2006) Author's notes, UNHCR Annual Tripartite Meeting on Resettlement, Geneva.

Pittaway, E. and Muli, C. (2009/2010) *The Settlement Experiences of Refugees and Migrants from the Horn of Africa*, Sydney: Centre for Refugee Research.

Pittaway, E. and Pittaway, E.E. (2004) 'Refugee woman: a dangerous label', *The Australian Journal of Human Rights*, 10: 119–36.

Pittaway, E., Muli, C. and Shteir, S. (2009) 'I have a voice – hear me! Findings of an Australian study examining the resettlement and integration experience of refugees and migrants from the Horn of Africa', *Refuge: Canada's Periodical on Refugees*, 26(2): 133–45.

Putnam, R. (2000) *Bowling Alone: The Collapse and Revival of American Community*, New York: Simon and Schuster.

Simich, L., Beiser, M., Stewart, M. and Mwakarimba, E. (2005) 'Providing social support for immigrants and refugees in Canada: challenges and directions', *Journal of Immigrant Health*, 7(4): 259–68.

Smyth, G., Stewart, E. and Da Lomba, S. (2010) 'Critical reflections on refugee integration: lessons from international perspectives', *Journal of Refugee Studies*, Special Issue on Refugee Integration, 23(4): 411–14.

Sydney Morning Herald (2007) 'Migration test on integration', 1 August. Available at: www.smh.com.au/news/national/migrant-test-on-integration/2007/07/31/1185647903342.html (accessed 27 April 2012).

The Ministry of Refugee, Immigration and Integration Affairs (2006) *A comprehensive integration initiative – and better integration*. Available at: www.nyidanmark.dk/enus/Integration/a_comprehensive_integration_initiative/a_comprehensive_integration_initiative.htm (accessed 18 August 2010).

United Nations High Commissioner for Refugees (UNHCR) (2010a) *Convention and Protocol Relating to the Status of Refugees*. Available at: www.unhcr.org/3b66c2aa10.html (accessed 26 April 2011).

United Nations High Commissioner for Refugees (UNHCR) (2010b) *Resettlement*. Available at: www.unhcr.org/pages/4a16b1676.html (accessed 28 October 2011).

United Nations High Commissioner for Refugees (UNHCR) (2011a) *Refugee and Internally Displaced People Figures*. Available at: www.unhcr.org/4dfb66ef9.html (accessed 28 October 2011).

United Nations High Commissioner for Refugees (UNHCR) (2011b) *Draft Survivors, Protectors, Providers. The Global Report on the Protection of Refuge Women and Girls*, Geneva.

Valtonen, K. (2004) 'From the margin to the mainstream: conceptualizing refugee settlement process', *Journal of Refugee Studies*, 17: 70–96.

van der Klaauw, J. (2009) 'Refugee rights in times of mixed migration: evolving status and protection issues', *Refugee Survey Quarterly*, 28(4): 59–86.

Yuval-Davis, N. (1991) 'The citizenship debate: women, ethnic processes, and the state', *Feminist Review*, 39(Winter): 58–68.

Zetter, R. (2007) 'More labels, fewer refugees: remaking the refugee label in an era of globalization', *Journal of Refugee Studies*, 20(7), 172–92.

Zetter, R., Griffiths, D., Sigona, N., Flynn, D., Pasha, T. and Beynon, R. (2006) *Immigration, Social Cohesion and Social Capital – What Are the Links?* York: Joseph Rowntree Foundation.

Index

Page numbers in *italics* denote tables, those in **bold** denote figures.

Abbott, Tony 10
Age, The 73, 74
Ager, A. 113, 173
Ahmed, Sara 66, 76, 77–8, 79
Alvarez, Vivian *see* Solon, Vivian Alvarez
American Association of Museums 51
Appadurai, Arjun 94
Arab Spring 128
Asociación de Padres de Pasadena Luchando por la Educación 99–100
asylum, number of applications 4
asylum seekers 12; abuse of system 18, 21–2; Australia 67, 74, 89, 109, 111, 118, 119, 170; commonality with illegal immigrants 25–7; deportation 18; dispersal policies 114; economic hardship 21; environmental factors 21; Europe 17–22; fear of persecution 19–20; gender-based persecution 20; image of 110, 117; insecurity issues 114–15; keeping a low profile 116–17, 122; labelling 108, 109, 111, 116; length of time dealing with cases 19; lip-sewing 75, 103; national identity of host societies 111; processes for dealing with 17–19, 91, 111; 'safe country' rules 19; 'safe third country' rules 19; sense of belonging 115–16; social connection 110, 121–3; traditional clothing 116; United Kingdom (UK) 109, 111, 114–17, 122, 123n1; work permits 18; *see also* refugees
Australia: assimilationist policies 34–5, 37, 39; asylum seekers 67, 74, 89, 109, 111, 118, 119, 170; Australian Multicultural Advisory Council (AMAC) 52; border security 8–10; citizenship rights 152–3;
Department of Immigration and Citizenship (DIMAC) 52; Department of Immigration and Multiculturalism and Indigenous Affairs (DIMIA) 68–72; fear politics 153, 156, 157–8; Greek migrants 13, 31–47; harsh security measures 153; Humanitarian Settlement Strategy 174; Immigration Museum, Melbourne 53–5; inequalities and historical injustices 121; integration criteria 172–3; Jewish Museum of Australia, Melbourne 56–7; migrant take-up of citizenship 52, 61, 170–1; migration legislation 8, 75; multiculturalism 9–11, 112–13, 155, 178; Museum of Brisbane 55–6; Muslims 133, 158; nation building 150–3; national identity issues 149, 152, 153, 155; off-shore processing centres 8; One Nation party 133; Operation Relex 8–9; 'Pacific Solution' 8–9; paranoid nationalism 133; public discourses on immigration 150; racism 155–7; refugees 109–10, 117–21, 122; Settlement Grants Program 121; social inclusion agenda 52; state border control 152; state sovereignty and security 152; women migrants, treatment of 64–83; *see also* insecurity, Australian case study; resettled refugees, Australian study; study on management of intercultural relations
Austria 157

Babacan, Alperhan 149–68
Babacan, Hurriyet 149–68
Barry, M. 154

Index

Bartolomei, Linda 170
Bennett, Tony 50
Bharatiya Janata Party 157
Blair, Tony 91
borders: responses to border crossers 88; securitization, effects on irregular migrants 90–2; security post 9/11 7, 92, 110, 134, 149, 163; statist approaches to control 6–7, 87–8
Bosnia 20
Brazil 21
Burnside, Julian 74
Butler, Judith 68, 79, 80

Caluya, Gilbert 79
Cameron, David 133–4
Canada 51, 88, 111–12, 132, 133
Castro, Brian 79–80
Cato Institute 23
children: *Children in Detention* (exhibition) 57; education 174–5; emotional burdens of parents 32, 41–2; family issues 175–6; sexual exploitation 6
China 21, 88
Christmas Island 8–9, 10
citizenship: birthright citizenship 25–7; contemporary forms of 101–2; ethical limitations 127; identity citizenship 10–11; intercultural 9–10; liberal citizenship 128; migrant take-up of 52, 61, 170–1; multicultural 163–4; resettled refugees 179–82; rights 127, 152–3, 162, 183–4; threats to 179
Clash of Civilizations (Huntington) 102
Clifford, James 95
Commission on Human Security 5
Commonwealth Ombudsman's Inquiry into the Circumstances of the Vivian Alvarez Matter 70–2
communicative ethics 49–50, 58–9
Crawford, C. 154, 160
Cresswell, Tim 81
cultural information flows 88

Dalziell, Rosamund 74–5
Damousi, Joy 31–47
'de-stating' 157
deportations 23, 24; unlawful 71–2
detention centres 8–9, 171–2; *Children in Detention* (exhibition) 57
diasporic communities: diaspora politics, role in global affairs 95; interference in politics of kin states 94; role in precipitating violence 94–5
displaced persons 4; gender issues 7–8; internally displaced persons 89; media portrayal 10; state responses to 5; *see also* asylum seekers; refugees

electronic media 60
Enlightenment period 128, 131
equal valued status 160–3, 181; identity, importance of 161; importance of status in achieving resources 161; social capital, importance of 161–2; status beliefs 161; status structures 160–1
Europe: asylum seekers 17–22; commonality of asylum seekers and US illegal immigrants 25–7; cultural development 51; riots and violence outbreaks 2005 93

Fall of Public Man, The (Sennett) 59–60
family relationships *see* resettled refugees, Australian study; war trauma
fear politics 153, 156, 157–8; harmful effects of 162; infeartainment 158
Ferres, Kay 48–63
films: *Narratives Across Cultures* 54–5
financial information flows 88
France 61; Paris riots, 2005 93; *see also* study on management of intercultural relations
From Stranger to Citizen 123n2

Genova, Nicholas de 92
Germany 133–4
global communications technologies 11
globalization: embodied globalization 88, 93, 103; impact on nation-state 150–1, 157
Gopalkrishnan, N. 157, 158
Greek Civil War (1944–9) 13, 32, 33–4, 43
Greek migrants, Australia 31–47; integration issues 37–9, 45; memory denial and identity 34–5, 37; personal reminiscences 35–44; post-war migration 33–5
Gurian, Elaine Heumann 51

Haider, Georg 157
Hallet, C. 154
Hanson, Pauline 133, 157
Harkavy, Robert 95
Harris, Kevin 51–2
Hayes, Anna 3–16
Healy, Chris 67
Hewitt, Jacqueline 74

Index

Holocaust 32
Howard, John 179
human rights 127, 163, 179, 181–2, 184
Human Rights Declaration (1948) 127
Human Rights Watch 19
human security: definition 5; gender issues 5–6, 7–8
Human Security Now 5
Huntington, Samuel 102

illegal immigrants 7; commonality with asylum seekers 25–7; United States 22–8
Improving Dreams, Equality, Access and Success (IDEAS) 98
India 157
infeartainment 158
Inquiry into the Circumstances of the Immigration Detention of Cornelia Rau (DIMIA) 68–70
insecurity, Australian case study 64–83; body image, importance of 77; Commonwealth Ombudsman's Inquiry into the Circumstances of the Vivian Alvarez Matter 70–2; Inquiry into the Circumstances of the Immigration Detention of Cornelia Rau (DIMIA) 68–70; national shame 74–5, 76; need for policy change 69–70; press coverage of cases 73–5, 81; sadness and insecurity 65–8, 77–8, 79–80; unlawful deportation 71–2
integration: assistance measures 120–1; conceptual framework 173, 174; criteria 172–3; definition 113; one-sided integration 120; and social connection 113–14, 121–3; UK policy 113; *see also* asylum seekers; refugees
internally displaced persons *see* displaced persons
International Network of Migration Institutions 48, 61
International Organization for Migration (IOM) 48, 151
Internet 11, 94
irregular migrants: citizenship 101–2; definition 89–90; education issues 101, Australia; effects of state securitization 90–2; and insecurity 102–3; involvement in worker cooperatives 98–9; and localized security 95–7, 104; policing against 91–2; seizure of public space 101; students 97–8, 101
Islam 120, 131–2, 133, 135, 141; *see also* religions

Italy 91, 92, 128

James, Paul 87–107
Jews 56–7

Kaldor, Mary 94
Kumsa, M.K. 111–12
Kurds: *Survival of a Culture: Kurds in Australia* (exhibition) 54

liberalism 128; neo-liberalism 157
Libya 91, 92, 128
Lin, N. 161
Los Angeles: *Asociación de Padres de Pasadena Luchando por la Educación* 99–100; Improving Dreams, Equality, Access and Success (IDEAS) 98; 'Justice for Janitors' campaign 96; Magic Cleaners (business cooperative) 98–9, 101, 104; measures to help irregular migrants 95–7; Pasadena 99–100; Pico Union neighbourhood 100; Pilipino Workers Center 99; University of California, Los Angeles (UCLA) 97–8

McNevin, Anne 87–107
Magic Cleaners (business cooperative) 98–9, 101, 104
Man, Paul de 76
Mansouri, Fethi 127–45
Marshall, T.H. 181
Mason, Robert 3–16
Massey, Doug 23
media: influence of 151, 157; portrayal of refugees and asylum seekers 10, 178–9; Rau and Alvarez Solon cases 73–5, 81
Merkel, Angela 133–4
Merleau-Ponty, Maurice 77
Mexico 22–3
Meyrowitz, Joshua 60
migration: as a cause of inequalities and insecurities 93–5; changes to 3; equal valued status 160–3; importance of memories 31, 32; statistics 4, 127, 151; transnational migration 127–8, 129–30, 151; *see also* sense of belonging
Migration Policy Institute (US) 24–5
Morocco 91
multiculturalism 14, 48–9, 128, 142; Australia 9–11, 112–13, 132–3, 178; backlash against 108–9, 112, 123; failure of 133–4; United Kingdom (UK) 112, 113, 133

museums 13, 48–63; *Australia's Muslim Cameleers* (exhibition) 54; Bable Project (community arts) 57; *Children in Detention* (exhibition) 57; *Cité Nationale de L'Histoire de l'Immigration* (Paris) 61; and citizenship 52–7; communication and inclusion 58–9; communicative ethics 49–50; *Communities of Faith Walking Together* (exhibition) 56; diversity, role in 49; Immigration Museum, Melbourne 53–5; Jewish Museum of Australia, Melbourne 56–7; late 20th century crises and changing role 50–2; migrant history, role in 48; *Moorooka Encounters* (exhibition) 56; Museum of Brisbane 55–6; *Narratives Across Cultures* (films) 54–5; *Small Object Big Story* (online resource) 55; social purpose of 50–2; *Survival of a Culture: Kurds in Australia* (exhibition) 54

Muslims: *Australia's Muslim Cameleers* (exhibition) 54; community security 7; global communications technologies 11; identity 128; post 9/11 hatred of 158; religion as obstacle to integration 120; transnational identification 14; transnational ties and migrant settlement 131–2; *see also* study on management of intercultural relations

Negotiating Existence 123n1
Neuman, Stephanie 95
New York Times 24
non-refoulement 12, 18

off-shore processing centres 8
online resources, *Small Object Big Story* 55
Operation Relex 8–9

people smuggling 9, 87
persecution, differences with discrimination 21
Pincetl, Stephanie 96
Pittaway, Eileen 169–87
private and public life balance 59–60
public space 10–12; and fear 158–9; and migrants' sense of security 13, 159–60

racism: Australia 155–7; definition 155; impacts of social exclusion 156; 'new racism' 111–12, 156–7
racist movements 151
Rainbird, Sophia 108–26

rape *see* women migrants
Rau, Cornelia 64–70, 67–8, 74, 81
'Redefining Security: the Human Dimension' (article, UNDP) 5
refugees: adaption to new cultural values 119–20; arrival experiences 171–2; Australia 109–10, 117–21, 122; camps 172; definition 19–20, 171; image of 108, 118–19; inequalities 121; insecurity issues 118–19; integration into host societies 109, 113, 118–19; labelling 108; legal obligations to 5; legal status 89, 91; rights to claim asylum 170; social connection 110, 121–3; statistics 4; *see also* asylum seekers; resettled refugees, Australian study
religions 103, 128; *see also* Islam
resettled refugees, Australian study 169–87; arrival experiences 171–2; challenges of resettlement 174–7; citizenship and security 179–82; education issues 174–5; family issues 176, 181–2; housing 175; integration 178–9; media image of refugees 178–9; need for policy change 182–4; negative identity markers 180–1; potential to contribute to Australian society 184; racism 176; rape and sexual abuse 175–6; social inclusion 177–9; social support within communities 173; study method 170–1; unresolved trauma 175–6, 182–3; work and qualifications 175; *see also* asylum seekers; refugees
Ridgeway, C.L. 160
Rudd, Kevin 9

St Denis (Paris) 136, 137, **138**
Saudi Arabia 21
Save the Children UK 6
Schech, Susanne 108–26
Second World War (1940–4) 32, 33–4, 43
secularism 61, 128, 131
Sennett, Richard 59–60
sense of belonging 10, 48, 52, 53, 129–30, 149, 156, 159, 179
sexual assault *see* women migrants
Sheffield 136, 137, **137**, 138
Silverman, Lois 52–3
social capital 119, 156, 161, 162, 173
social cohesion 49, 52, 109, 112, 153
social connection 113–14, 121–3
social exclusion 9–10, 51–2, 177; changing relations with inclusion 60–1; definition 154–5; negative identity markers 180–1; racism and fear 154–8

Index

social inclusion 14, 164; changing relations with exclusion 60–1; definition 154; and equal valued status 160–3; resettled refugees 177–9; state policies, impact on 8, 52
Solon, Vivian Alvarez 65, 67–8, 70–2, 74, 81
Somalia 20
Spain 91
Spinoza, Baruch 131
Sri Lanka 94
Steiner, Niklaus 17–28
Stokes, G. 162
storytelling 58–9
Strang, A. 113, 173
strong states: border security 87–8; effect of policies on irregular migrants 90–2; sovereignty 87; tensions between states and citizens 88–9
students 97–8, 101
study on management of intercultural relations 134–42; background 134; data analysis 135–9; data collection 134–5; feelings of community inclusion **140**, 141; local and transnational ties with other Muslims 136–9, **136**, **137**, **138**, **139**, **140**, 142; relationship between local and transnational ties 138–42; summary of data *135*; ties with local Muslim groups **139**
Sudanese 118–19

Tamil community 94
Taussig, Michael 75–6
Toqueville, Alexis de 59–60
Touraine, Alain 49, 60–1
transit processing centres 91
transnationalism 11, 31–3, 45–6; migration 127–8, 129–30
Tunisia 128

Ukraine 91
United Arab Emirates 88
United Kingdom (UK): asylum seekers 109, 111, 114–17, 122, 123n1; Immigration and Asylum Act 1999 111; multiculturalism 112, 113, 133–4; refugee integration policy 109, 113, 122; social exclusion agenda 51–2, 177; *see also* study on management of intercultural relations
United Nations Convention Relating to the Status of Refugees 92, 127, 171

United Nations Educational, Scientific and Cultural Organization (UNESCO) 48
United Nations High Commissioner for Refugees (UNHCR) 4, 5, 6, 151, 169, 171; human security, definition of 5; refugees, definition of 19–21
United States: 287(g) program 24–5; Arizona State Bill 1070 24; birthright citizenship policy 25–7; border with Mexico 22–3; Constitution, 14th Amendment 26; deportations 23, 24; illegal immigrants, commonality with European asylum seekers 25–7; illegal immigration 22–5; irregular migrants 90, 91; legal status of immigrants 27; museums 51; policies to discourage illegal immigrants 23–5; Proposition 187 (California) 24; students 97–8, 101; tensions between state and citizens 88; *see also* Los Angeles
University of New South Wales Centre for Refugee Research 170

Vico, Giambattista 131
visas 8, 10, 23, 91, 111, 118, 119, 122
visibly different migrants 3–4, 7, 9; identity citizenship 10–11; media portrayal 10

Walker, H.A. 160
war trauma 12–13, 31–47; depression, incidence of 32; executions 35, 40–1, 45; family silence 32, 40, 42–3, 45; memories 31, 32; personal reminiscences 35–44; survivor guilt 44; and transnationalism 45–6; unresolved grief 43, 44
Washington Post 26
Wazana, R. 154
Weber, Max 87
Weekend Australian 76–7, 81
whiteness 9, 10
Whittlesea (Melbourne) 136–7, **136**
Will, George 26
Wills, Sara 64–83
Wiseman, Hadas 45
women migrants: identity issues 7–8; rights 182; sexual assault 6, 172, 175–6; transnationalism 11; *see also* insecurity, Australian case study

Young, Iris Marion 49, 58–9

Zelinka, S. 155